9/14

The LOVE of Your LIFE

D1372759

What we learn from
living in the grip of passion

Susan Baur, Ph.D.

SOURCEBOOKS CASABLANCA™
AN IMPRINT OF SOURCEBOOKS, INC.®
NAPERVILLE, ILLINOIS

This publication is designed to provide accurate and authoritative information in regard to the subject matter covered. It is sold with the understanding that the publisher is not engaged in rendering legal, accounting, or other professional service. If legal advice or other expert assistance is required, the services of a competent professional person should be sought.—*From a Declaration of Principles Jointly Adopted by a Committee of the American Bar Association and a Committee of Publishers and Associations*

Published by Sourcebooks, Inc.
P.O. Box 4410, Naperville, Illinois 60567-4410
(630) 961-3900
Fax: (630) 961-2168
www.sourcebooks.com

Library of Congress Cataloging-in-Publication Data
Baur, Susan.
    The love of your life: what we learn from living in the grip of passion / by Susan Baur.
       p. cm.
  ISBN 1-57071-871-7 (pbk.)
  I. Love. 2. Man-woman relationships. 3. Intimacy (Psychology) I. Title.
 HQ801 .B345 2002
  306.7—dc21

                                                      2002003400

Printed and bound in the United States of America
VHG 10 9 8 7 6 5 4 3 2 I

For Inte L. Fatih

Acknowledgments

Many old friendships got a new lease on life when I asked, "What does the term 'love of a lifetime' mean to you?" I would like to thank my old friends Dr. Robert Blanchard, Nancy Butler, Stella Thomson-Miller, Mary-Pat McKenzie, Brett Cimino, Jane Walker, and Pamela Hunt. Each of these men and women practically shouted, "I know *exactly* what you mean!" They told me their stories and gave me the benefit of years of thinking on the subject. New friends, including Barbara Sulzberger, Bobbi Keane, Miriam Bronstein, and Karen Marlatt, read the manuscript with such obvious relish that I was encouraged to tailor my ideas to the needs of women and men who were teetering between doubt and belief. Barbara, in particular, was a source of insights.

Over the course of several years, Judi Gyovai brought arms full of books, tapes, questions, and ideas to the local coffee shop every week and slogged through all the detours and dead ends that one must explore on the way to workable ideas. Friend, mentor, editor, heckler, her advice was valuable, her affection priceless.

My agent Miriam Altshuler worked so hard on this book, it gives me a headache to think about it, and my editor Hillel Black was forced to use his X-ray vision to see what I was getting at in the first drafts. To both, thanks.

It goes without saying that when I write of love, I think of the love of my life.

TABLE OF CONTENTS

To change how we see things takes falling in love. Then the same becomes altogether different.

—James Hillman, *The Soul's Code*

Author to Reader

When I was over forty, a man I had dated in college picked up my book *The Dinosaur Man* at a distant Border's Bookstore and then, as I had been fantasizing for decades, picked up the phone and called me. We had not been in touch for years, and although I had married, raised children, started two careers, and divorced during that time, I had also begun to long for this love the way a compass yearns for north. Whenever I thought of love, I swung toward the place I'd last seen him and asked a hundred questions beginning with, "Are you alive?" I did not kid myself into thinking I would ever know the answers. Then on that evening when the phone rang, his voice with its heavy freight of memories hit me like a truck. My image of myself and the world—an image that had both protected and constrained me—cracked in a thousand places. I am sure I have never been more surprised in my life.

Were we twenty years old again? I wondered as I stood weak-kneed at the phone. Had nothing of importance happened since he and I were lovers? Or were we mature adults, with so much unshared experience that we could not possibly know who was on the other end of the line?

"Did you ever join the Peace Corps?" he asked. "Have you become a doctor? Where exactly do you live?"

"I don't believe this," I thought, as I began filling in the blanks and opening my own storehouse of questions. "But it's happening! It's happening at last!"

During most of that electric conversation, we exchanged memories as if the first order of business was to reestablish the relationship that had flourished briefly between two teenagers long ago. We called each other nicknames that no one had used for decades, we teased each other about traits we no longer possessed, told ancient, outdated jokes, and laughed until we choked. "You haven't changed a bit!" we said to each other, and indeed the longer we talked, the more the old feelings came racing back across the broad, dark fields of memory, and the more I felt that perhaps I had not been living a real life since leaving college after all. I wondered if my whole adult life had been a detour.

As our conversation continued, we moved gradually closer. It felt as if we stood shoulder to shoulder, then cheek to cheek with no hundreds of miles in between. I wondered if I would still recognize the smell of his hair and skin. I wondered what he was wearing, and realized with a disagreeable jolt that I had no idea how he dressed, what he did for a living, or even what he looked like now.

Eventually there was a slight pause, and the conversation shifted.

"Are you married?" he asked casually.

"No longer," I answered. I took a deep breath. "And what about yourself?"

"I'm married," he said, and my heart contracted.

"Why did you call?" I asked quickly, giving myself time to fit this serious information into our teasing and flirting. "Why now?"

"I have been thinking about you for several years," he said carefully, his voice dropping. "If you're ever out this way, I want..." He stumbled over the word, and my heart opened again in spite of itself. "I want...to take you to dinner."

For a moment, I considered answering his words instead of his voice, but no.

"Dinner!" I shouted. "Dinner! You fool!" And we both began laughing so hard I thought I might cry.

"Stay in touch," we told each other after trying to end the conversation a dozen times. "Stay in touch."

After hanging up, I wandered aimlessly through the house. Nothing was as it had been an hour before, and not a single thing could be taken for granted anymore. Yet even as the familiar became strange, the strange grew oddly familiar. When I went to bed and lay beneath my skylight gazing up at the Milky Way, I felt I had something in common with the stars. I couldn't say what it was, but it seemed that everything I had ever cared about was spinning together through that clear, black night.

After two more phone calls, my college love and I made plans to meet. Although in each of our conversations he guarded the privacy of his family with discretion, it had become clear that parts of his marriage had ended. Was he almost free? Was he looking? I couldn't tell what lay behind his decision to meet, but mine was simple. I had walked away years before and regretted it. I wasn't going to make the same mistake twice.

As the date of our reunion approached and my excitement rose, I became aware of how unlike a real decision my supposedly simple decision was. Behind our meeting lay a web of choices that I had made with so little thought that they couldn't be called choices at all. Yet now this web held me and seemed to be directing my life. I reflected on one of the threads in this web as I drove through Boston on my way to the airport. As I passed the mental hospital where the experiences related in my book *The Dinosaur Man* took place and thought back to the profoundly ill patients I'd cared for there, I found myself thanking them for inspiring me to write the book that prompted my lover to call; especially the Dinosaur Man himself, a schizophrenic who had mistaken me for the dinosaur who had been the love of his life 130 million years before. Was it possible that my willingness to stand in for his lost love, a seemingly inconsequential decision made years before, was responsible for the reunion I was moving toward now? Did life really unfold in such a bizarre way?

When my plane finally took off, I could not will it to fly fast enough. If standing in the aisle flapping my arms would have hastened our arrival by one minute, I would have done it. Finally we landed, and the moment I had pictured for years arrived. I was face to face with a middle-aged version of my college lover—a curiously familiar stranger. We stared at each other until, released by some invisible signal, we rushed into each other's arms. One of the oddest sensations I have ever had was recognizing the glorious, heart-pounding arrival of love but having only the vaguest idea of who I was in love with. "What is happening to me?" I asked myself helplessly. "And who is this person?"

To find out, the attentive stranger and I took off to a quiet resort and there spent several sleepless nights and days together. If the image of my old life hadn't shattered completely when he first called, it shattered during those long, ecstatic days. On our last morning together, I lay like a pile of diamonds in his arms, and from that perspective, life looked miraculously good. He was indeed the same exuberant, over-the-top, difficult, loyal, generous, lightning-fast man I had run away from in college, and from his point of view I was the same quintessentially desirable woman. End of detour. Beginning of life.

By the time we said our reluctant good-byes, I had begun making major rearrangements in my thinking. For one thing, I was inexpressibly grateful for the unambiguous arrival of love. There was no cell in my body that was not leaning toward this man, and I had never known this wholehearted willingness before—neither from myself nor from a man. How would I act and think as a woman swept away by love? In fact, who was I now? For another thing, love itself surprised me; it had not come to me as I had imagined it should. My perfectly matched partner, my complement, was not free to love me, and I wasn't sure how we were going to work this out. I thought of the play and movie *Same Time Next Year*, where two lovers meet once a year. Even one meeting a year would be enough for me, I thought. This was love at last, and we would find a way to preserve it.

Very quickly, however, the price of a secret love became apparent to both of us. We tried meeting, we tried parting, we tried calling, we tried silence, but nothing gave us the clear space and the clear conscience we needed to be our best, and less than best was unacceptable. Of course, I hoped he would start talking about divorce, yet I also admired his unwillingness to consider it seriously when he thought of the consequences. Perhaps we had gotten back together too late and with too many prior commitments. After a year, we agreed to say good-bye, and it was then that I discovered a whole new meaning for the word "shattered."

For one brilliantly illuminated year, I struggled through the nights and days as if my life depended on seeing every shadow, hearing every whisper, feeling every breath of air, and tasting all the flavors in water. I clung to the belief that somewhere in all that is usually overlooked lay a balm for my heart and an answer to my questions. And there were so many questions. Was our romance what people call the love of a lifetime? Or did smart people dismiss what, for me, was an earthshaking experience as a mistake? Would this love affair continue to influence my life? Had he already moved into my heart? Or could even this much joy and sorrow sink into some dark recess of memory and be lost?

I think it takes a lifetime to answer these questions, but over several years I untangled a few of them and arrived at a decision. Regardless of what others might call our romance, and even regardless of how my college love might label his memories of me, this man is the love of my life. We chose each other as college sophomores, kept each other alive in our hearts for years afterwards, and chose each other again. No one will replace him—or me—as the original first choice, as our spirit's best companion. This man is also the one who gave me the opportunity, at last, to lose myself in love and thus to dive into the deeper world that lies like an ocean beneath the archipelago of fact and reason. If he were to remember only one thing about me, I would want him to know that it was because of him that I finally gathered the courage to dive into life.

After this love had rearranged my thinking, I began asking my friends what the term "love of a lifetime" meant to them. At some point, I realized I wanted to write a book on the subject. I then interviewed two hundred people—family, colleagues, students, waitresses, bartenders, lifeguards, housekeepers, doctors, dog trainers, professors, and the staff and residents of a nursing home. I gave seminars on the subject at a local library and bookstore, and I asked a few of my patients as well. Although I am a practicing psychologist, my quest was more personal than professional. I wanted to know what the love of a lifetime did to people and how they made sense of it. Giving myself over to love so helplessly and willingly had transported me to a new place. I wanted to meet my neighbors.

I quickly found that unless people had a happy, straightforward story to tell (in other words, a story that fit the Hollywood model of the love of a lifetime), most were initially guarded. They gave me a simple definition of the love of a lifetime and left it at that. "It's your initiation into love." "It's the person you'd want to be with if you had only thirty minutes left to live." Others cited great lovers from movies, history, or stardom—*An Affair to Remember, Romeo and Juliet,* Humphrey Bogart and Lauren Bacall—and a few argued that the love of a lifetime was a publicity gimmick or that "in reality" there was always more than one. But eventually most of my respondents told me a story either about themselves or a relative. Especially from women, who are the keepers of family legends and the great weavers of tales, came intricate accounts of secret passions, treasured heartbreaks, and difficult journeys. Although men told stories too, the ones they were willing to share with me tended to be simpler: here was the woman who sustained or inspired me; here was the one who broke my heart long ago.

It became increasingly clear to me that what people call the love of their lives is not always a relationship that lasts. It is, instead, a passion that draws them into life and teaches them important, difficult lessons. It is, many told me, the true beginning of their adult life, the experience that stands between "before" and "after." Each lover emerges from this relationship, or this phase of a lifelong relationship, a different person—less the innocent observer of life and more the experienced participant. Although I could not yet say how these changes came about, it was already clear that the value of the love of a lifetime is not how long it lasts or even how sweet it is, but how thoroughly it shakes us up. It is the love that opens our eyes and sets us on a new path.

About a quarter of the love-of-a-lifetime stories I gathered were successful, long-lasting relationships—some marriages, some long-term affairs—that were obviously treasured by both lovers. These romances had started as grand passions and made the transition to quieter, more stable kinds of love.

Another quarter were important, but abbreviated romances—love affairs that were either prematurely ended by death or dislocation, or impossible loves that could not have been sustained under any circumstances. Not surprisingly, the very power that enables a love to shake a person up also makes it a difficult relationship to hold onto. Some of these shorter love affairs were treasured, but others rested uneasily in memory. Could they be as good as a love that lasted a lifetime?

The third quarter of the accounts I heard included a mixture of mistakes and mismatches, as if to make the point that great love is also compatible with all the mean and miserable things we hope affection will exclude. I heard of several people who committed suicide when they lost the love of their lives. One took an overdose on his estranged wife's birthday. As the historian of love Irving Singer observed, "Love is not always beneficial to those who experience it—anymore than life is." Or as Joan Crawford put it, "Love is a fire. But whether it's going to warm your hearth or burn down your house, you can never tell."

The remaining 25 percent of my respondents had no stories of love to tell, but rather anticipation or regret. They had not experienced a great love, either because they had not yet met the right person or because they had run away the instant they did.

As I listened to more and more stories, I realized that classifying them as "happy" or "sad" obscured a more basic criterion of success. For many people, what seemed to count more than contentment was how the romance changed their view of themselves and the world. I was amazed by how many lovers remained grateful for a love that had been studded with painful problems, but led nonetheless to personal transformation. This was the category that intrigued me most. How did some people learn so much from such a difficult love? Was there an active ingredient or an essential insight that could turn even the most confusing love affair into an opportunity?

~

At the heart of every love-of-a-lifetime story I heard, I found at least a moment of unexpected and uncontrollable passion that shocked the lovers into seeing the world with new eyes. In the grip of ecstasy, with their awareness heightened to an almost unbearable level, the extremes of joy and sorrow, personal power and vulnerability, and certainty and uncertainty became apparent. This, I learned later, was the first of three phases of a great love. Whether the romance began as a brief, dramatic affair that swept the lovers over Niagara Falls or a carefully crafted relationship that more resembled an ascent of Everest, each was an extreme experience that propelled the protagonists into a passionate engagement with everything—themselves, their beloved, the whole world. It was regarded as the greatest emotional gamble of their lives, and the lovers found themselves 100 percent involved in a drama they had no control over, one that could not be negotiated by reason and intelligence alone. To care so much and have so little control was a shocking combination, yet the resulting vulnerability seemed to release in them a vitality they hadn't known they possessed. Unless so terrified by the power of their own response that they ended the relationship immediately, they wanted more of this fully-alive feeling. In its grip, they seemed to resonate perfectly, not only to each other but also to the slow immensity of the natural world with all its greatness and danger. Passion didn't merely light up their lover and themselves, it lit up everything.

Some, excited and relieved, said, "My secret fear had been that nothing could move me." Others, "The world holds a beauty I hadn't seen before." Or, "Love pulled everything apart and rearranged me. It's a miracle I'm still standing." And from a few, "Never again!"

Passion revealed more to the lovers than exhilaration. It showed them a more potent version of themselves. It magnified their strengths and their weaknesses, too. They discovered just how fearful, angry, jealous, and shamefully irrational they could be when confronted by the helplessness they sometimes felt. After all, their happiness lay in someone else's hands. Could they live with the understanding that they couldn't control what counts most, and that this situation brought out the worst as well as the best in them? Could they tolerate seeing that under the influence of desire they were fully capable of thinking murderous thoughts, and at least contemplating, if not committing, mean, self-serving deeds? Having been stripped of the illusion that they were sweet people in control of their destinies, the lovers learned one final lesson from their ecstasy. Suddenly aware that every plant, animal, and person strove to be as happy and bursting with life as they were, they began to suspect that the whole blooming, buzzing dance of existence was more important than anything else, even than the individual dancers. Powerfully felt but only vaguely articulated, these revelations set in motion a number of changes.

"Passion by itself is nuthin'," a white-haired, tattooed man told me at the laundromat. "It's the gas without the Harley."

Which brings us to the second phase of the love of a lifetime—the work. In simplest terms, the question shifts at some point in every romance from "Can we stand the heat of this passion?" to "Can we put into practice what we learned in the grip of ecstasy?" In other words, regardless of where we go or with whom, can we hold onto the new perspective that passionate love first gave us and change our lives to reflect this new vision? Or will we decide that love is a misleading madness that has made us look foolish and taught us nothing? If this is our answer, then the passion has been futile.

I remember asking a young woman if she had experienced the love of a lifetime. Initially, I was confused by her answer. "Every relationship sweeps me away," she told me sincerely. "They all begin as the love of my life, and I think, 'Oh, this is the one. If I lose him, I'll die.'"

"And then?" I asked.

"And then it ends, and I start over. I guess I've had three or four loves of a lifetime."

What was going on here? I wondered. Her description of the passion she felt for each lover seemed real, but something was missing, which made these love affairs seem more like infatuations. They didn't satisfy, and she repeatedly dove back into another passionate engagement. Eventually, I realized that for a romance to be remembered as the love of a lifetime, the work that follows is as important as the ecstasy. The initial explosion must lead to a new way of feeling and doing, and this was missing from the young woman's love affairs. Each passion shook her, but she was not ready to live with the extremes—or the lessons—it revealed, and she went back to her old way of seeing things. Here was the difference between infatuation and the love of a lifetime. Both were genuine passions, but the first did not have a sufficient grip on the lovers' minds and souls, as well as bodies, to sweep them away. The affair either fizzled out or was renounced without anyone being significantly transformed. Undoubtedly, Cupid will return to the young woman, I thought, with a stronger bow and arrow. However, she will only find a series of infatuations until she can tolerate what passion reveals and can throw her whole self into the romance.

When passion does its job, it separates us from what has gone before. For some, the changes that love prompts come quickly, for others extremely slowly and with great effort. For some they arrive all at once, for others one after another. Reflecting on the work involved, people say:

- "You don't fit into your old roles anymore. You have to start a new life."
- "Even when you might lose, you play to the last pitch."
- "You give it everything you've got."
- "You respect the parts of life that can't be understood."
- "You learn to believe in yourself."

The list varies from lover to lover, but all the changes revolve around what he or she learned at the height of the storm. Although some of the people I talked to stayed with their partners while they learned to put love into practice, others experienced only the initial passion with someone that forever after they thought of as the love of their life. Then they put their demanding new understanding into effect with others. Either way, all had the chance to try to build a life that used love for fuel—and all were grateful.

Those who were even minimally successful at incorporating the lessons of ecstasy into their lives entered the third phase of the love of a lifetime and reaped its rewards. Now, rather than skating over the surface of life or only occasionally glimpsing the emotional and spiritual complexity of the world, the lovers became experienced participants and vital contributors. "Before, I lived in my mind, now I live in my heart as well," said one. "The mystery always reappears," said another, "and spring returns." "I'm up to any challenge, because I'm part of the world now, not separate from it." Whether in pairs or alone, old or young, rich or poor, the process of growing into the love of a lifetime leads lovers to a lifetime of love.

Clearly there are other ways to discover the underlying complexity of the world and the self, and to discover the power of active caring versus cautious observing. Several men told me that experience in combat started them on the same path. A priest said it was his discovery that Jesus loved him more than he loved Jesus. Men as well as women said it was the birth of a child. Nevertheless, I believe that romantic love is both the most common and the most fitting initiation into life at full force.

That, I learned, is what the love of a lifetime can do for some people—but not for all. A disturbing number of the men and women I spoke with admitted that they were still confused about the love they couldn't forget.

"I've thought about this guy every day for eighteen years," one woman told me, "but he was so awful to me that it's hard to believe he really loved me."

"I still have her picture," more than one man confided, "but I don't think she thinks of me. I'm daydreaming."

Can the husband who cheats be the love of a lifetime? Can the woman who walks out without a word be the one you hope to meet in Paradise? And what if *you* are the one who broke off The Romance? What if *you* couldn't or wouldn't let passion sweep you away or change your life? Many people with an unforgettable romance wonder if what they experienced was really love, or something else. Although there is never much solid information when it comes to love, and there is always the temptation to "fix up" the story with wishful thinking, an intelligent appraisal must be made of what many regard as an essential turning point in life. In private musings, in conversations with sympathetic friends, in hearing of similar romances, the story of the love of a lifetime must eventually be worked out.

Making sense of the love of a lifetime takes time and often seems to lead to a blank wall. A graduate student explained that each time she dated the love of her life, a curtain went up revealing a world of surprising vitality. Conversations took on more meaning. Mountains seemed higher. The sea bluer. However, neither she nor her lover could live for long in such an intense world, and after trying repeatedly over the course of four years, they went their separate ways. Now she thinks she has fallen in love with someone else—a wonderful man—but the curtain doesn't go up and the world doesn't shimmer. "What am I to do?" she asked. "Try to forget that beautiful world or try to go back? There must be a third choice, but I can't see it."

In a scenario that sounds different but is similar in some respects, one lover backs out, leaving him and his partner stranded on separate islands of doubt. "Was our love ever mutual?" at least one of them wonders. And, if not, "Can unrequited love be cherished as the love of a lifetime? Why should I treasure a beautiful love that didn't work?" As with the graduate student, the brokenhearted need to realize that their job is to say good-bye to the impossible partner without turning their back on the passion they experienced and that has begun to change them. *If* they loved with all their heart and were shaken by passion, there is a great deal worth holding onto after the final good-bye. There is sadness to acknowledge also. My guess is that the graduate student has not yet found a way to live with passion. Although she knows that the shimmering world is important and is wisely reluctant to leave it behind, she can't handle a great love right now. The third choice she is searching for is to cultivate as much passion as she can bear in her new life, not only with her new man, but in art and nature, with children, and in church if she's religious. It's not a perfect choice, as we will see, but no one can command passion to arrive on cue in manageable amounts. Every time we respond to love, we are trying to let ourselves be initiated by passion. Sometimes we don't get very far. But to say, simple-mindedly, that if love ends it must not have been real love, does not help us either to see what we have already done right or to draw closer to the experience of losing ourselves in love.

~

When it comes to making sense of our most passionate and complicated love, we receive little help. The popular culture tells us simplistically that the measure of love is its outcome. If the love is real, it will overcome all obstacles and last; if it's not real love, it will end. "It wasn't meant to be." This is not true as we can see with Elizabeth Taylor and Richard Burton, and their two divorces, or with Katharine Hepburn and the married Spencer Tracy, or even with Prince Charles and Camilla Parker Bowles and their lifelong, on-again—off-again relationship. We may not personally want a love as intense or demanding as any of these, but we would not dismiss them as being something other than extraordinary loves of a lifetime.

When we turn to experts on love, we find the same confusion between feeling good and being in love. We are told that the "healthy" romance that ought to be cherished as the love of a lifetime is a committed, well-behaved affair between people who are kind and sensible, and indeed this kind of love may foster lasting unions *after* a grand passion has opened our eyes. But "kind" and "sensible" isn't where love begins its most important work. A quiet love may teach, but it does not transform. Nor do "kind" and "sensible" haunt. You don't pick up the phone thirty years later to talk to the kid in high school who you considered your most reasonable classmate. But wildly exciting? Crazy for you? Ruthless and out of control? That's a different story.

So who do we turn to for an appreciation of the intense romances that introduce people of all ages to the full force and complexity of life? Who have worked to understand their complicated passions and found that leaving does not necessarily mean losing? Lovers themselves, of course. They've been through the experience, and they have worked for years to make sense of it. Admitting their own shortcomings as well as their partner's, they have tried not to delude themselves about their love affairs. But they have also realized that they will lose the vitality released by their great love if they renounce their heart's version of the story. To call the romance that still lives in their hearts a second-rate attraction because it doesn't fit the happily-ever-after mold is to break faith with themselves and pretend that nothing important happened when the curtain went up. Here, then, are complicated love stories that real people have learned to treasure. As passionate and beautiful as they are difficult, they continue to generate the wonder that keeps life vital.

The chapters that follow are divided into three sections. The first, "Invitation," is concerned with what it takes to get a great love affair off the ground. Does this fateful encounter begin with the right person or with a readiness for love? And what do lovers do when they first feel the undertow of this powerful attraction? Because all love-of-a-lifetime relationships are fueled by passion, we will look at what compulsive desire does to people—both the pain it inflicts and the opportunities it affords.

The second section, "Work," describes the changes that the love of a lifetime sets in motion. When passion reveals that such states as happiness and sadness or connection and separation invariably go together, lovers must find a way to live with these contradictions. Can we recognize that love has changed our view of everything and make a break with the past? Can we commit to those we love after realizing how painful the loss of love can or could be? Can we give everything even if this means taking our hands off the controls and driving blindly into the future? Trust the parts of the world that cannot be understood? Believe in our picture of the love of our lives—and of life itself—regardless of how others see it? These are the kinds of questions or lessons that the love of a lifetime presents.

Finally we come to "Rewards." In this section, lovers describe a strength that is called by many names. Some say that the love of a lifetime leads to a lifetime of love, or to a life that has meaning—to a rooted life, a connected life. No matter how it is expressed, the lessons taught by extreme love lead to what all of us hope for—a meaningful life that is stronger than death.

Part One

The Invitation

CHAPTER 1

A Dangerous Proposition

WE ARE SHAPED BY
WHAT WE SEIZE AND
WHAT WE REFUSE.
—John Tarrant,
The Light Within the Dark

Tucked into the crypt of a chapel in the pink marble town of Verona lies the tomb of Giulietta, the Italian girl who supposedly inspired Shakespeare's *Romeo and Juliet*. Every year thousands of visitors—most of them women—come to the chapel that sits behind an archway of vines to stare and dream. Do they really want the kind of love that burst on Giulietta? And if they received her invitation, would they jump for it or run? Shakespeare himself understood this kind of love to be a dangerous proposition: "too rash, too unadvised, too sudden;/Too like the lightning which does cease to be/Ere one can say it lightens." Yet in the Western world, this apparently ill-fated invitation sets in motion a story we consider one of the most perfect examples of the love of a lifetime.

Triggered by a look, a laugh, or a kiss planted on an unsuspecting cheek, something catches our heart's attention, and a love affair begins. Although every beginning is an invitation, how, lovers wonder, can they tell if it's *the* invitation to the love of a lifetime? Do certain characteristics distinguish this beginning from others? In this chapter, we will look at the various kinds of invitations people receive to start a relationship that will change their lives. We will watch men and women from their teens to their seventies as it dawns on them, after several hours or several decades, that they may be embarking upon an unpredictable and uncontrollable experiment. Not until their feet lose contact with the sea floor does the invitation really arrive, and it is at this moment that they will go for love, scramble back to shore, or flounder in the shallows. Lovers who know in their hearts they can't swim are remarkably sensitive to the first signs of the love of a lifetime. Most manage to get out of the water before they get hurt, even before they consciously recognize the distinctiveness of this love. But whatever reason people have for declining, if the invitation to a great love is not acknowledged and accepted, the experience never begins. The first step of the love of a lifetime is having the strength to accept your own powerful response to another person.

~

It is quite a shock to see someone you know fall headlong in love. There is a sudden loss of balance, some frantic teetering, and then a plummet into an exciting but unknown state of mind. It reminds me of the reckless boys who try to kayak across Woods Hole passage, a dangerous waterway in Massachusetts, when the wind is slamming the sea in one direction and the tide is sucking it in another. A forest of ten-foot waves rises on the back of a roaring torrent so strong that it pulls three-ton channel markers underwater and holds them there. Seeing a white-faced kayaker return from the Hole during flood tide is like seeing a person who has just fallen for the love of his life.

When my twenty-nine-year-old son—blond and athletic—bumped into an Australian girl at a pizza shop in the Alps two days before his ski vacation ended, he returned home a wreck. Pale and badly shaken, he stood stupidly in my living room trying to explain why I had to lend him six hundred dollars so he could fly back to Europe that evening. "No," I said, but I was smiling. The signs were unmistakable. He had received the invitation.

"I have a picture of her," he said, pulling an undeveloped roll of film from his pocket and holding it in his hand as if it were the Hope Diamond. "Mother, she's...I just can't explain it."

What I think my son couldn't explain was the emotional turmoil that made him suspect that this beautiful, spirited, funny-sounding Australian was the right woman for him. From his toes to the top of his head and from his mind to the center of his heart, he was being flooded by unfamiliar yet instantly recognizable signals that she was the one. As far as he was concerned, the invitation to fall for the love of his life was delivered when her blonde head popped over the booth where he sat eating pizza. But was it the arrival of the right girl or was it my son's readiness for love that finally opened the door? Lovers always say it's the person. Onlookers often think that the timing is just as important. As King Lear says, "Ripeness is all."

My son did not fly back to Europe that night, nor did he die on the spot. Instead, he rang up the most outrageous phone bills I had ever seen until summer finally rolled around and the Australian flew halfway around the world to visit. The two made a handsome couple. Both slim, athletic, and perpetually tan, they swam, sailed, cycled, and generally carried on. She was so in love that she was willing to leave family and job, finagle a working visa, and move to the United States.

"But I can't ask her to do that," my son anguished. "What if it doesn't work out? Of course I want her here, but maybe I'm being selfish. How can I ask her to give up so much?"

My son's girlfriend pointed out that the only question he had to answer was, "Do you want to see me this fall?" She'd figure out the rest. Still, he could not bring himself to let her take such an enormous gamble after so short a time. Just before her two-week vacation ended and she prepared to return down under, the two agreed that they would make a decision by September 30th. Either she'd move to the States or they would break off the relationship.

The weeks ticked by. The phone bills mounted. By the end of August, my son was taking long, solitary walks. By September, he was talking earnestly with friends. When I saw him on the twenty-eighth of the month, however, the tension was gone from his face and he was beaming from ear to ear.

"What's the deal?" I asked curiously.

"Roses," he whispered. "Lots and lots of roses."

Later I learned that on September 29th, the lovely Australian went to work as usual and did not notice that the receptionist in her office was purple with excitement. At ten o'clock, this same receptionist assembled everyone except my son's girlfriend in the company's conference room, where to their surprise they saw a bouquet of five dozen red, yellow, and pink roses tied with a blood-red ribbon from which hung a small pink envelope. Then, completely unaware of what was going on, The Right Girl was called into the conference room. A moment of confusion, a split second of surprise, and then three months of longing and uncertainty dissolved in tears. She wept as she tore open the envelope, and sobbed as she took out the card.

"I love you. I need you. Come to Boston!"

When the applause died down, she smiled through her tears and said simply, "How soon can I leave?"

This is the way love's invitation is supposed to come to us—directly, unambiguously, and dramatically. And this is how it is supposed to be answered—"Yes!" But how often does it actually happen this way? As Myrna Loy was fond of saying, "Looking for love with all its catastrophes is a less risky experience than finding it." In the stories that follow, we will see what happens to people who have a harder time with love's invitation. Some accept a riskier and more complicated proposition; others postpone their acceptance for decades; still others reject the invitation, cleanly or sloppily; and finally, some people never receive one.

~

One day, a dark-haired woman of perhaps fifty arrived at my door with a carpet cleaner slung over each shoulder like Coachman handbags. A strong, well-proportioned woman with a broad face and olive skin, she was dressed in a smart black pantsuit. She had come to shampoo my rugs. Introducing herself as Mrs. Tavares, she gazed past me and sized up my mismatched carpets. She was already at work. As she set down her machines, I said matter-of-factly, "I'm writing a book on what people mean by 'the love of a lifetime.' Are you familiar with the phrase?" Without looking up from the floor, she nodded and started to smile.

"I'm the right person to ask," she said. "The love of my life has prompted me to do everything with love." She bent gracefully to lift the edge of the nearest carpet and peer underneath. "Even cleaning."

Completing her inspection, she explained that she would shampoo both sides of my rugs at no extra cost. That's what she meant by doing things with love, and whether she was cooking, cleaning, or caring for her family, she paid attention and did a good job. "For me," she emphasized, tapping her chest. "I work with love for me."

Mrs. Tavares was a natural storyteller, and as foam bubbled over the first carpet, she went back in her mind to the triple-decker houses in the Portuguese neighborhood of Fall River, Massachusetts, and told me about her childhood. In those days, everyone worked in the knitting mills, she said, and the dream of every mother and father was to help their children escape. It soon became clear that young Lena had the best chance of escaping of anyone in the parish.

"I don't mean to boast," she said modestly, "but I had good grades, and I could finish high school. That was a first in my family. I won a beauty pageant, too." She smiled and gave a quick little waltz step behind the softly whirring machine. "Another first. It meant I would marry well."

Imagining the dignified Mrs. Tavares as an eighteen-year-old, I pictured a Mediterranean beauty—strong features, long black hair, curvy figure, and a sexy way of walking. She probably drove boys to commit sins against the church just by sauntering past them in a wispy summer dress.

"By the time I left parochial school," she continued, "I had the reputation of the perfect girl. My mother bragged that I was never any trouble, and my father said I would support them in their old age."

When the young Portuguese girl moved to Boston to attend nursing school, however, Lena was unprepared for the slick ways of city boys, and at the end of the first semester her grades were poor and, far worse, she was pregnant.

"I was so afraid of my father's reaction," she said earnestly, "that I hid my...my condition for six months, then married secretly. The child's father had just finished his freshman year in college. I was in for misery, and I knew it."

Sent to western Massachusetts to live with her new husband's parents while he completed his degree, Lena took in washing to support herself and her new baby. For her board, she cleaned her in-laws' house and taught herself to cook by making their Sunday dinners. So lonely that she routinely cried as she scrubbed clothes, she was not unhappy to learn she was pregnant again. The next year, another child was born. When her absentee husband finished college, the whole family moved to Fall River to open a restaurant. They bought a triple-decker house in Lena's old neighborhood. Lena, her husband, and the children established themselves on the top floor, and her in-laws lived beneath them. The taverna was on the ground floor.

"I was still lonely," she said, "but busy. I had some family around, and I did all the cooking at the restaurant. My husband handled the rest, except...the one thing I insisted on was that we hire waiters, not waitresses. He had the eye, my husband, and he would look every woman up and down. I wasn't going cook in that kitchen and watch him undress each waitress as she took a plate from my hand. No."

One day when Lena's children came home after school and threw themselves into chairs in the restaurant's kitchen, where they could watch her chop vegetables while doing their homework, she overheard a new waiter talking with them. He was a lean, wiry man with black hair and dark eyes. He was quick, Lena noticed. He looked like an acrobat.

"I was thirty-one years old at the time," she recalled, "young, hair down to my waist, ready for life, and starving. I wasn't sure for what, but starving. Gradually, I realized that this man, this acrobat, was really listening to my kids. He was paying attention to what they said. Looking them in the eye. And suddenly I wanted that." She stopped pushing the carpet cleaner and straightened to her full height. "It was all I could do not to throw myself between this man and my children. 'Me!' I wanted to shout. 'Pay attention like that to me.' By the time I finished the onions, I was weak in the knees, and after I'd done ten pounds of julienne strips, I was madly in love. Attention. I wanted that man's attention more than I'd wanted anything in my life."

Love issued no formal "invitation" as far as Lena was concerned, and there was no period of wondering if this man was the right one. He was.

The interest she could hear in his voice, the directness of his dark gaze, the way he'd tilt his head when she spoke to him—his attributes all plowed into Lena like arrows into St. Sebastian.

"Within a month we were having an affair, which we knew—I knew—we couldn't hide for long." She smiled ruefully. "You can't hide that kind of love. It comes out your pores, your eyes, the ends of your hair. My particular problem was clothes. If you're lonely, clothes hang on you like a rack, but in love..." She shrugged elaborately. "When I stood in the kitchen in a cotton-knit dress, that fabric would start to slide over my skin like my lover's hand. I couldn't stop it. It just slipped and slid every time I moved, and when that happens you light up. You look like you're hearing dance music."

Apparently, the glowing, swaying Lena poured so much sexual energy into chopping her vegetables that green and yellow and carrot-colored jewels came flying out from under her fingers. Her tomato sauce shimmered like red silk, her specials sold out every night, and a swelling river of compliments flowed back into the kitchen from the diners.

"What's goin' on with you?" her husband barked. "Look at me!"

But Lena was convinced that anyone who looked in her eyes could see she was having an affair. She looked at no one. Her husband became openly suspicious, and even the waiter began to feel that their love was too dangerous.

"No," Lena said to her lover, "you shot the arrow. We're not turning back. I'm not impulsive," she insisted, "but once I make up my mind..."

"It was a dangerous situation," she admitted with a shudder, remembering nights in the restaurant when her husband took the cash upstairs and left her to hose down the kitchen floor and lock the doors. With the whole house quiet, it was at this late hour that she could sometimes manage ten minutes alone with her lover, who would sneak in the back door and silently clamp her to his chest with his strong arms. But her husband was right over their heads, a stairway away. They kissed noiselessly. They didn't dare speak, not even in a whisper.

In the middle of winter, Lena overheard her husband making plans to stuff her into the trunk of his car, transport her to New Hampshire, and put her in a mental institution. Someone had told him that his wife must be having a nervous breakdown and needed shock treatments. Within a matter of hours, she sent her two children to her sister's home, and at midnight on that icy, starlit night, she lowered herself and one suitcase out a third-floor window on a knotted rope. She and her lover picked up the kids in a car with a broken heater and were several states away before the sun rose.

"I left everything but my children for the love of my life," she said proudly. "My home, my job, my friends. Everyone thought it was so out of character for me, but it wasn't. It was the first thing I'd ever done that was truly *in* character. Me, that's what I mean by the love of a lifetime."

For several years, Lena suffered as news came back from her family that they disapproved of her irresponsible flight; they believed she was mentally unbalanced. Her children were upset about losing contact with their father, grandparents, aunts, uncles, and cousins. "But they liked having a happy mother," she added quickly.

As soon as she was officially divorced and remarried, the family moved back to Massachusetts and were gradually reconciled with her relatives. A year later, she had a son by her second husband. Always a hard worker, she began running a cleaning service and working for her parish. It was not an easy life financially, but it was, and still is, the right one for her.

"I'm a lucky woman," she said, as a thick layer of foam bubbled out over the last carpet. "At fifty, I'm more alive than I was at twenty. That's what love did for me. It said, 'What are you willing to jump out the window for?' It got me to pay attention and gave me the life I was meant to have."

Mrs. Tavares accepted love's invitation with a fierceness that matched her own passion for life, and I wonder if it is not always so—if we don't say "yes" or "no" to love in much the same way we answer the other questions that life presents. Once the young Lena had outgrown her childhood role of cautious obedience, she became something of a gambler. She took a gamble when she went away to school, gambled when she had sex before marriage, and gambled when, without training, she started cooking for a restaurant. Her greatest gamble by far was stealing off in the night with the love of her life. Risking her children's future, her reputation, perhaps even her life to be with the man who listened, she said "yes" repeatedly in spite of doubts and complications. As a result, she found herself learning the lessons that a great love can teach. After many years, she grew into a way of living that takes everything she's got and fits what she thinks of as her true character. Big risk, big gain. It is always so.

The invitation to fall for the love of a lifetime asks us to take the greatest emotional gamble of our lives. The enormity of the risk and the apprehension that accompanies it distinguish this invitation from ones where we know instinctively that much less is at stake. On the surface, this invitation may "merely" demand we leave our homeland and family, risk our reputation, or jettison our career. On a deeper level, it asks us to risk our very identity. Do we see our destiny unfolding in this love? Specifically, are we willing to be the product of this adventure no matter how long it lasts and how it turns out? No wonder the invitation to fall for the love of a lifetime is accompanied by moments of fear. "I'm not going to come out of this relationship in one piece," we say to ourselves, and with good reason. "I'll never be the same."

~

Nancy said, "Yes," to the love of her life when she was nearly seventy, and her love illustrates why this invitation feels different from others. Unlike even the most violent physical attraction, the charming flirtation, or the sensible pairing, this invitation involves all of us.

When I first met Nancy in her airy, book-lined home, she was eighty-four years old. Short, gray-haired, and always on the verge of smiling, she led me up a flight of stairs lined with photographs of sailboats, dogs, and authors. Upstairs, her living room looked out over a sedgy cove, and she quickly pointed out her trim day sailor riding quietly at its moorings.

"Takes skill to sail these waters," she stated, and I knew she was referring to Cape Cod's hidden rocks and rushing tidal currents. "I wasn't really comfortable until I was in my fifties. That's me on the *Quissett*," she continued, pointing to a silver-framed photograph that showed a younger, but equally engaging woman in short shorts. Smiling slyly under a jaunty sailing cap, she was seated on the rail near the stern of her sloop operating the tiller with one bare foot. A little vixen, I thought to myself.

As a young woman, Nancy admitted, she had been quite a flirt. She loved the intricate rituals of courtship—the suggestive looks, the double meanings, the first dates—and she assumed that when the right man came along, she would fall in love with ease. To her surprise, this did not happen. Men lined up at her door, but she was never satisfied with the ones who fell for her. It was not until she was almost forty that she met her future husband. A worldly man, he offered Nancy what she called "superior companionship." The two spent a satisfying twenty-seven years together running a bookstore and traveling. Nancy was the buyer, and over the years she cultivated a taste for British and American fiction. Book clubs adopted her choices, and for years she wrote a weekly article on books for a local paper.

Everyone who met Nancy and her husband at the bookstore or elsewhere remarked on how genuinely courteous they were to each other. They were widely admired as a pair. Then Nancy's husband died. She missed him terribly, and at the urging of a friend, resumed her travels to take her mind off her loss. On the first trip after her husband's death, she and another gray-haired woman packed up their favorite Ann Taylor pantsuits and flew to Bermuda. They stayed with a retired British writer and his wife in a house surrounded by gardens that tumbled down a steep hill to a pink-shell beach. Although their hosts were "to the manner born," Nancy recalled, their home was tasteful rather than lavish. The writer had taken up the cultivation of roses in his later years, and Nancy could still picture his lean, elegant form bending over, eyes closed, to inhale the fragrance of an enormous bloom. He often wore a soft, navy-blue blazer, she remembered, and he carried a small pair of silver garden clippers instead of a handkerchief.

"I met the love of my life among those roses," Nancy stated. "My host and I were attracted to each other immediately, you see, and we spent a great deal of time in conversation. We talked of books and plays and music—the kind of talk I was used to. He was a married man, and I recall that his wife bustled about importantly with one of those little basket pocketbooks. She was chic, a beautifully cared-for woman—fingernails like sea shells—but she didn't have much to say about books.

She wasn't a thinker like her husband. But he, *he* had a mind that ran like a racehorse. He was a beauty.

"It is such a thrill," she continued eagerly, "to recognize your own passions in another person. It's like wandering through the Sahara Desert and suddenly coming upon a person who speaks your language and comes from your hometown. It's a reunion of spirits."

She paused to look out over the cove where sailboats shimmered in the summer sun. "There are few pleasures in this world as utterly delicious as finally meeting your match."

The only time that Nancy and her host were alone was the last evening when they went strolling through the gardens. Big, cabbage-like roses were in full bloom, she remembered, and the perfume seemed to drift out to sea in ribbons. One moment she would smell only the salt air, but by moving even a few inches the smell of roses would surround her. Nancy declined to say exactly what happened in the garden except that the writer with a mind like a racehorse took her in his arms and held her... and held her. These two old beauties with their matched passion for ideas stood silently in the garden and just held on. Eventually, he told her when to expect his letters and a visit.

Nancy and her friend flew back the following day, and it was only when she was alone in her own house that she began to feel all the doors and windows in her body flying open in a way they had never done before.

"It was a new sensation for me," she said carefully. "I didn't even know these feelings existed. Yet every new opening felt like a 'yes.' 'Yes, you can come in, and yes, I will come to you.' I felt an overwhelming willingness. Even when only one of the promised letters arrived...followed by silence, I remained willing to do or feel or think anything. I had finally said yes to a truly passionate love, a whole love."

Several months later, as Nancy was debating whether or not to send a letter of her own, her traveling companion called with the news of their host's death. He had collapsed suddenly not long after their departure.

"I wish he had known how much our meeting meant to me," she said sadly. "That's my only regret. I wish I could have told him what a difference our meeting made.

"I never wanted romance after that," she continued, "because I don't believe I could ever be as willing with anyone who didn't fit as perfectly. Besides, I have the experience inside me, complete." She thought for a moment. "No, I think the experience gave *me* a sense of being complete."

When Nancy embraced love, she disrupted everyone's picture of her earlier life, including her own. Her traveling companion insisted that she could not possibly be in love, and other friends said the same. It was a reaction to grief. It was a fantasy, not a love affair at all. She was already so securely paired in everyone's mind with her late husband that there was no room for another love. Her twenty-seven-year union was supposed to be the love of her life—period. Nancy found herself quietly but persistently disagreeing as she went about the business of rearranging her memories to accommodate this unexpected experience. She had to admit that what she'd shared with her husband was closer to friendship and farther from love than she had originally imagined. Further, she had to admit that the charming, flirtatious self she'd been proud of as a young woman had really been a person afraid of finding love. But with the writer, she finally met her match. Their passions were similar; their minds worked the same way; they were equally determined. Much more than a pair of lonely bodies in need of comfort was involved.

Did she wish she'd met the love of her life sooner or been ready to accept love's invitation in her twenties?

"He was the cherry on top that was saved for last," she said with a charming smile, "but no, I don't regret not having a steady diet of cherries."

~

Nancy said yes when she was ready and so did many others, including a grandmother who found and married the love of her life at sixty-four and a man who made his first and, he is sure, only trip to the altar when he was fifty-two. "All's well that ends well," these contented lovers seemed to say. While the love of a lifetime gave Lena Tavares, and others who jumped for love at the beginning of their lives, the right future, these much older lovers found that a great love made sense of their past.

Stories of delayed love were more common than I expected. I met lovers who, before finding a great love, annoyed their dates by saying, "I don't think I'm ready for a real relationship yet," and others who put the romance on hold while they went back to school or took a job thousands of miles away. Still others married someone who, like Nancy's husband, provided companionship but did not start a forest fire. Many of these individuals subconsciously sensed that with the stakes so high and their resources low, they did not have the skills to handle love's invitation. They weren't ready for a great love. Most of us are reluctant to admit this, even to ourselves, because it looks like failure. Regardless of how well or poorly our childhood has prepared us, society tells us that we are all supposed to be ready for love by the time we reach eighteen, the official age of adulthood. Some are, but many aren't. There is a traditional Persian story that describes one of the paths taken by those who need more time.

A long time ago there lived a young man bursting with energy and ambition. Morning and night he rode his father's horses through the pale green valleys that surrounded his mountain home. He hunted game. He practiced calligraphy. He played the sitar. One day as he went galloping through the wild hills, he spotted a cave. Dismounting, he cautiously went inside, and deep in the cave, he saw a dim light. When his eyes grew accustomed to the dark, he moved farther into the cave until he saw that the light came from a luminous pearl the size of a melon. It was beautiful beyond description, and on the spot he was struck by a wild desire to possess it. However, the pearl seemed set in a tangle of scaly ropes, and when he bent down to pick it up, he realized that the gem was resting in the outstretched claw of a sleeping dragon. Straightening immediately, the young man backed out of the cave, jumped on his horse, and went clattering off.

For days he was in the foulest mood imaginable. Restless and irritable, he drove himself crazy with longing. Why couldn't he have what he most wanted in the world? Should he return to the cave, he wondered? He pictured the dragon in his mind. That was certain death. Eventually, the young man put the pearl out of his mind. The demands of daily life reclaimed him, and within a year he was married. Then for the next thirty years, he generally did his best to be a good husband and father. He did not torment himself very often with thoughts of the pearl.

When his children were grown, however, and he was getting on in years, the man found himself thinking a great deal about the beautiful pearl, and decided to satisfy his soul by looking at it one more time. Again he rode through the wild hills, up and down the valleys, and at last he spotted the cave. With cautious anticipation he entered, and very quietly inched his way forward. It took much longer for his eyes to get used to the dark this time, but finally he saw a dim glow. There was the pearl, fully as beautiful as it had been thirty years before, and what a deep sense of satisfaction he felt to see it again. But something had changed. Abruptly he realized that the dragon guarding the pearl had shrunk to a creature the size of a cat. Filled with unexpected joy, the man bent down and took his beloved pearl.

For young, unprepared lovers, a delayed invitation will far more often arrive after they have gained enough confidence in other areas of life to face the dangerous aspects of love. Most typically, this invitation will arrive when they are about fifty years old, but it can come anytime. It may be offered by a person that the would-be-lover has already tried to love, but more often it comes from somebody new.

~

Unfortunately, "yes," and "later, please," are not the only two responses given to *the* invitation. A number of people told me that they met their great love, recognized the invitation, and, for reasons they could not fathom, took half a leap into the air. There are more of these sadly botched love-of-a-lifetime stories locked away in people's hearts than I had imagined, and for me they cast a particularly poignant spell.

A young woman told me about her grandmother, who, she said, had been in love only two times in her long life. "But not because she was cautious or serious," my informant insisted. "She was a big, strong woman with blond braids across her head and crinkled eyes that were always smiling. Grandma lived to laugh."

The grandmother had been happily married for many years to a man who had a cherished childhood friend, a schoolmate who had entered a religious order and become a monk. Many stories of the husband's early years included this fine friend, and his wife came to feel a certain affection for the man. Eventually the husband died, and his widow, now about sixty, wrote to Father B. and told him of his friend's death. By return mail came an appreciative reply and several wonderful stories of the boys' early adventures. The widow wrote back expressing her delight and asking for more. Soon, she and the monk were corresponding—perhaps fitfully at first, but eventually with regularity. For ten years, they wrote back and forth.

In the not-too-distant past, letter writing between members of the opposite sex was considered a natural prelude to intimacy, and to some degree this was the case between these two literary friends. The grandmother savored her private hour every evening when she would continue her written conversations with Father B., and she often laughed out loud as she described the events of her happy world.

Father B. clearly cherished the relationship, too. Perhaps carrying each newly received letter with him throughout the day until he could retreat into the monastery's garden or a corner of the library, he grew to anticipate the arrival of each letter. By reading and rereading the bold and by-now-familiar handwriting, and in crafting thoughtful replies, over the years these two contented souls grew to care for each other in an unusual way. Only their bodies were strangers.

Ten years into this correspondence, Father B. was selected to receive a high honor. There would be a rare public celebration at the monastery, and Father B., as recipient of the honor, would give an address. In one of his next letters, he asked the grandmother if she would attend with her granddaughter. She agreed, and with considerable anticipation, the seventy-year-old woman and the twelve-year-old set off on a two-day drive to meet the wonderful Father B. at last.

The granddaughter remembers the excitement of arriving at the monastery. Driving slowly through heavy stone gates and stopping in a silent courtyard, her grandmother explained to her that the monks in this order did not speak unless absolutely necessary. Soon she could see that this was true. Silent shapes in long black robes floated along the spring green paths, their heads bowed. One of these shapes met them at the front door. It was the first monk the granddaughter had ever seen, and she bent her head to peer into the shadows of his hood. There she saw a long face with sad eyes that reminded her of Obi-Wan Kenobi in *Star Wars*. The solemn figure bent near the grandmother and softly whispered in her ear. Father B. would meet them presently, he breathed. "Why, thank you," replied the grandmother and favored the monk with one of her wonderful smiles. The monk gestured quickly to a large sitting room on the ground floor and was gone. At dinnertime, the grandmother and granddaughter were still waiting. The same monk ushered them into the refectory and again whispered that Father B. would soon arrive. He did not.

The next morning, the entire community gathered in the church to honor the monk, and it was only when a single figure rose from the ranks of the brothers that the widow finally realized that Father B. was the monk who had greeted them and whispered in her ear. Seeming smaller now, he stood and gave his speech in a voice that seemed both sad and old. Immediately after the ceremony, he retreated into some holy corner of the monastery where visitors could not go.

What happened? Was Father B. hit so hard by love's invitation that he feared he would leave his calling? It is hard to imagine another response that would render him unable to tolerate the two or three conversations that the grandmother expected to have with him. Apparently, the monk was so shaken by the vision of a new life filled with love and laughter that he ran back to his old one. The correspondence ended shortly after the meeting, and so did the friendship. What did it feel like for Father B. to live out his quiet life with an alternative running through his imagination? Did he sit in the refectory imagining the grandmother laughing or singing as she moved about her kitchen? Did he picture her alone, then imagine the two of them deep in happy conversation? Whatever form the haunting took, it seems probable that Father B. lived with the memory of an unanswered invitation for a long time. The granddaughter was more concerned with her grandmother. What did she feel when she lost her intimate correspondent in such a mysterious way?

Although we have no way of knowing what it felt like for either one of them to carry an unanswered invitation in their pocket, the aborted love affair of Bob Walsh shows what is likely to happen.

A family man and the owner of a wire company in Toronto, gruff, heavyset Bob Walsh could not understand how a lost love of a lifetime could hover benignly in the mind as a "lovely memory" or how it could serve as an inspiration. Ushering me into his office, he gestured to a chair, then dropped heavily into an old swivel chair that sat behind his desk. I knew he had been a hockey player in high school and college, and he looked it. Dressed in a black, collarless knit shirt with sleeves pushed halfway up his powerful forearms, I guessed he still did a fair amount of physical labor—and desk work. A pair of red-framed reading glasses was perched jauntily on his balding head.

"If you're a realist," he told me somewhat wearily, having gone over this material in his mind many times before, "meaning if you're smart enough to know the facts and strong enough to face them, then you gotta admit that losing the love of your life is a tragedy. That's what the phrase means after all, it's the one woman in the world who releases every ounce of the love you have inside you. If you lose her..." He paused and pursed his lips. "You lose."

He resettled himself awkwardly in his squeaky chair as if to show me that losing his love had made it impossible for him to get comfortable.

"And I lost more than a girl," he continued. "I lost a whole family."

In his youth, in winters past, Bob and his three brothers skated every minute they weren't in school. They skated along a broad canal before classes began, they skated at recess on a flooded parking lot, and they skated long after dark on any surface that was even dimly lit and covered with ice. All four of the powerful Walsh boys made their mark in hockey. On weekends, when families skated after church on the waterway that winds through the city, Bob's family and Tess's always met at a certain bridge right after mass. When Bob was thirteen, he started bumping Tess as she skated along the canal, and by fourteen he made sure she was on the end of the line of skaters when they "snapped the whip," so he could watch her fly off her feet and go sliding at ninety miles an hour across the ice. Two years later, he was skating hand in hand with her.

"We made a comical pair," he recalled, his face relaxing. "I weighed almost two hundred pounds, and she was a ninety-pound string bean with a mop of curly red hair. I used to kid her that she weighed less than the family dog."

Bob Walsh looked dreamily out his office window. "We had bonfires along the canal in those days, and when we'd come off the ice at night, I'd just tuck Tess under one arm and carry her into the shadows. That's where we practiced kissing—and we got good." He smiled in spite of himself.

There was never a time when "Bobby 'n Tess," as they were called then, formally became a couple, because they had always been part of each other's lives. He was as welcome in her house as she was in his, and they simply relaxed further and further into the rhythm of each other's routine without giving it a thought. Even when they left for separate universities, they got cookies from two mothers, came home together over vacations, and spent summers being counselors at neighboring camps.

"I guess I was in love with her family as well as with Tess," Bob said. "I especially liked her father, and I remember his characteristic way of saying, 'It sure is!' I'd ask if it was OK if Tess and I went skating or walked to church together. 'It sure is!' he'd boom. I began saying it too, and I still find myself saying it occasionally when I'm in a rare good mood. Everyone in her family expected yes, and once you began saying yes…well, it became a habit. I liked who people became in her house."

Yet in spite of all these good things, the couple broke up in their last year of university. "I can't remember why," Bob said in a puzzled voice. "I have thought and thought, but I can't recall what we broke up over. I play our lives back, and it's like there's a piece of film missing. It just breaks. I'm pretty sure it was my fault. At least it was my fault that I didn't see the importance of doing whatever it took to…But she didn't ask me to do or give up anything. We just broke up."

Bob sighed and ran a big hand over the back of his neck.

"We just broke up," he repeated with a shrug, and I was reminded of the Persian story of the boy who leaves the pearl. Bob Walsh may have sensed the dangers of love before seeing them clearly and run without ever knowing why.

"A year later I learned that Tess had moved to the States," he continued. "I wasn't surprised or even…just irritated, I think. Annoyed in a restless kind of way."

"How did she take the breakup?" I asked.

The big man almost blushed. "I don't know. Several years later, I got married," he continued quickly. "The night before…this is hard to say…the night before I was sitting in Charlie's room, that's my younger brother, when Mom called down the hall that the phone was for me. It was Tess. 'Hey Bobby, congratulations,' all that stuff, chattering away. 'Why didn't you invite me, good luck, where are you two going'…On and on, laughing, and believe it or not that's when it hit me, like…like the first time I got my nose broken in hockey. I thought, What's happening? How did we get, you know, on different tracks? How did I *do* this?

"'Bobby? You there? Hey, why didn't you invite me?' I only remember feeling hit in the face, but Charlie told me that I said, 'If you come to the wedding, there won't be one.'" He let out a long breath. "She didn't come. I got married, and later she did, too. But I started hurting on the night before my wedding day.

"My mother died five years ago February and everybody in Toronto came to the funeral. I knew Tess's family would be there, but I hadn't thought about seeing Tess herself." He sighed again. "When I was told she was coming to the wake as well as the funeral, I became extremely upset—raising my voice, pacing, the whole scene. My wife tried to calm me down. My brothers thought I was a jerk. I remember Charlie yelling, 'She's not the enemy!' but that's exactly what she was—the evidence of my stupidity, the prize I lost."

Bob Walsh took a deep breath. "Tess had aged well," he said carefully. "She had filled out some, but the energy, the curly, sorta red-gold hair, the happy chatter, they were all just like before. When I spotted her, I felt my knees go.

"Actually, I couldn't bear to look at her. It was too painful. I was stripped by my mother's death. I'd never lost anyone before—tapped like a Sugar Maple. Whatever I felt poured right out of me and I couldn't stop it. If I had looked at Tess for more than two seconds, I would have scooped her up in my arms and bawled." He paused, perhaps imagining what it would feel like to hold her again in his arms. "I would not have let go. They'd have to call in the Jaws of Life."

"Does your family understand how you feel?" I asked.

"Of course not. My sisters wanted Tess to *talk* to me for God's sake, as if that's what I needed. They still wonder why I haven't gotten over her because—and they're right about this—she has certainly gotten over whatever she felt for me.

"But how in hell do you get *over* a love of a lifetime?" he asked, his voice rising. "A whole life missed out on. How can anyone say...how can *she* say that she has 'lovely memories'? I have pain."

"Perhaps she remembers how wonderful it was to love you," I suggested. "You were her first love, after all, and she may be glad she had the experience—glad she said yes and gave it everything she had. That's a wonderful experience to look back on."

Bob Walsh rocked back in his chair as if slapped. For a full minute he said nothing. "You think *she* remembers loving," he said slowly, "and *I* remember getting cold feet?"

In a novel by Haruki Murakami, two childhood sweethearts part and years later discover that they have lost touch with the painful beginning of life—the plunging in all the way that Bob Walsh never quite dared to do. In the novel, the man discovers to his surprise that what he misses most is neither the innocence nor the sensual promise of the early relationship, but the misery he experienced when he was "tossed about by some raging, savage force, in the midst of which lay something absolutely crucial."

Why this appetite for trouble? Why does a successful, middle-aged businessman like Bob Walsh, who remembers the innocence and the kisses of his first love, feel robbed by having missed out on the heart-breaking parts of love—the parts his girlfriend endured?

"What have you missed?" I asked. "Besides Tess, I mean."

"The chance to jump in and give it everything I had," he said, looking me straight in the eye. "The chance to become me."

~

How often I heard this. A friend returned from a playground where she had been chatting with another mother who had said no to the love of her life and was now stuck in an unsatisfying marriage. "All she could talk about was how she'd missed her chance…over and over. It was pitiful." No storm for her, nothing crucial. No dropping out of a window on a rope on a bitter night, dangling with a single suitcase above the frozen ground. No crashing, no burning, and no finding one's unique character, place, and purpose in the world. No wonder Father B., Bob Walsh, and others are haunted by regrets. They never accepted the invitation and started the process that in hindsight seemed like the path they were meant to travel.

~

Finally, we come to people who have not even glimpsed an invitation. Among the fifty or so men and women I talked with who had not experienced a love of a lifetime, many told me they had not yet met the right person. Some didn't want to.

A man who runs an experimental farm where he raises goats and llamas said he was relieved he had not been invited to fall for the love of a lifetime because, "I'm not a people person. I'm not comfortable getting that close to anyone." Although he had married and remained married for twenty-five years until his wife died, he did not describe their relationship as love. It was respectful and intellectually stimulating. "I'm lucky," he concluded, "I didn't get in over my head." Today he tends his animals, is lulled to sleep each night by their soft sounds and warm smell, and spends one long weekend a month with a woman who lives fifty miles away. "It's a perfect arrangement."

Of course, other people can't wait for love's arrival. Every party, every night on the town may be the beginning of the one adventure they really want. "What about us people who haven't found the love of a lifetime yet?" challenged a forty-year-old friend of mine. "Am I supposed to feel deficient or just sorry for myself? I mean, good Lord, when I'm lying on my deathbed I want to remember the time I went for it, hit the wall, surrendered. It makes me sad to think I might not have that experience—whatever 'that' experience is."

As she spoke, I found myself thinking back to a conversation I'd just had with a man who had won and then painfully lost his great love in his twenties. They had been so in love, he told me sweetly, so confident, so beautiful together. He was a handsome Finn, and it was easy for me to picture him as part of a tall, stunning couple. Yet if I had not had a great love of my own, I don't think a painful longing would have squeezed my heart as he spoke. "You lucky man," I thought. "You didn't waste time getting to what counts. I wish I'd been ready in my twenties." Knowing exactly what he was talking about made me miss the experience grievously.

Could my friend miss what she hadn't had?

"When I read a particularly tender love story," she was saying, "I think I catch glimpses of what love could be, and it makes me so lonely. Music too, and sometimes a movie. But can I do anything about it?"

"I think you can," I answered, reminding myself again that all of us get glimpses of everything—the best life has to offer and the worst.

"You can do several useful things to get ready for the love of a lifetime, but they aren't very exciting."

I explained that although people have no control over love and cannot will the perfect person to appear, they can influence the timing of the event by getting ready for love. In other words, they can become acquainted with, and tolerant of, the parts of themselves and the world that love will someday force them to confront. For example, do they even recognize their own strong negative feelings? Or do they channel their anger into a migraine so fast they never realize they're in a rage? Do they let music, a love story, or a rippling willow tree take them away from the world of getting and spending for more than two seconds? Or is the newest new thing more important than the life of the heart? If they don't bother to learn the tough but beautiful language of love, how will they manage when an arrow pins them to the office wall?

Another thing you can do, I told my pal, is to become more confident by getting good at whatever you do. In my years of psychotherapy, I have come to believe that the strength that comes from doing something well is one of the best preparations for love.

Finally, it's good to pay attention to the often subtle signals that love sends. Although we all know someone who returned from a first date and announced that this was the person he or she was going to marry, most invitations are far less clear and can, unhappily, be missed or dismissed. It took one woman thirty years to recognize a particular man as the love of her life. One man I spoke with didn't know he'd been invited until the woman who was trying to love him died. From a would-be lover's point of view, the main question is, "Is this *the* person for me?" But I would say the question of readiness is equally important.

"Will I ever be ready?" a never-married woman asked. "I'm hoping love is like cooking," she continued. "If you learn to cook really well, people find you."

The invitation to love often seems misleading and difficult to evaluate. Frequently, it seems poorly timed, although I suspect that it is perfectly timed, and it is mysterious, pairing just these two people together in an unforgettable way. Before it arrives, we wonder if we will recognize it, and we guess what it will feel like. Afterwards, we laugh at ourselves because it is so unmistakable. No one I spoke to had forgotten meeting the love of their life, although quite often the two lovers did not agree on when and where the fateful meeting took place.

If all I had to go on was my sample of love's invitations—not the whole story, not lovers' later reflections—I would have to conclude that what we sometimes call the god of love is a trickster. He doesn't come how or when he is expected, and he doesn't even tell the two unsuspecting mortals the point of this most delightful tribulation—doesn't tell them that the love of a lifetime is not only or even primarily about "happily ever after," but about risking their present direction and identity to find a new way of living. They are being invited to jump into a relationship with everything they have and live at full strength. The cost of saying no, or of delaying too long, is to be trapped in a flirtation with life that doesn't go very deep.

When women go to pay their respects to Giulietta in the river-ringed town of Verona, they descend silently into the small underground crypt at the center of which is a crumbling sarcophagus. There are two surprises. The first is that the tomb is empty. The old stone tub holds only a nosegay of herbs—rosemary, thyme, lavender—twisted together and faintly fragrant. Whatever remains of Giulietta is now somewhere else. The second surprise is that in one of the shallow niches in the wall of the crypt there is a mailbox surrounded by notepads and stubby pencils. Scraps of paper like white petals spill from the mailbox onto the stone floor. We know exactly what to do, and as fragmented memories of the unforgettable invitation rush into our minds, we know exactly what we want to say.

"*Cara Giulietta,*" "*Ma chère Juliette,*" "Dear Juliet..." we begin, "I will never forget the first moment when I *knew*. We met when I was..."

CHAPTER 2

Passion

Possibly the most haunting love story in Western literature concerns the adulterous passion of Launcelot and Guinevere. Before this story was told, the central question asked of a romance was "Is the union legitimate?" After Launcelot and Guinevere, the central question became—and remains—"Do they love each other?" So shocking was the idea that passion might be more important than society's rules or the mind's reason, and that passionate, adulterous lovers might therefore be the heroes rather than villains of a story, that when Chrétien de Troyes was commissioned to put the story on paper in 1177, he refused to write the ending. He could not bring himself to put in writing that desire could exempt a person from being a good Christian. When pressured by his patron to complete the poem, however, he reluctantly agreed to dictate the final verses to a scribe. Thus he told of Launcelot and Guinevere talking all through the night, she inside her room, he standing in a frenzy of desire outside her window. Each had believed the other dead—their greatest love lost forever— but after months of frustration the knight had at last found his lady. Did she feel the same relentless compulsion? Launcelot wondered. Would she break all the rules for love? As the first light of morning slipped over the horizon, Launcelot at last took King Arthur's wife in his arms and held her "as if she were more precious than the relics of a saint."

When men and women say yes to the love of their lives, they discover passion. The extreme form of every emotion roars through them like a chimney fire, and although they may be able to control their actions, they are helpless when it comes to their feelings. They feel everything. Without exception, every person who described a love of a lifetime agreed with "The Song of Songs." Love's passion is as intoxicating as anything in the world that we see, hear, taste, smell, or feel. "Its flashes of fire are the very flame of God."

A grand passion is not merely the urge to go to bed with someone. Nor is it an infatuation that is a brief lurch toward love with no follow-through, no transformation. A full-blown passion is a far more intense and overwhelming experience. When the focused desire of a person's mind, body, and soul yearn in unison for another person's mind, body, and soul, the result is staggering. Triply intoxicating, the love of a lifetime is a romance that occurs between all of a person and, temporarily, all of the world. The experience is unforgettable. No grand passion: no love of a lifetime.

In this chapter, we will see passion sweeping lovers toward three revelations. The ecstasy that drove Sir Launcelot will strip them of their innocent, self-contained picture of themselves. It will give them more power than they imagined possible. And it will force them to shake off their insularity and join the turmoil of life without handicap or protection.

The word "passion" comes from the Latin word *pati*, meaning "to suffer"—not suffer meaning to be miserable, but suffer as in the Biblical phrase, "suffer the little children to come unto me." The Latin root suggests patience and endurance. Passion is the capacity to let feelings come into the heart. It is the willingness to feel everything intensely. In the love of a lifetime, this capacity to feel is given free rein, or rather love snatches the reins from our hands and sets off with our emotions like a runaway horse. There is no way to slow this kind of passion down or steer it away from danger, except to fall off and end the ride. If a person hangs on, the destination is unknown. In *Tales from Ovid*, the poet Ted Hughes singles out the kind of passion that attends the love of a lifetime and speaks of it as "not just ordinary passion...but human passion *in extremis*—passion where it combusts, levitates, or mutates into an experience of the supernatural."

Lovers suddenly feel their hearts beating in unison and burst into tears. Painters see flames coming out of their beloved's head. Music sweeps lovers away.

"Will this wreck my life?" they ask in alarm, and "What kind of a person will I be when the constraints of common sense and convention are so severely strained?"

~

Big, handsome, and at the height of his career at one of Boston's best hospitals, Dr. Niemeyer met me at the door of his office, barely convinced by a friend and colleague that it would be good for his health to talk to me. As the doctor ushered me into his large but surprisingly simple office, the first thing I noticed was the real art on the walls. Two seascapes in the manner of Winslow Homer were prominently displayed, and hanging above a low, built-in bookcase that ran around three sides of the room was a series of rural scenes depicting both farming and fishing.

"My father's influence," he said, noticing my interest. "He was a physician—and he collected art."

Dr. Niemeyer gestured to a wing chair and as I settled between its blue-gray arms, he swung into his own chair and started in.

"When love comes too late," he began, "or when you put it off until middle age...it takes a toll." He smiled grimly. "A friend of mine said it was like trying sex, alcohol, and drugs for the first time on your fiftieth birthday." He paused, reflecting. "He underestimated."

The doctor, who was well over six feet tall with very short, salt-and-pepper hair, swiveled his chair to look out over the adjoining hospital buildings. "Even here, no one knows much about this kind of love. I think..." he swung back to face me, "I think it's a biochemical storm, a freak event. I have a better chance of figuring out why men get prostate cancer than of discovering why they fall in love."

Planting his hands palms down on the desk, Dr. Niemeyer presented his own case history succinctly. He had been what his family called, "a good Jewish boy from Brooklyn." The bright, oldest child, the serious young man with no time for girls, he had raced through high school and college focused on attending the medical school of his choice. From his mother, he had inherited an ear for music and a talent for languages, and from his father, his love of art and his drive to be an outstanding physician. Everything in his life had gone as he thought it would, and that did not surprise him at all. Marrying the proverbially devoted wife and having three beautiful children was, like moving to the top of the heap in Boston, the easy part. Outwitting cancer was the hard part. That's why he'd chosen oncology and the surgery that went with it.

"And then when everything was going well," he continued, a touch of surprise entering his voice, "Leslie arrived and I fell in...into this addiction. If you haven't experienced it yourself, you can't understand. Even if you have," he corrected himself, "it's not...I mean, it's rare. It's one in a million."

Apparently, love ambushed Dr. Niemeyer one balmy spring day when golden buds swarmed in the trees like bees, and sailboats drifted lazily across the Charles River—details the doctor was not yet in the habit of noticing. Into the hospital walked a young, immensely bright physician who, he said, looked like a John Singer Sargent portrait. Like the beautiful blue bloods Sargent painted, Leslie was blonde and slender with an aura of confident femininity that moved with her like the scent of perfume. A classically beautiful woman, her skin was perfect, her nails were perfect. She moved and dressed perfectly. And in her, all this perfection seemed natural and unstrained. In the doctor's opinion, she was a work of art endowed with a brain like his own.

"*And* she was a perfectionist," he explained, leaning forward. "No detail was overlooked before surgery, no source of information that might help us was passed over. A dynamo. And with the patients? Ah, Leslie's history-taking was better than mine. Everyone loved her. It was a pleasure simply to be in the same room."

Leslie had come to Boston to find a mentor, and she was eager to work with Dr. Niemeyer in spite of his frightening reputation. Because he was both ambitious and a perfectionist, he was exhausting to be around. Nothing was ever good enough. Although he was unaware of the great pressure that his talents put on others, his colleagues and family had learned to manage him by giving him a wide berth. They kept their own projects as far from him as they could, and treated him like a valuable but dangerous source of power. Leslie was familiar with the isolation that being the best involved. Like Dr. Niemeyer, her career came before everything, including her husband and young children, and she too felt that her relentless need to fight for every life entrusted to her kept her working long after others had gone home.

Dr. Niemeyer and Leslie fell for each other in a brief period of time. In her second week, they had scheduled a surgery together, and for the first time the two would be standing across from each other separated by a narrow, draped body but joined by the exciting job of eradicating a cancer. They were going into combat together.

Dr. Niemeyer was not "a joking surgeon" or even a talkative one. He wanted his O.R. silent. The anesthetist sat out of sight on the far side of the screen, listening through earphones to the patient's heart, the scrub nurse placed instruments into the surgeon's gloved hand, the circulating nurse came and went quietly, and often the only sounds in the room were the soft beeps and burbles of the machines. Leslie knew this, and so when she heard her favorite piece of classical music softly swell from the speakers in the corners of the O.R., she looked up in surprise at her partner.

"You can tell when someone is smiling with a mask on," the doctor told me, and for the first time his shoulders relaxed and a wide smile spread across his face. "You see, there's lots of real eye-to-eye in surgery," he continued. "'Leslie, do you *see* this?' '*Look* at how it's attached.' 'Can you *spot* that?' Every time we'd contemplate a move, we'd check each other's eyes. And we could tell everything just by looking. Standing in that small space, the music playing, my hands moving better than they'd ever moved before, I thought my heart would burst through my chest."

He smiled again less broadly. "And I didn't even know it was love."

Glowing with exhilaration and babbling nearly incoherently over the fine job they'd performed, the two doctors waltzed into the surgeon's lounge and replayed the entire surgery from start to finish.

"We sat there in our scrubs, our heads getting closer and closer, and we couldn't talk fast enough to keep up with our thoughts. We were juggling a hundred ideas in the air, and suddenly I realized I would never get enough of this. 'It's her intelligence,' I thought to myself. 'It's her energy.' Finally it dawned on me. I was happy. And the next minute..." He took a deep breath and let it out. "I was in love in a way I'd never been before."

Soon the doctors were locked in a passionate, addictive affair. For the first time in his life, the senior physician experienced tidal waves of happiness so powerful and irresistible that they scared him. In the habit of relying on his intellect, he searched his mind for explanations. But what came swimming up from the depths instead were memories. He remembered watching cowboy movies in Brooklyn, specifically one in which a stampeding herd of buffalo thundered across the grainy screen just as the subway passed beneath the theater and shook the building. How excited and disturbed he had felt then. How he hoped it would happen again. He also remembered wearily waiting for the elevator one midnight in college. The red "Down" arrow blinked silently, the doors slid open, and he slumped inside before noticing two students locked in a passionate embrace. Throwing himself out just as the doors closed, he had walked down the stairs and out into the night feeling that same anxious excitement.

He'd never been what you'd call a man of torrential lusts, he admitted wryly, but when Leslie arrived, every desire he had ever postponed came stampeding back. The closest he could come to explaining what had transformed him from a classic workaholic to a man who thought only of making love to Leslie was that with the sudden release of so much passion, the chemical balance in his brain had been thrown off. He didn't know which neurotransmitters were flooding him with unmanageable desire, but if he had another life to live as a doctor, he'd choose to study the brains of addicted men.

Of course there were dozens of reasons why the affair with Leslie should not be pursued. Both were married. Both had children. Both cared a great deal for their reputations as trustworthy, not to say exemplary, individuals. Almost as soon as they had rushed together and experienced the intoxication that had eluded them all their lives, they began trying to break apart. They stopped performing surgery together. They agreed not to stay late at the hospital on the same night, and for a few days, even a few weeks, they would manage to avoid each other. Inevitably, however, they would catch sight of one another in the broad, marble-lined hallways of the hospital, and one look was all it took. Hating himself for going back on his decision and adoring the thought of crushing Leslie in his arms again, the handsome doctor would lock eyes with her as he had in surgery. That night or the next, he would hear a tap on his office door.

The doctor turned his chair again to look out into the fading light of evening. "The happiness was leaving," he said simply, "and what took its place was compulsion. I really believe this kind of attraction does something terrible to the brain."

When the destruction of both families seemed imminent, the doctor took his family on vacation, and, as agreed, Leslie wrenched herself and her family out of Boston—far out of Boston.

"It was awful," Dr. Niemeyer stated flatly as he turned back to his desk. "You can't imagine what a racking, pervasive kind of pain it was. There were times when I thought I would arrest or stroke out. I often hurt so much I couldn't speak.

"But I kept working," he said, as if in answer to my unspoken question, "and over time...well, it did *not* get easier but I got used to it. I calmed down."

Abruptly he looked me straight in the eye.

"No matter how many years go by," he said angrily, "if she walked into this room right now, or next year, or ever, I'd be out of this chair before she crossed the threshold."

Some time after Leslie's departure, Dr. Niemeyer's wife insisted they see the movie *The Bridges of Madison County*. Although apparently unaware of her husband's affair, she had her heart set on seeing this particular film. To the doctor's embarrassment, he found his hands twitching as he tried to warn Clint Eastwood not to stop in the town where he would meet Meryl Streep and fall in love.

"But people cried at that movie," I told him. "Some of them cried when they realized they had never experienced a love like that and weren't likely to."

The doctor looked at me so sharply that I flinched, and for a moment I glimpsed in his tired eyes just the edge of the sadness that Leslie had left behind.

"How *long* did they cry?" he asked.

I am willing to bet that the doctor thinks he will cry over Leslie forever, and the odd thing is, I think he wants to. Although part of him certainly wishes he had never discovered his capacity to feel so intensely, another part tends the grief that surrounds his memories of Leslie as if it were a hedge of orchids. He seems to treasure the unexpected biochemical storm that put him in touch with a great source of inner vitality, but also collapsed his innocent model of the world. He knows now that he is not the emperor of his own brain. He has inside him a defiant force that can topple him any time it chooses—any time Leslie walks through the door. This realization has tempered his arrogance, slightly, and continues to change his thinking. Even now, many months after her departure, he is still getting used to the idea that there is a civil war being waged inside him between passion and what he calls integrity. But I don't think he'd trade this state of affairs for anything. He is as passionate a man as he is intelligent. He wants both these forces in his life now, and to have both is to struggle.

Of course, not everyone I spoke with came to the same conclusion regarding the value of passion. One woman who fell helplessly in love discovered that passion led both to great sex and humiliating obsession. Although it quickly became apparent that her lover was blatantly unfaithful, she craved his presence no matter what he did. Like Dr. Niemeyer, she felt addicted, but unlike him, she couldn't part with the "drug." Even after her lover moved in with another woman, sexual dreams of him remained to torment her. She would wake in despair as if she were an overeater who had just wolfed down a chocolate cake against her better judgment. Why couldn't she control her appetite for this man? she wondered. What a weak, stupid person she must be to crave what hurt her. How ashamed she felt. For years, this woman couldn't bear to think about her passionate affair unless it was to blame her partner or vow never to fall in love again.

"I fall too fast and feel too much," she used to say, "and I pick men who take advantage of me. Never again."

Although the first thing that struck this woman about passion was its force, the lesson I wish to draw both from her and Dr. Niemeyer's experiences is that in addition to being overpowering, passion reveals personal weakness as well as strength. By igniting our negative emotions as well as our positive ones and revealing how little control we have over either, a passionate love collapses our innocent picture of ourselves. We are more afraid, angry, lustful, jealous, unreasonable, and all the rest than we wanted to believe. We are more likely to break the rules or hurt those who love and trust us than we thought possible.

This brings us to integrity. Just as a person with a passion for chocolate cake must have greater-than-average self-discipline if he or she is not to become overweight, a passionate lover must have unusual integrity to balance his or her desires. In other words, it takes remarkable strength of character to be a truly passionate person. If this is missing, passion turns into the self-destructive states of indulgence or obsession, as it did for the woman who loved like an overeater. Although Dr. Niemeyer may not realize it, he continues to value his passion for Leslie precisely because the two of them found the strength to do what they believed was right. In their case, it was to end the affair, but for another pair it might be to find a way to be together. For everyone, however, to be a passionate lover is to feel intensely and act honorably. Great lovers are not weak people.

Shakespeare explored the tension between passion and integrity in his play *Antony and Cleopatra,* and concluded that the distinction between self-indulgence and passion depended on whether or not the lovers eventually took responsibility for their actions—whether they "owned it," as we would say today. Shakespeare pitted Caesar's belief that the nobleness of life lies in controlling all emotions and never letting them ignite, against Antony's and Cleopatra's belief that a good person lives passionately and takes the consequences. "Burn," the Queen of Egypt seemed to say, "but take responsibility for the damage your fire may cause—to yourself as well as to anyone else."

While challenging our integrity and often bringing us to our knees, passion also pumps us full of jet fuel. Some say it is the source of all vitality.

When the French novelist André Gide, who was a homosexual at a time when this was considered both a crime and a sin, found himself burning with desire for young men, he wrote prayers to God asking

Him to remove this passion, which he experienced as humiliating. Years went by, Gide grew old, yet still he suffered attacks of desire that embarrassed him. Finally, when Gide was in his eighties, God answered his prayers. Desireless at last, the writer discovered to his dismay that he was not content. He hadn't realized, he told God, that when the barely controllable passion disappeared, so did his interest in life.

~

Half German, half Irish, half seduction, half trouble, Marta O'Sullivan had plenty of passion and plenty of interest in life. Her parents had emigrated to Youngstown, Ohio, just after her birth, and when World War II began, the white-skinned girl with the mane of wavy auburn hair was tall, bright, difficult, and seventeen. She came from a family of haters, she admitted. Her family members carried grudges for years, and each had perfected the art of hating something or someone in a marvelously flamboyant way. Marta's way of hating was to be rebellious, and the butt of her attacks was the working class she belonged to and the city she lived in. It was the city in particular that she loathed, and she vowed so often to leave Youngstown that it became a kind of trademark. When the war started and soldiers began moving through the steel town, Marta saw her ticket out. Pretending to be eighteen, she got a job in an officer's club seating men in a small dining room. Her first real challenge was to keep everyone happy as they waited for a table for Thanksgiving dinner. One of the men who came late and waited longest was Clifford Martin.

Clifford, or Cliff as he was always called, couldn't have come from a more dissimilar background. Born in Hartford, Connecticut, he grew up in a starchy New England family with lots of money. Sent first to private schools, then to boarding schools and expensive colleges, Cliff brushed off learning the way the family maid brushed crumbs off the table. He was expelled from Trinity College, then Yale, and finally Brown. No more money for wasted education, said his parents, and Cliff found himself in the Officers Training Corps. He became a second lieutenant just before Thanksgiving, and was stationed in Youngstown.

When the two rebels met at the entrance to the Officer's Club, the attraction was immediate. Cliff was six feet one, slim, dark-haired, and as clean cut a young man as Marta had ever seen. In his trim, khaki uniform with a single gold bar on each shoulder and his visored hat, he could have been a poster boy for the armed services. When Marta stood at his side or guided him to his table, everyone who saw them smiled— a smashing couple, a leggy, high-spirited pair. Marta swayed provocatively as she left his table, sure that many eyes were traveling up the lines she'd drawn on the back of her legs with an eyebrow pencil—she couldn't afford silk stockings. By the end of dinner, Marta had Cliff's address tucked in the pocket of her blue shirt-waist dress—she was embarrassed to give him hers—and they were on their way to falling in love. In the following weeks, the handsome couple went dancing, drank Manhattans, and smoked cigarettes. Because she would never let him escort her home, they said their good-nights at a bus stop. More than once, the bus drove off as they kissed so hard their lips bled.

For Marta, Cliff was a first-class ticket to dreamland, and for Cliff, Marta was the hot ticket he had only read about in books. By Christmas, they had taken the scandalous step of becoming sexually intimate, but they weren't able to stop. In those days sex was supposed to mean marriage. Cliff received orders to report to San Francisco. He was heading for the Pacific. Knowing that neither he nor Marta was the patient, faithful type, Cliff refused to marry her. Marta was astonished not to get her way. After a huge fight, she stomped off vowing to marry him eventually no matter how long she had to wait. Her resolve began to weaken by the end of the week.

For the next several years, Cliff slogged his way through the Pacific islands becoming increasingly disillusioned by the barbarism he saw, while Marta dated other soldiers, though never for long. Finally the war came to an end, and after Cliff helped to liberate a prisoner-of-war camp, which left him deeply embittered, he returned to Youngstown to see if Marta had married. No longer young kids, they had exchanged their fresh good looks for character. Leaner and deeply tanned, Cliff seemed more wary and vigilant, while Marta, still a bombshell, seemed more grimly determined to better her situation. She was desperate to leave town. Fueled by their considerable anxieties, their reunion in the dark streets of the steel town was as fiery as the furnaces. As one used sex to forget the war and the other to forget Youngstown, the two misfits fell back into each other's arms. "Save me—now!" each seemed to be demanding, but the words that came out of their mouths were, "Marry me."

Once Cliff and Marta married and moved to California, Marta never saw nor spoke to a member of her family again. "My family's crazy," she told her new husband. "So's mine," he replied.

Over the next seven years, the couple had one of its few good times. As Cliff put himself through school to become a mining engineer, Marta gloried in their sunny rented room—with kitchen privileges. Then they had a daughter, and moved into a one-bedroom apartment. Four years later, a son arrived and they moved up again. Cliff and Marta were still much attracted to each other and their dreams were coming true. Both had broken decisively from their families and were starting life over. When little Clifford was diagnosed with a rare and untreatable form of cancer, however, the family came under such tension that it fell apart. By the time the toddler died, Cliff was drinking heavily and Marta was trying to kill herself with sleeping pills. Miserable, Cliff jumped at the chance to work in South America nine months of the year to help establish copper mines. Increasingly cared for by her precocious daughter, Marta was left alone to imagine her husband's drinking and carousing. She knew her slim, handsome husband had a woman in every mining town he worked in, and the thought worked on her like poison. When Cliff returned each summer, the two would tear into each other like alley cats. Alternately making love and arguing, Marta would soon be screaming that he was seeing other women.

"Great! Wonderful!" Clifford roared sarcastically. "My mother was crazy and my sister. Now you! What's next, Marta?"

Their fights were truly horrible, the daughter remembered—loud, frightening, and physically abusive. Often she believed they would kill each other in their fury, and alone in her bed, she would wonder which one of them she should hope would survive. "Why don't you get divorced?" she pleaded many mornings as they limped to the breakfast table.

"It would have made my job easier," she recalled.

At last Marta and Clifford did divorce and life calmed down enough that the daughter, relieved of most of her caretaking duties, dared leave for college. Clifford spent almost all his time in South America now, and Marta used her alimony for clothes, manicures, and weekly visits to the hairdresser. Their passion had apparently burned out, and they had both turned to the mechanical details of daily living. There was a fall weekend at their daughter's college designed to honor parents, and without knowing each other's plans, both Cliff and Marta showed up for the event. Alarmed, the daughter wondered how she was going to keep the peace, but she didn't have to worry. Her father had cut back on his drinking, and her mother looked smashing with a new blond hairdo. The two seemed quite taken with each other, the daughter noticed. When her parents appeared again two months later to take her out to lunch, the daughter was again vigilant. "What's going on with you two?" she asked at the end of the meal, when she caught them smirking at each other.

"We got married this morning."

This time Clifford and Marta went to South America together. There they became high rollers, learning the tango, betting on the horses, and eating at the best restaurants. At last the two were living the good life that Marta had envisioned since her dreary days in Youngstown. Yet neither was content. Marta at sixty was still an attractive woman, but not a head-turner who could make her husband jealous. And Cliff was aging in a more dangerous way. In the course of six years, he had three bad accidents. "We're slipping, Marty," he would say to her. "We can't keep up."

As Cliff was recovering from his third accident, one that involved a cable that nearly decapitated him, cancer was found in his jaw. In spite of treatments, it soon became clear that he was dying. "One of the terrible things about being in great physical shape," Marta kept telling her daughter, "is that you linger."

Clifford and Marta returned for the last time to California and there, to the astonishment of everyone who knew them, they finally let love overtake them.

"Something was released by the illness that we had never seen before," the daughter said. "Dad became affectionate for the first time in his life. He was stooped now and painfully thin, but he held hands with Mom. He stroked her hair. He looked at her, I mean *really* looked at her, and there was so much love in his eyes that I would start crying and have to turn away. He complimented everyone, but not mechanically. He thought carefully about what he said. He became this powerful, loving man, and his passion...his passion for Mom and me and everything around him ran like a river through our lives. The sicker he got and the more pain he was in, the more loving he became. Pure spirit. 'This is great,' I told Mom. 'It makes up for everything.' I hoped it would last for years. 'No,' Mom said. 'We have to let him go.'....and so we did."

The social commentator Christopher Lasch, author of the well-known book *The Culture of Narcissism* and the lesser-known *Women and the Common Life*, would have seen in this story support for his contention that passion, rather than shared interests and values, is the more reliable, and therefore more valuable, force in holding a marriage together. Passion is reliable? Lasch thought so. He believed that the essential ingredients of a lasting union are mutual esteem and desire. As dangerous as passion may be, with its ability to override decency and common sense and in other ways reveal personal frailty, he felt that it is the only fuel that can keep a couple like Cliff and Marta moving over rough terrain. In other words, Lasch believed we need the experience of being flooded by emotions in order to bond solidly with another person. This may be what Stendahl meant by "the only unions that are legitimate forever are those ruled by genuine passion." (Interestingly, research shows that other emotional landslides besides love forge unshakable bonds between people. Survivors of hotel fires, for example, are much more likely to marry than people who share a weekend at the beach. Like lovers, these people are 100 percent involved in an experience they have no control over.)

There is a tendency today for lovers to try to sidle into love without experiencing "a sudden, overwhelming attraction." Lasch implied that it can't be done. The experience of being swept away must come first, then love can be seen and appreciated for what it really is. Initially, I found this to be a an odd thought, but whether I asked the wisest clinicians I could find or read the oldest legends I could lay my hands on, the idea that we must *first* be swept into the storm of life before we can become an experienced human being came up again and again.

"When my eldest son was about to be engaged," a psychologist told me, "I wasn't sure if he'd really fallen for this girl—and I knew he'd never fallen before—so I told him, 'Bart, don't marry her if you aren't crazy about her because if you do, one of two things is likely to happen. Either the two of you will go along OK until one of you finally falls head over heels in love with somebody else, or you'll spend your whole lives feeling restless. You'll wonder why you feel so disconnected, as if you've missed out on something somewhere along the line.'

"You see," he continued, "I was telling him not to marry until he'd experienced a great love. Each of us has to experience an impossibly perfect love before we can settle down to the reality of a less-than-perfect relationship. It doesn't matter whether the love of a lifetime is the person you marry—the perfection will depart soon enough and a real partnership will follow—or whether your great love comes before you marry. But what is important is that your moment of perfect love arrive before you try to establish a real partnership. I told Bart that no real relationship can satisfy a person who's still looking for perfection—nor should it. That's why the love of a lifetime should come first. It's the love affair that makes ordinary life acceptable."

A Hindu legend makes the same point. It says that passion is necessary not just to reveal lovers to themselves and to supply energy for the vital life, but to get every living thing involved to its fullest capacity in day-to-day life—to force, if necessary, every man, woman, animal, and plant to join the eternal dance.

Early on, as the world was being made, Brahma, the creator of the world, sat with his eyes closed looking deep inside himself. Every time he discovered a feeling or an idea, it leapt into being. As he continued to meditate, surrounded by the gods he'd already thought into existence, there suddenly appeared from his mind the first female—a beautiful, naked, brown-skinned woman. At first, no one knew what she was for. As Brahma gazed at her in wonder, however, feelings for her began to form, and these feelings jumped from his head and took on the shape of a gorgeous young man equipped with bow and arrows. "What is my name?" the new creation asked brashly. "What am I here to do?" Brahma replied, "You are Kama, the god of love and desire, and your job is to wander the world shooting your arrows through the hearts of men, women, and gods, causing bewilderment and delight and thus ensuring the continual creation of the world."

To everyone's horror, the youth immediately let fly his arrows at the assembled gods, and one by one they shivered, shook, and went mad with desire. "You are stronger than Brahma the creator of the world, Vishnu the preserver, and Shiva the destroyer," said one of the gods. "We are all in your power." Only they weren't. Shiva, the god who destroys so that life may continue, wasn't interested in falling in love. He preferred to meditate and remain serenely in control. Brahma realized that unless Shiva too fell under the power of love, he would remain aloof from the world and would not do his job in the best possible way. In order to destroy life well, Shiva first had to care for it. The Destroyer had be drawn into the eternal dance so that everything would matter to him.

It was not easy to find the destroyer a mate, but after much discussion, the gods convinced the great goddess of illusion to take on a human form and become Shiva's wife. Many adventures followed, but finally Shiva was married. He was so deeply in love with his black-skinned, black-haired bride, so completely ruled by desire, that their honeymoon lasted nine thousand years during which time nothing died. Death himself had finally bowed before passion and felt the full and uncontrollable force of desire. Years later, when the human incarnation of his wife died, he felt the power of grief. Through these two great emotions, he learned to care for every living thing. He shared a great and mysterious bond with all of them and did his job of ending their lives compassionately. To be connected to life requires passion.

~

"I have sought love," wrote the philosopher and Nobel Prize laureate, Bertrand Russell, "first because it brings ecstasy—ecstasy so great that I would often have sacrificed all the rest of my life for a few hours of this joy. I have sought it next, because it relieves loneliness—that terrible lone-liness in which one shivering consciousness looks over the rim of the world into the cold, unfathomable lifeless abyss."

Insight, ecstasy, and connection are the gifts that passion confers, and sorrow and struggle are the cost. The triple intoxication strips lovers of their innocence, fills them with vitality, and sends them whirling into a world where they feel connected to a life force that resides in everything and connects each to all.

~

In spite of all the ecstasy and excitement, however, I wonder if a grand passion is actually something people want today. Is "submitting to the inevitables of destiny," as the mythologist Joseph Campbell called this kind of experience, considered an essential adventure or an optional detour? Not surprisingly, the answer depends on who you ask.

In the popular culture, music, movies, and magazines make it clear that we have a nearly insatiable appetite for romantic passion. Several years ago, columnist Ann Landers began running a series of letters called "How We Met" that described the odd, difficult, or delayed meeting of true lovers. When she tried to end the series, there was an outcry, and she agreed to continue to publish the letters intermittently. They are always greeted with enthusiasm. A great many people hope for the kind of passionate, single-minded love described in these letters, and they are proud of themselves if they find it. Like the people I interviewed, they would agree with novelist Virginia Woolf's statement: "At some time or another nine out of ten people passionately want love more than they want anything else."

But not everyone agrees. According to historians of love, the age we live in does not put a high priority on passionate love. Among the reasons advanced for the decline are affluence and opportunity. The more a person has, it seems, the harder it is to gamble everything for love. Bent on conserving career, hard-won rights, interests, property, friends, and plans for the future, the would-be lover holds on to all that he or she has acquired and is not willing to be swept away. When a recent Harvard University graduate made a survey of typical undergraduate romances for her alumni magazine, she concluded "today's students have a savvier, more cynical perspective [on love]...Students are increasingly more concerned with constructing lives around résumés rather than romances."

They are looking for a "partnership-marriage," she continued, which will not interfere with their career. They hope that friendship will sustain their relationship while they invest long hours at work or travel to opposite ends of the earth. They like the "mutual respect" half of Lasch's formula for a great love, but not the uncontrollable "desire." As the historian of love Irving Singer puts it, "we are living in a period in which large numbers of people have renounced their faith in love."

Another reason given for not valuing a grand passion is that men and women in a secular-materialist society like our own have a hard time taking seriously the mystery that is part of romantic passion.

"It is precisely the belief that a sudden, overwhelming attraction establishes unshakable bonds that the modern mind...finds so shocking," wrote Lasch in *Women and the Common Life*. "We dislike mystery. We crave what we can control."

Turning to the new experts on love—therapists and brain scientists—we find still another opinion. "Healthy love" is valued. Passion is considered a process or a problem. It is not hard to see why this division occurred. Therapists have concerned themselves with the social interaction part of love, which can be studied using the interactions of therapy, while scientists have investigated the parts of love like infant bonding and passion, which, they believe, can be reduced to a physical process and studied using scientific methods. At least for the past hundred years, science has reduced passion to physical attraction in the service of reproduction and equated it to genes, hormones, and brain functions. "Love emanates from the brain; the brain is physical, and thus as fit a subject for scientific discourse as cucumbers or chemistry," argues a recent book on love by three psychiatrists.

Sad to say, therapists, with the notable exception of Jungians, have accepted science's stripped-down model of passion-as-reproductive-drive and have largely decided that Eros, "the god who breaks limbs," has almost no place in "healthy love." A roaring passion is not seen as a valuable experience unless it stays on the happy side of the emotional street. When powerful ground swells of jealousy, fear, obsession, heartbreak, and confusion break on the scene, passionate love tends to be redefined as dysfunction. Someone is impaired. In an average clinic, the same star-crossed lovers who inspire our favorite films and novels would be seen as people in need of therapy, the goal of which would be to prevent them from experiencing the trials and tribulations that we so love to hear about. When passion is taken out of love, however, what remains is "healthy love." Described in terms such as "music that varies endlessly in pleasant ways," it has comfort and reliability as its only goals. This form of love can support and teach, but it does not transform a person the way passion does. Therapists apparently hope that the insight, ecstasy, and connection that passion so roughly confers on lovers can be gained in less disruptive ways.

I don't think they can. I think we are smart to hold onto our appetite for passion and to keep pictures of its joys and sorrows fresh in our minds. I don't believe that a friendship or a partnership-marriage can do what a grand passion can do, and I don't believe that an explanation of passion in Darwinian or neurochemical terms comes anywhere close to the heart of the matter. As for therapy's cautious views, I think it's a shame if we are so afraid of pain and frustration that we would sooner redefine a star-crossed love as a series of impairments and mistakes than suffer through a major heartbreak with our patients. Whether we look at larger-than-life couples like Katharine Hepburn and Spencer Tracy, Richard Burton and Elizabeth Taylor, or consider ordinary people like

Dr. Niemeyer and Leslie or Cliff and Marta, I don't believe any life is profoundly shaken and rearranged except by passion *in extremis*.

I am certainly not saying that romance is the only form of passion that pushes us out of ourselves and into the eternal dance. The object of our passion does not have to be a lover, perhaps not even a person. I heard stories of passionate attachments to children, parents, Jesus, war buddies, causes, and ideals. But passion is essential. In the following chapters, I will demonstrate that passion transforms people in a way no other experience does. To avoid a grand passion is, to a greater extent than many imagine, to avoid becoming a full-fledged member of the human community.

Once a grand passion is experienced, a series of changes begins. One of the first is the need to break away from an old life that no longer fits the new person.

Part Two

The Work

CHAPTER 3
Breaking Away

DEEP LOVE ALWAYS
SEPARATES US FROM
WHAT HAS GONE
BEFORE.

—Ethel Person,
*Dreams of Love and
Fateful Encounters*

I WONDER, BY
MY TROTH, WHAT
THOU AND I
DID, TILL WE LOVED?
WERE WE NOT
WEANED TILL THEN,
BUT SUCKED ON
COUNTRY PLEASURES,
CHILDISHLY?

—John Donne

One of the first things I noticed as I began collecting love-of-a-lifetime stories, was the antipathy that married and single people feel for each other when they compare stories of the love of a lifetime.

"Marriage is the *real* school of love," claimed one of my friends. "When the honeymoon is over, that's when true lovers get to work. In the end, it's the follow-through that counts."

"Not so," chimed in another. "Every great love story in the world involves people who *can't* get together. Think of *Casablanca, Dr. Zhivago, Love Story*— me and Bob! Obstacles fuel passion, and passion is the key. Keeping house is not love with a capital *L*."

Clearly, both are right although not, perhaps, in the way they would imagine. Passion starts the love of a lifetime, and we have seen that it is the total, unqualified, unprotected giving of ourselves that sweeps us into a new frame of mind. This is an indispensable initiation. But if the passion goes nowhere and teaches nothing, then it hasn't done its job. Kama or Cupid will have to try again. Everyone knows someone who has one romance after another. It's a soap opera of a life with every episode circling back to the beginning, and we suspect this person knows nothing of love. In a true love of a lifetime, passion starts lovers doing things differently. Although men and women who have married for security or convenience don't understand this, lovers who marry the love of their lives do. Combining passion with an ongoing relationship, they are the experts on the ways in which love separates us from what has gone before. In this chapter, we begin to look at the work that the love of a lifetime asks us to perform. Giving lovers a new view of themselves, a grand passion makes lovers realize they don't fit into their old roles any more. Having lost their innocence, it's time to leave home.

~

Early one morning, I drove in the pouring rain to a small town on Cape Cod to serve on a jury. When the usual courtroom delays presented themselves and a recess was called, everyone in the jury pool pulled on their raincoats and left, except for myself and two other women. When one asked what I was writing in my notebook, I described my interest in the love of a lifetime, and soon we were deep in conversation. One of the women tentatively suggested that her husband and their three children might collectively be the love of her life because her family gave her more pleasure and frustration than anyone else. The other woman, Ali, who introduced herself as the daughter of a well-known local portrait photographer, asked if anyone ever named a parent as the love of a lifetime. Yes, I told her, very occasionally a son named his mother, but quite often a daughter pointed to her father.

"I guess I'd have to say my father is the person who's done the most for me," Ali told me. She cocked her head for a moment and a shock of straight blond hair fell across her eyes. "No, he's the one," she said, brushing it back. "He's definitely had more influence on me than anyone else and has made my life the way it is."

It took no prompting to get Ali to describe her wonderful father. Not only was he handsome and kind, he was very, very good at what he did.

Everyone loved him and his photographs, and he was viewed in the community as highly successful. "A dream of a man." Sadly, he had been diagnosed with Parkinson's Disease, but being ill made him, if anything, sweeter. When he first learned of his illness, he approached Ali and her two sisters individually and offered to take each anywhere in the world she wanted to go. Ali chose India, and the photograph she cherishes above all others is one of her and her father nested together like spoons astride an elephant. She pulled out a wallet-sized copy of the photo and passed it to me with a smile. There she was on an elephant, her athletic body enfolded in the arms of a man twice her size. I could see that both father and daughter had straight, yellow hair that fell in their eyes. It blew across their rosy, wide-awake faces and gave them a rough and ready look—two colonial adventurers exploring the jungle. Dressed in what looked like white linen shirts and khakis, they made a good-looking pair.

"He's such a backer," Ali said as she returned the photo to her wallet. "I can trust him completely."

"It must be difficult to find men to date who are as wonderful as your father," I suggested, having noted she wasn't wearing a wedding ring.

"Yes," she said slowly, and, as she looked off into space, I wondered if she were the kind of woman who had a particularly hard time breaking family ties and leaving the favored relationship she had with her father. I had already talked with other women who named their fathers as the love of their lives, and I had the impression that having a parent in this position made falling in love and leaving home either a bit easier or a lot harder than usual. When it was easier, the father provided such a fine model of a good husband and father that his daughter formed the expectation that she would find a man just like him. And she did. In the difficult cases, however, the father gave his daughter some portion of the affection that usually goes to a wife. Such a young woman unconsciously formed the expectation that her most precious relationships would always be with a man whose allegiance was divided. One woman told me that she became her father's confidante by the time she was nine. Although aunts and uncles all admired their close bond, she felt it had inadvertently prepared her to be "the kind of woman you have on the side."

"He called me up the night before he died and said, 'You are the person I've loved most in my life.' How do you break out of a bad pattern you're grateful for?" she wondered.

Although later we will see that parent-child devotion can be a mixed blessing, this woman has continued in the pattern her father introduced her to. She only falls for men who are unavailable, nor does she fall all the way. If Ali was like this woman, I thought, she too was probably having a hard time falling for someone so hard and so completely that she'd leave home and start life on her own.

Our conversation shifted then to the various forms that loves of a lifetime take. I mentioned that a sizable number were kept secret either because they were adulterous, seemed too short to count, or were so wrong-headed and impossible as to be embarrassing. The first woman shook her head sadly. "What a waste," she murmured. Ali began to smirk.

"So a really stupid love affair can be the love of a lifetime?" she asked.

"Oh, yes," I assured her. "But it must be unforgettable. One man was misled, robbed, and abandoned not once, but twice by the same woman."

"Did he feel like a jerk?" Ali wanted to know.

"Of course."

"But did he regret...you know, forever?"

"For years he thought of himself as a dupe, but he also realized that he had been more alive and energized with her than with anyone else. He was humiliated all right, but eventually he decided it was worth it. He said it woke him up."

Ali burst into ripples of laughter and turned quite pink.

"You're telling my story," she said. "I don't believe it."

Ali then explained that she had lived close to her childhood home and the influence of her wonderful father until she was almost thirty. Her family's way of doing things had seemed the right way, and she remembered thinking that people who did things differently, like putting liquor in the refrigerator instead of in a proper bar, lacked refinement. Finally, she found a man who did things like her family. She married him, and found herself in a "serviceable relationship with an OK guy." A year or so later, Ali made plans to open her own studio and follow her father down the endlessly fascinating road of art. But instead of being excited, she was restless and annoyed. She was missing something.

"This is so embarrassing," she continued, shooting me a quizzical look. "When I was thirty-four, I met a man who was...well, so magnetic and charged with energy, so attractive, that within five days I was ready to run away with him. This was not like me. Five days. Totally unreasonable. Unforgivable!

"So I dumped my marriage and took off with this guy, or rather I followed him across the country. Very soon I discovered that I couldn't trust him—not about women, money, the truth, anything. Trust became the central issue between us, and there was none. But, my God, there was attraction by the truckload. He was the sexiest man in the world and we struck sparks. Riding in his truck, smoking a toke, showering in a cheap motel—there was no place and no time of day that we didn't want each other more than we wanted anything else. Put that kind of passion together with no trust, and I can't tell you how bad it got before I came limping home. He was a total con artist, and I was a fool."

"But," I said for her.

"But a swept-away fool," she continued with a wistful smile, "a happy fool, a 100-percent-in-love-and-falling-over-the-cliff fool."

"Quite a break from the family routine," I suggested.

Ali groaned. "Total rebellion, total disaster."

In spite of the exhilaration she had felt with this untrustworthy man, Ali did not appear to have the strength to profit from her passionate rebellion. She had discovered passion all right, and she had shattered her former image, but now she was a wreck. Confused and lonely, she pulled into her shell and vowed to stay there forever.

"I had become the kind of woman people read about in tabloids in the checkout line of the food store. I'd been unbelievably irresponsible and self-centered. No one was going to get me to act that crazy again. No more love for me. I was sure of that."

"So you went back home?" I asked.

"Yes and no," she said slowly. "It sorta looked like I was home, but I'd done too much damage to fit back in, especially with Mother. That's partly what made it lonely."

For six years, Ali remained in limbo. Throughout the rest of her thirties, this lovely young woman with the rugged good looks of an explorer hardly dated, and when she did, she didn't notice whom she was seeing. "I was still at the bottom of the cliff, hurt and closed off."

At the same time, she started her own studio, but that didn't go well either. She dabbled with photography, tried painting, made a quilt that traced her route across the country, but couldn't get herself in gear. Then, about a year after her tear across the States, she took up pottery.

"I had no idea what I was doing," she admitted, "but I was a little less miserable when I was up to my elbows in clay. At first I made bowls and stuff, but pretty quickly I branched out into free-form sculpture. I used all different kinds of clay, and I let their 'personalities' come through. I'm not a glaze person, but I'm crazy for form."

"What did your father think of your new career?" I asked, trying to picture the rugged man I'd seen in the photo caressing the big, sensuous forms that Ali was describing.

"Oh, he loved it," she replied thoughtlessly, then stopped herself. "Actually, he's better with bowls. I don't think many people get the shapes. I mean, either they do or they don't. But I make them for me."

When Ali turned forty, she met a divorced man her age with a daughter. He lived nearby, and the two shared similar interests. Ali emerged from her fog enough to notice her dates, and decided she rather liked him. For one thing, he loved her pottery and said she put more feeling into clay than anyone else. And for another thing, he considered her a great lover.

"If only he knew how I learned that," she groaned.

As soon as Ali found herself looking forward to his nightly calls, she got scared and suggested they see each other less often. He didn't agree. "You're still looking for Mr. Right," he told her over the phone, misinterpreting her caution. "Well, how about Mr. Right around the Corner?"

"He was 'right' about one thing," she conceded. "I was being a coward, and thank God he was mature enough to call me on it."

The two continued dating, and as Easter approached, Ali gathered her courage and planned a huge Easter-egg hunt to introduce Mr. Right around the Corner to friends and family. She dyed eggs. She hired a trio to play music. She practically bought out a bakery. On the eve of the great party, her boyfriend came over to help decorate the house.

"At the end of the evening, he sat me down," Ali started to giggle, "looked me straight in the eye, and told me that his high-school sweetheart had just flown in from Ohio and they were leaving on Easter morning for Bermuda!"

"No!"

"Yes! What a shock, but that wasn't all, I mean that wasn't the *big* shock." She sat up straight in her chair and looked at me proudly. "I raced into my bedroom, threw myself face down, and started to cry, but you know, I couldn't get into it. 'I've been dumped again,' I reminded myself. But I still couldn't get the tears to come. 'I *cared* for this guy,' I wailed, and that was it—that was the shocker. 'My God, I care again,' I said to myself. 'I'm back.' I started laughing *and* crying really hard then, and I felt so much relief. I was alive again.

"It was strange," she continued. "I felt a ton of loneliness lift right off my back like a crane was removing a suit of armor. Yes, I've been dumped again, but look what I've gained."

"What had you gained?" asked the third woman, puzzled.

"Well, I'd been stuck," Ali explained. "I'd jumped off a cliff and ruined my Ms. Perfect costume, but I was afraid to get up and...well, start being somebody else. And then..." she shrugged her shoulders and gave a big smile, "I don't know. I guess Mr. Right around the Corner saw the new me before I did. But there I was, put back together again and ready to go. It was such a good feeling."

"Mmm," said the other woman, nodding sympathetically. "But both those men left you. Who's the love of your life?"

Ali threw back her head and roared. "Mr. Wrong…of course!"

Well, not exactly "of course." The quiet woman asked a good question. Is Ali's destructive affair with a con artist really a good example of a love of a lifetime that triggered a break with her old life? Or was it merely a mess? Years from now, will she still remember Mr. Wrong as the love of her life?

My guess is she will. I heard many stories like hers from people who, when asked to consider the love of their lives, did not hesitate in naming an irresponsible heartbreaker even after they had paired up with someone who suited them much better. The double leap from the safety of a closely guarded heart and the protection of a tightly knit family was remembered by them as the most remarkable and dangerous experience of their lives.

"So wrong, but such an impact," said a friend of mine who quit college to run away with a man from South Africa. "I knew he was not the man I wanted to marry, but he was the one who broke into my heart. He was always breaking into things. Our relationship was stormy, and we left and came back together a dozen times before we finally parted. It was awful, and I literally thought my heart would break. But then, well, I got better, and a couple of years later I met my husband. The day before my wedding, he handed me a newspaper clipping, and I learned that my first love had been killed in a gunfight. I remember crying uncontrollably. The next day I stuffed that scrap of paper into my wedding gown and carried it down the aisle. I sobbed all the way through the ceremony, and everyone except my husband thought I was crying for joy.

"As the years went by," she continued, "our marriage had its tough times, and I often asked myself, 'Would I have run back to my first love?' I hope my answer would have been 'no,' but I'm not sure. He was a bad man in many ways, but he brought me to life. I know it sounds terrible to say, but it's better that the love of my life is dead."

~

Sometimes it takes a thug to break into a well-defended heart and steal it away. Whether the protective walls have been built in response to hurt or as a form of allegiance to a wonderful father or mother doesn't matter much. A lover must come along who is dangerously powerful, unscrupulous—or at least unhesitating—and not at all what the family wants. This is the man or woman who will get the job done for Cupid and be remembered as the love of a lifetime. It was the con man who got Ali to let go and dive off the cliff, and it was he who inadvertently turned her away from photography and toward pottery, where she could express her new and passionate understanding of the world in clay. She will almost surely remember him as her great and desperate love even as she shares better times with a good man.

Both Ali and my friend wrenched themselves away from their families before they knew what they wanted or had the resources to build it. Not everyone has such a difficult time. Some young men and women are less entangled in their families and don't have to start a major rebellion to find love and leave home. Others know more clearly what they want out of life, and no matter how hard the leap from home is, they land in a workable new life. They don't have to spend time at the bottom of the cliff, as Ali did. But regardless of how it's done, the old life is left behind. "Deep love always separates us from what has gone before," Ethel Person observed. Few realized this more clearly than the nineteenth-century poet Elizabeth Barrett as she struggled to leave her tyrannical father for the love of her life, Robert Browning.

~

Elizabeth Barrett enjoyed an enchanted childhood in rural England, and it seemed to her that God had given her a loving family, a beautiful home, and the wit to appreciate both. When she was fifteen, however, she fell ill with what is variously described as a combination of tuberculosis or spinal injury and emotional problems. She was confined to her bed most of the time and never recovered fully. As she settled into the life of an invalid, she formed the idea that God had given her a great talent for words as a consolation prize for the disappointments her illness entailed. She would succeed as a poet, she believed, but she would never marry or have a life in society.

A few years later, Elizabeth Barrett's mother died, leaving eleven children to the care of a husband who was not temperamentally suited to handle them. Increasingly bitter and depressed, he withdrew into a joyless religion and expected his children to follow. No matter how sick Elizabeth Barrett felt, every evening she knelt on the floor and prayed with her father.

Mr. Barrett did not encourage any of his children to leave home, least of all his sickly daughter. He would not give any of them his permission to marry. Although several of the children left home against his wishes, Elizabeth never doubted she would remain. There were several reasons. One was that a decision of hers had inadvertently robbed her father of a son. One of her brothers had accompanied her to the seaside, and when Mr. Barrett commanded he return home, Elizabeth had insisted he stay. Soon after, he was drowned in a sailing accident. Elizabeth felt she was to blame, and after the accident, found it increasingly difficult to meet people or even leave her bedroom. In addition to guilt, she was too sick to marry. Tuberculosis—if that is what she had—was a serious illness at that time, fatal for the poor and only slightly less serious for the rich, who could slow down the disease by escaping to a cool, dry climate. Barrett knew that sooner or later she would waste away. By the time she met Browning at thirty-nine, she was painfully weak. Her dark hair lacked luster and her skin sometimes looked waxy. With heavy features and an extremely wide mouth, she did not imagine herself an appealing woman. Poor nutrition took an additional toll. Existing on little besides clear broth and bread, she rarely had the strength to get out of bed, and she never went out of the house in winter. Still another reason for not considering marriage was the unreliable nature of love itself. Love rhymes with glove, she liked to say. Both slid on and off easily.

Then into her darkened sickroom walked the thirty-three-year-old poet Robert Browning, prepared to worship both her and her work. Barrett was appalled by his delusions. Couldn't this healthy young man with the kind face see that she was a bedridden, middle-aged invalid? For many months she held him at arms' length and severely limited his visits. Once, when he declared his love for her, she became so outraged that she announced she would ban him altogether if he mentioned the word "love" again. She was a sick woman on intimate terms only with death, she told him grimly. She would never be anyone's wife.

Browning continued to court Barrett without using the word "love," and the invalid grew a little stronger every day in spite of herself. She also grew more confused. Browning urged her to go south for the winter with him and write poetry in Italy. When her physician agreed that the warmer weather would prolong her life, Elizabeth asked her father for permission to travel with one of her sisters. He would not answer. Elizabeth tried again. Indicating that she would stay in England if her father insisted, she asked for an answer, but he remained silent. Finally a brother interceded, and Mr. Barrett bellowed, "Go! But I don't approve."

"He is a madman, and you are his slave!" Browning thundered when he heard the news. But Elizabeth could not bring herself to break with her father. She owed him too much and she was too weak.

Gradually, the invalid poet began seeing herself more as Browning saw her and less as her father saw her. She found she could walk around her room without getting exhausted. She discovered a certain beauty that shone from her dark eyes. Her feelings changed, too. As she later wrote, one day as she lay in her bed, she was seized by a strange and powerful emotion. It came on so suddenly that it seemed to grab her by the hair and pull back her head.

> Guess now who holds thee!
> "Death," I said, but there the silver answer rang...
> Not Death but Love.

Thoroughly shaken, Elizabeth Barrett had to admit she was in love. Plain, sickly, and thirty-nine, she hadn't expected it and couldn't explain it. "He cares for me because he cares for me," she told herself, and to Browning she wrote, "I stand by a miracle in your love."

Of course, Elizabeth Barrett in love was quite a different person than the invalid. She wanted to get out of bed, walk outside, travel, and care for her new love. She wanted to kiss. She wanted to grow strong. She even wanted to get away from her father, which was not a side of herself that she felt comfortable considering. But even as she tentatively put her new ideas into practice, she wondered if she was pulling the wool over her own eyes. Was she really changing? And could she actually leave her father who, of course, saw no changes in her at all?

After more than a year of courtship, the two lovers formulated a plan. In early spring, she would quietly walk back and forth in her bedroom to try to build her strength up so that she could stand on her feet and walk short distances. If successful, she would then take her maid into her confidence. In the summer she would take short trips in town, and in September she and Robert would elope. Although the couple's plan had to change several times to accommodate Mr. Barrett's erratic activities, Elizabeth and Robert finally snuck off to church on September 12, 1846, and were married in a matter of minutes. When the minister suggested Browning kiss his new wife, the answer was, "No time." The two poets hopped into separate carriages, and hastily returned to their respective homes.

The following week, Elizabeth summoned all her courage and, with her maid and her dog, walked out of the house as casually as she could manage. They went to the neighborhood bookstore where Browning waited. Before Mr. Barrett knew what was happening, the little entourage had taken the train to the English Channel. There they safely boarded the night boat for France before the furious father realized that his daughter had escaped. He never forgave her, and for as long as he lived returned the letters she sent him remained unopened. Elizabeth Barrett Browning and her husband were on their way to Italy where they set up their household and, in spite of her age and illness, had a son. The Brownings' marriage flourished until Elizabeth's death fifteen years later.

"I love thee with the breath, smiles, tears of all my life!" she had written, "and, if God choose, I shall but love thee better after death."

Although most love affairs are less dramatic than the Brownings', the periods of doubt and guilt that Elizabeth Barrett suffered as love changed her picture of herself and drew her away from her family are, in fact, common. The love of a lifetime initiates such sweeping changes that it inevitably breaks former ties in ways that are unexpected and painful. It is not only that a person's primary allegiance shifts from the family of origin to the adored man or woman, but that it shifts from the family's previously accepted values to new, experimental ones. Priorities of all kinds are turned upside down and lovers seem bent on developing new personalities. Good girls run away from home, talkers fall silent, the cocktail set gets religion, and the brainy join jazz bands. When a passionate love of a lifetime forces a person like Ali or Elizabeth Barrett to see life in a new way, it also starts them thinking and speaking in a new way. To their families and friends, what comes out of their mouths sounds like a foreign language. Everyone is genuinely mystified. Even when a great love sandbags a pair of fifty-year-olds, the lovers must incorporate their new understanding of how life works into their old relationships. After my college love reappeared—and disappeared—one of the greatest surprises for me was how profoundly the changes he initiated affected my old friendships. Over the course of some five years, I found myself readjusting my relationships. In addition, I formed new ones with people I had previously ignored, and lost a few as well. These unexpected changes convinced me as much as anything else that a great love changes us at the core.

∼

I spoke with a woman who was raised in an academic household in which everyone was judged by how much he or she knew. After falling in love, the woman gradually decided that kindness meant more to her than education. When she became formally engaged to a good-hearted

ran an aquarium and wore tall rubber boots, her family was
curious. Did this man read? At least about fish? Was he doing
research? "You can do better," they told her repeatedly. "A professor's
daughter can't marry a fish keeper." The woman herself had had serious doubts until she went camping with him. At the end of their
weekend, they broke camp and trudged several miles down the mountain in a warm rain. After they had slung their backpacks into the
trunk of her car, the woman reached for her keys but couldn't find
them. Suddenly she felt sick. She had hung the car keys from a short
branch on a tree at the campsite so they wouldn't get lost. They were
still there.

"He didn't yell," she remembered. "He said, 'Anyone could make that
mistake. I'll get them.'"

Hours later as she saw his light flicker through the misty darkness,
she thought of a story she had heard as a child about religious
pilgrims. Each had to leave home in the dark and climb up the side of
a mountain until he or she arrived at a rustic shrine. There, each
pilgrim lit a candle, said a prayer, and returned with the flickering
light. The whole town turned out to watch the lights come trickling
down the mountain.

"When I saw his light come flickering down the trail, a feeling of certainty settled over me. I wanted the man with the kind heart because I
wanted to be like that myself. Love had changed my priorities."

I also had a client who fell in love with a tall, skinny forty-year-old who
lived with his parents and boasted of having a computer in every room of
their split-level ranch. My client adored this impossible man for three years
with no visible results. Then she crashed her car. She awoke in the hospital with this man at her side chanting, "Thank you. Thank you." Much

later, he told her that on that day he finally realized he loved her, and he also knew he would soon break his parents' hearts by moving out.

Romantic love is not the only experience that takes people from their old homes and pushes them into the dark to find their own way. One woman explained that the birth of her first child and her conversion to Christianity, as well as her first love, all ranked equally as transforming loves of her life. Each was a revolution, quiet or dramatic, which broke with the past. Two men admitted that the first sight of their newborn babies sent a wave of love through them that nearly knocked them to the floor. They had both thought they were familiar with love—knew all about it—but the power of their reaction astonished them and still does. One freely admits that his son is the love of his life, and I wonder if this won't make it difficult for the son to break away when it's time to find a love and a way of his own. But none of us chooses the love of a lifetime. It simply arrives, and whether it's easy or difficult, we remember the romance that sets us on our own path as the love of a lifetime. Such a love gives people a much needed *incompleteness*. By surprising and confusing them, it enables them to change their minds and expand. It is the rough emotional equivalent of molting, that dangerous process in which a crab sloughs off its protective shell and grows larger before forming a new home.

"No human creature can give orders to love," wrote novelist George Sand, who knew this from personal experience. But once its shock troops arrive, we can supply them with food or starve them out. It takes enormous courage to let one's old world be shaken apart by a grand passion, and it takes strength to remain uncertain and uncomfortable while the whirlwind destroys the familiar picture we have built of ourselves. It takes effort, intelligence, and patience to discern the new version of ourselves that has been revealed and to distinguish it from wishful thinking. As happy and exhilarating as a great love affair can be, it is also a demanding journey into the unknown that is taken alone and not completed quickly.

While traveling with his companions across some vast and uninhabited stretch of land, Lawrence Durrell wrote, "We had become, with the approach of night, once more aware of loneliness and time—those two companions without whom no journey can yield us anything."

Strange as it may sound, the love of a lifetime is, among many other things, the lonely, uncertain journey of the brand new revolutionary on her way from a hometown she has outgrown to a place and a way of her own.

CHAPTER 4
Staying in the Ring

THE HERO'S CODE:
SHOW UP, PAY
ATTENTION, TELL THE
TRUTH, AND LET GO
OF THE OUTCOME.
—Angeles Arrien,
The Four-Fold Way

When mathematician, philosopher, and Nobel Prize laureate Bertrand Russell described passion—an experience he sought relentlessly— he said that it brought him two distinct states of euphoria. One was physical ecstasy, the other, connection.

"It relieves loneliness," he wrote of the latter, "that terrible loneliness in which one shivering consciousness looks over the rim of the world into the cold, unfathomable lifeless abyss."

In this chapter, we look at the connectedness that passion introduces us to and the difficulties lovers have in maintaining it. "The same blood was flowing through both of us," one lover told me. "We would melt together," maintained another. "Even our dreams merged." When the love of a lifetime strikes, it brings moments of near-perfect connection, a level of togetherness that every lover secretly believes has never before occurred in the history of the world. It also brings the possibility of a heartbreak that is equally extreme. In a grand passion, lovers are so vulnerable that they are sure all the blood in their body will run out of them if their beloved leaves. What can be done? Stay in the ring and hope that misunderstandings and disappointments won't kill you? Or run, and save what little of the old self remains? We all do some of each, probably on a daily basis, but until a person can tolerate the loss of love, he or she will be terrified of connection.

There are no easy love affairs in this chapter. Although the two marriages and one relationship I use as examples all lasted many years, they were undertaken by people who were ill-prepared by their childhoods to tolerate the fears and uncertainties of intimacy. All had particular trouble remaining connected to another person. Of course, when life went smoothly they were enthusiastic lovers, but when a problem reminded them of love's fragility, they leapt out of the ring. They jumped into bed with another partner, worked fifteen hours a day, drank heavily, or moved. In spite of bad habits bred of insecurities, however, these skittish lovers eventually managed to commit to love. They were amazed. As Ram Dass, an American who has brought much Eastern philosophy to the west, put it, "my heart closes all the time and I have to open it again." When love hits, a lot of hearts fly open, but not all learn how to keep on opening when trouble arrives.

Leah Blackman's marriage might be seen by many as an excruciating form of warfare, but her definition of the love of a lifetime is a touching one. Such a love, she believes, is found in the person who finally proves to you that you can be a devoted spouse. How do two people do this for each other? Forty-some years ago, Leah was a miserable eighteen-year-old in major trouble in central Florida. A thin girl with hazel eyes and waist-length brown hair, she had gotten a rotten start in life by anyone's standards. Raised as an only child, she had witnessed the constant drinking and fighting of her parents until, in an effort to escape, she had married and moved out at age sixteen. The union almost immediately faltered, and two years later the usually rebellious Leah had slunk back home so depressed she wouldn't speak. For several weeks, she picked at food and only left her room to go to the bathroom. Her father screamed, her mother cried, and after three weeks with no improvement, the police were called in to take the stringy-haired girl to a mental hospital. There she was cleaned up and given old-fashioned electroshock treatments—where she felt like she was going to choke to death while all the bones in her body were broken. Thankfully, she remembers little from her two months of treatment except the ineradicable sense that she was being punished for being alive. She also remembers the presence of a serious young man named Daniel Blackman who seemed glad she'd been born.

Leah first met Daniel in the hospital, where the twenty-nine-year-old graduate student was a part-time volunteer. In some respects, the dark-haired, bespectacled student seemed as shy and uncertain as she was, and even with her mind addled from the electroshock, she noticed he had a habit of touching his glasses repeatedly when nervous. When he played Ping-Pong with her in the poorly lit hospital basement—and always won—she discovered he was more agile than he looked. And on Wednesday evenings when staff and patients gathered in the old gym to dance, she further noticed that he held her just a little closer every time. He wasn't the best-looking partner she'd ever danced with, she decided; his nose was too big and he frowned too often, but he was "earnest." Occasionally, he shook off some of his seriousness and tried to make her laugh. "Champagne?" he would ask as attendants in white coats passed among the dancers handing out sweetened orange juice. The drink was intended for patients who were coming out of an insulin-induced coma, which was one of the treatments. It was a funny place to fall in love, but that's where she met Daniel.

Once Leah left the hospital, the two embarked upon a short but stormy courtship. Daniel too had been married before, and, like Leah, his confidence had been shaken by the magnitude of his mistake. "Neither one of us was easy," she remembered, "and we knew it. I was too much, and he was too little. There were times when we couldn't stand each other." But they did indeed marry.

Leah was still experiencing large ups and downs in her moods, and either she danced in the kitchen as she prepared a candlelight dinner for Daniel or she lay in bed for a week and wouldn't get up. Daniel, on the other hand, was as regular as a clock. From the age of fourteen when his mother died and his father disappeared, he had brought himself up according to a strict and unwavering schedule. He got up at the same time each morning, ate the same breakfast, and now dressed in suits that were so similar Leah was sure his patients believed he had only one.

"What you call 'control,' I call reliability," he would tell her with infuriating calmness.

"And what you call calm, I call frozen!" she would scream back.

"He kept people out," she recalled, "and that drove me crazy. Sometimes we'd go dancing, and when I felt his hand pressing into my back or sliding a little further around my waist, I knew for a fact that he loved me and I could feel us melt together like a couple of candy bars left on the dashboard. But he wouldn't say it. I'd look up at him as the music played and sing along with the words, telling him, you know, how much I cared, and sometimes I'd feel him pull back. It's a terrible hungry feeling to want love from someone who is locked up and silent. I felt helpless. For years, I didn't know if he would ever love me. He didn't know either."

For her part, Leah had an urgent need to bestow affection lavishly and have it received enthusiastically. It was her way of reassuring herself that she was indeed connected. To Daniel, it felt like attack. When he needed to study, she needed to sing him a song. When he was late for class, she needed three or four good-bye hugs. And when he settled down to read, she would invariably start a conversation.

"Honey, do you remember what were we doing *exactly* one year ago today?"

"Yes," he would answer coldly, readjusting his glasses, "trying to read."

"I badgered him pretty bad," she admitted. "When he was angry he used to shout, 'You're like a glass that can't hold water,' and I would think to myself, 'He's right. Who would want a glass like that?'"

After Daniel received his degree in clinical psychology, the couple moved out of the city into a fine brick house on the grounds of a private hospital. Two children were born, and Leah embarked on a career she called "wife and mother," but her children referred to as "small-town royalty." Not only did her husband serve her—he did all the driving and shopping and most of the cooking—but patients from the hospital were hired to care for the house and lawn. A woman wearing six strings of pearls did the ironing, skinny men with tremors raked the yard or washed windows, and a dozen others dropped in at odd moments to give Leah a bunch of lilacs or leave Daniel a long, rambling letter. Leah, meanwhile, ate chocolates and taught herself to play the piano. She looked "womanly" by thirty, and enjoyed the status that her flowing dresses and lace collars gave her in the hospital community. After a few years at the piano, she began giving impromptu recitals for the neighborhood children as well as the window washer and the ironer. The Blackman house was the most entertaining place to be in the entire hospital complex. There was food, conversation, and abundant sympathy for everyone except the Blackmans themselves. For the four of them, there was the old and neverending fight over whether Daniel could reach out to his wife and establish a connection, and whether Leah could believe she was lovable.

By the time the children were in grade school, they realized that their father had two distinct personalities. At the hospital, everyone loved Doctor Daniel because he was so kind and above all so patient. "You are lucky to have such a husband," the nurses and receptionists said to Leah, and to the children, "I hope you appreciate your father." At home, however, Dr. Daniel shut himself up in his den and bellowed if his endless reading was interrupted.

"Why don't they get divorced?" the children asked each other when they were old enough to understand the concept. "Why don't they grow up?" they asked as teenagers. They were always relieved when their father, now grown gray and portly, went away for a conference, and they were always appalled when he called a family meeting and presided over it like a detached therapist. Predictably, both children developed dramatic ways to force their parents to stop feuding and pay attention to them instead— asthma for one, school difficulties for the other. Both were out of the house by seventeen. It seemed to them that their parents must have agreed to be miserable. Both complained. Neither changed. Obviously there was something safe and familiar about disappointment, and something dangerous and unpredictable about love.

Not long after the children had left home, Daniel reduced his hours at the hospital, and Leah persuaded him to take ballroom-dancing lessons. It was, she said, the best thing they ever did.

"Dancing finally taught him how to melt," she said. "The children say it was a miracle, but I say he finally got over the hump. He began to thaw."

For nearly three years, the couple danced, Leah with her copper-colored hair and big, colorful dresses, and Daniel in his serious gray suit made quite the pair. At home, they slept in separate bedrooms and took vacations alone—he to conferences, she to visit the children—but every week they danced together. He continued to serve her like royalty, and she, more gracious now, poured him a little sherry, played the piano, and let him read. To the children, they seemed almost happy.

At sixty, Daniel died.

"Mother was helpless," the daughter said. "I mean quite literally, she had no idea how to take care of a house or herself. She couldn't drive. She couldn't imagine sleeping without hearing him snore in the next room, and she couldn't eat without him. What about breathing? Speaking? She had lost the one person in the world who really knew her. We were sure she would 'accidentally' kill herself."

Leah remained so deeply depressed for two years that her children felt forced to call her daily to see if she was alive. There were emergency trips to her home, the hiring and firing of homemaking help, and the shock of seeing Leah's dyed hair turn gray.

"Hopeless," Leah called herself, but she was not lost in the same way she had been at eighteen. The question back then was whether or not she had what it took to build and sustain an intimate connection: the question after Daniel's death was whether she was able to live without the one sustaining connection she had indeed been able to make.

In the third year after Daniel's death, Leah tentatively rejoined the living. She dyed her hair apricot and elaborately "put on her face." She started to cook and went to temple.

"I always wanted Daniel to show me how much he loved me," she reminisced. "That was the water I needed in my glass to stay alive, and I wanted him to keep on pouring. But you know," she continued, shaking her head in surprise, "that's not the way it finally worked out.

He didn't convince me I was his sweetheart, I convinced myself. The day came when I knew for a fact that I did a good job of loving my stubborn, hard-headed husband, and then...well, I knew that I was lovable myself. Do you see what I mean? A person who can love... is lovable."

As if to test this insight that to her was so novel and refreshing, Leah "took up with" a sixty-five-year-old man who had been orphaned in Germany during the Holocaust and who rarely spoke.

"This is good," she said, "because he doesn't interrupt my thinking."

Naturally, her thinking is about Daniel.

"Believe me, I always knew where Daniel was when he was in the house. I was always listening for him. I used to say I couldn't live with him or without him, and that's still true. We still argue and..." she paused for a second and shrugged, "and we still dance. After he died," she continued, "it took a while to figure out how to stay in touch, but now...now I know right where he is."

I heard a lot of stories like Leah's and Daniel's: two difficult people, strongly drawn to each other by loneliness and desire, get together and slug it out. These are sometimes called "rescue marriages" or "recovery relationships," but I think of them as romances that give vulnerable lovers chance after chance to connect. In these love affairs, they gradually learn to trust their partner and themselves in spite of their insecurities. Prince Charles's twenty-five-year reliance on Camilla Parker Bowles seems to be this kind of love affair. During a phone call that was recorded, Charles told Camilla how proud he was of her. "Don't be silly," she replied, implying she had done nothing special and not understanding that he regarded her love as proof of his intrinsic worth. He quickly set her straight. "Your greatest achievement is to love me." And his greatest achievement, it seems, is to believe at last that he is worthy of being loved.

~

The terms "committed partner" or "staying in the ring" can be misunderstood to mean that a lover must endure forever the miseries of a failed or failing relationship. Nothing could be farther from the truth. "Staying in the ring" means the willingness to remain awake and available for as long as the relationship lasts. It also means that no one partner unilaterally determines the moment when a marriage or romance is over. There is no pretending the relationship is fine, then blindsiding the other by asking for divorce. The surest way I know to stay in the ring is to follow a device from Angeles Arrien's *The Four-Fold Way* called "the hero's code": show up, pay attention, tell the truth, and let go of the outcome. The Blackmans had trouble with all four steps. Reading alone in the study when his wife wanted to talk was not showing up. During those endless hours, Daniel was out of the ring, and the romance suffered. Even when the two were together, neither did a good job in the early years of their marriage of paying attention. Leah didn't say, "I can see you're lost in thoughts of work." Daniel didn't say, "I can see you're lonely."

Telling the truth comes next. This refers to one's own true feelings and beliefs, not to a judgment passed on another person. "I feel cornered when you badger me," is a truth. "You talk too much," is an opinion. Telling the truth is unbelievably difficult at times, but unless it's done, the relationship cannot be sure of its foundations or even its true size and shape. In other words, its outcome will always be in doubt and remain hidden unless both partners tell the truth. When they do, the relationship will follow its own course like a brook. It will meander all over the place reflecting the partners' ambivalence; it will sink into the earth and end; or it will, as with the

Blackman's marriage, gradually cut a clear bed for itself and flow more surely. Once Leah and Daniel showed up together on the dance floor, the two paid attention to each other, sang the words of the songs that expressed the truth, and let the dancing move their love forward—at last. Love is tough, and only heroes learn to stay in the ring.

~

When two young kids, Dora and Len, decided to marry many springtimes ago, it was not at all clear if either one of them could become a hero. No one had taught them that all this difficult truth telling and showing up paid off.

"Because spring was unusually warm this year," Dora told me shakily, "and because springtime has always been for me a time of miracles and heartbreak, I awoke the other morning and said out loud, 'I want him back.'"

She paused a minute as if confused.

"I wish I believed that," she said. "I mean, I wish I knew for sure *what* I wanted."

The "him" that Dora may or may not want back is her husband, Len, who is the love of her life and the man from whom she has been separated for ten years. The time is at hand, they both agree, when they must decide once and for all whether to remain apart or try one last time.

As often happened when a person volunteered to tell me her story, Dora and I spent the first ten minutes beating around the bush. An athletic woman who dressed and moved like a college kid, Dora was sitting backwards in her chair tossing out the buzz words. "You know the routine," she said cheerfully, glancing past me out the window, "I met this guy named Len and we started dating. He was handsome. I was beautiful." She laughed. "Seriously, we looked great together. I was the energetic cheerleader; he was the quarterback. We could have been the homecoming king and queen of any Small Town, U. S. A." On she went with the background, how compatible they were, what they did together, how he loved his cold beer, perhaps too much, until she reached the point where she and Len were married on an unseasonably warm spring day. Quite abruptly she looked me in the eye and began to cry.

"I'm crying because spring is unusually warm this year," she said through her tears, and I sensed that now she was going to tell me how it felt, not just how it happened.

Year by year, project by project, binge by binge, Dora told me what it was like to weave a bond of great love with a man who felt as alone and unprepared as she did and then to see their beautiful tapestry of shared intimacy begin to unravel.

"We built a house for ourselves out of love, neither one of us knowing how it was supposed to go, yet both of us being so helpful and willing. I was constantly amazed that two people who had not received much love growing up could do such a good job together, but with Len I had the unshakable feeling that nothing was insurmountable. I don't know *how* I knew that we could do anything we set our minds to, but the feeling was bedrock under my feet. For the first time in my life, I had leverage. I was sure I could make things happen."

"Len and I always washed storm windows together," she continued. "We worked together well, and I can still see him standing on a ladder, his tanned face and baby-fine brown hair framed against the blue September sky. Or we'd hang out the laundry together in summer...and winter." She laughed happily at the memory of huge frozen sheets hanging from the line like the blades of a windmill. "I loved the feeling of being a team.

"I keep several old snapshots of Len in a shoe box mixed in with pictures of the kids, paper clips, rubber bands, and the warranties on my kitchen appliances. The jumble reminds me of the way we lived, all mixed in with the daily chores of living. Warm. Connected. Deeply in love. But this is only half the story.

"Over the years, Len would stop drinking intermittently, then start again," she went on. "We had three kids, our circle expanded. We weren't going to let anything hurt them the way we'd been hurt. I remember trying to picture our family as others saw it, and I liked to think they envied us. All three kids looked exactly like Len, square little faces and flyaway hair. I think we looked like one of those happy, on-the-go families you see on television. But that's not the way it worked out. Len's drinking disrupted the team. We never knew if we had five players or four—or two opposing teams. I found it hard not to pay him back in kind, not by drinking, but by going off with the kids and forming our own team or by paying more attention to my friends. He'd keep me waiting hours for a movie date—me and the babysitter waiting at home together, and me making up stupid excuses about how my husband must be working late. I remember taking a sitter home on Valentine's Day after Len simply disappeared. It broke my heart to see our house come down."

Dora gazed out the window behind me. She didn't cry over the sad parts of the story, I noticed, only over the achingly lovely memories of love—the beauty of the man, the promises he fully intended to keep, the warm spring days of their young lives. I have walked into churches that made me cry in that same sudden way, perhaps because they pull pain and beauty so unbearably close together—because they express in a single image searing loneliness and unremitting hope.

"I will never stop being 'the woman who loves Len.'" Dora continued. "I could no more stop loving him than I could stop being Dora. But I was watching the kids get all messed up."

Dora said that making the decision to leave Len "was like losing a pint of blood a day." She knew she had to get away from this unreliable man, but she didn't know how to do it without losing the precious confidence she had gained in herself. Her mother and her friends screamed, "Cut the sucker loose!" But no one told her how to leave without erasing all the good they'd done for each other.

Luckily, Dora was in no rush. She waited for a brief period of sobriety, told Len she wanted to stay married but live apart until he stopped drinking, and when he raced back to the bottle, moved herself and her kids to a safer place.

"The kids are grown now," I said. "Are you going back?"

Dora heaved a sigh.

"Once Len said to me that when he dies, I will still be the only woman he has ever loved. I can say the same to him. In this lifetime, I think I've gotten all I'm going to get, but I feel sure I'll be with him after death." She paused a moment. "As I listen to myself, I realize all over again that no one can live with a person who keeps pulling back, and that's what alcohol does, it puts him out of reach.

"We're supposed to call each other next week," she continued in a low voice, "and he'll ask, as he always does, if there's..." She sighed again. "...if there's any chance."

Dora's arms slumped over her chair and she looked up at the ceiling. "I am his forever," she said to the spring air, "but no, I won't try again."

I do not think that Dora wasted her time with Len, and she herself would be horrified at the idea. The two were together for nearly thirteen years, and for most of that time they were learning to connect—she on the fast track, he on the slow. Dora reminds me of one of those huge, tropical amaryllis corms that require eight or more years to gather enough strength to bloom. I don't think she spent the last ten years recovering from the heartbreak of losing Len to alcohol. I think she has been working on the hero's code. When I spoke with her, there was a clarity about her sadness and a conviction about the worth of her love for Len that made me think that for Dora their marriage was not the end of her travels along the road of love but a long beginning.

Two years later, I overheard Dora talking endearingly to "Honey" on the phone.

"Was that Len, honey?" I asked when she hung up, "or Somebody New, honey?"

"That was New," she answered, beaming. "Actually, we've known each other for years and then oh, about eighteen months ago…well…you know."

"And Len?"

"The love of my life, without question. I almost died, but it was great." She thought for a moment, still smiling. "Len and I completed a tough course together and I know a lot more about love now." She winked. "This one's easy."

Several months later, Dora was married to her new love.

It is a wonderful thing when people like Dora and the Blackmans learn after a rocky start that they are capable of staying in the ring. Challenges remain, of course, but several forms of self-doubt are over. They know they can fall in love all the way, they know they can love well, and they have learned that as a result, they are lovable. They stayed together long enough to learn these immensely useful lessons. But staying together by no means guarantees good results. Many relationships go nowhere as the partners lurch in and out of the ring and finally stop expecting intimacy. No matter how long these passionless unions of convenience last or how smoothly they run, low-risk relationships teach superficial lessons. They do not prove that we can connect or tolerate the loss of love, only that we can put our own lives on hold and live without intimacy. We assume that these lightweight duets exist outside marriage, and that active, committed partnerships develop inside some form of monogamous relationship. But neither love nor its lessons are reserved for the unattached. Transforming love presents itself to anyone. Sometimes disguised as distraction or indulgence, love pushes open any door it finds. It invades.

~

When Kermit was sixty—a tall, wealthy man with a shock of white hair and a charming touch of a brogue—he wasn't sure he had ever fallen flat on his face in love. He knew how to remain married—he'd been with his wife, Alice, for thirty years—and he knew how to start passionate romances on the side, but they never lasted. Either he had never really been in love, or "real love" always faded. Sometimes he identified with the protagonist in the musical *Stop the World, I Want To Get Off,* who sings "Why Can't I Fall in Love?" And other times he agreed with an article in the *Washington Post* that said passion never lasts and even very good relationships make do on mutual interests and a sense of loyalty. OK, he said to himself, that's the way it is. When he met a sophisticated, forty-five-year-old opera critic at a cocktail party, a Greek woman with the exotic name of Delphine, he thought, as usual, it would be fun to flirt, but he wasn't expecting much. The tall, black-haired woman with the dark eyes and a wide, red mouth reminded him a little of soprano Maria Callas. Obviously a spirited woman, she was married, he noted, to a humorless hulk. She would undoubtedly respond to a little blarney.

Although mutually and immediately attracted to each other, Kermit and Delphine got off to a nervous and rather tentative start. She seemed flattered by the African daisies or birds-of-paradise he sent to her office, and pleased to be escorted by such an urbane gentleman to intimate restaurants with gurgling waterfalls. But Kermit could not be sure whether she was interested in him or only bored with her marriage. Because he was in the habit of managing the emotional distance between him and his lady friends, the uncertainty made him anxious. The real problem, he decided, was that Delphine was fifteen years his junior. He spent the first two years of their relationship wishing that her smooth olive skin would wrinkle so that he wouldn't worry so much about the fifty-year-olds who materialized around her like mosquitoes on a summer evening. Someday, he feared, she would notice the darkening constellations of moles on his skin or his shrinking muscles, and then she would leave him for a man her own age.

More than once when their lunch was interrupted by a friend of Delphine's who stopped by their table and stayed too long, Kermit found himself suddenly more interested in his career. Working had always made him feel better, he admitted. It put things in perspective. Flirtations came and went. Work stayed. He was never going to retire.

Then, some three years into this dalliance, Kermit and his wife moved from Washington, D. C., to Princeton, New Jersey, as they had planned to do for decades. He was devastated to be separated from Delphine. Although they had plans to meet every two weeks in Philadelphia, he was thrown into a panic that mortified him. Every night he had dreams of missing his train. Every day he forgot his keys or lost something or sat in his car in the garage not knowing where he was supposed to go. He suffered, he said, as he would hate to suffer again. Delphine's absence made his heart ache, and it also prompted embarrassingly adolescent behavior. Whether striding along a trail in the woods with his polished walking stick, he found he could not stop himself from scratching her initials on rocks. He pictured the charming village of Princeton covered with her initials—carved into trees, spray-painted on buildings, and lovingly scratched onto every rock.

Clearly this was the moment to join a book club and charm someone new. Time to travel. Time to work. Instead, Kermit fretted his way back and forth to Philadelphia. He said he felt pushed forward by an unknown and unexpected force. A hand placed squarely between his shoulder blades shoved him out of the house and onto the train. It pushed him up against his worst anxieties.

Kermit continued seeing Delphine, and in less than a year she separated from her husband and moved permanently to Philadelphia. Kermit was both relieved and alarmed. Now he could see her more often, but would she be content with only two or three lunch dates a week? The answer was, "No."

Delphine began going to operas, concerts, plays, and dinners with unattached men. Kermit knew what she looked like in black, backless dresses or flaming silks. She would sweep her black hair into a bun, hang diamonds from her ears, and glow with pleasure. He was beside himself. Again he tried to take a step back, but the hand that rested against his shoulders kept pushing. Was he more in love with Delphine than the other women he'd romanced? Was the timing finally right for him? Perhaps, he said, it was the rather desperate courage that comes with age. At sixty, he hadn't yet "lived hard enough" except in those moments when he was starting a new romance. He got something from that thrill that he needed on a more permanent basis. It was time to hold on and see if he could get it.

But it wasn't easy. For months, Kermit tried to appear reasonable concerning Delphine's dates. Finally, he went to her apartment and confronted her. He knew it wasn't fair to ask her not to go out with other men, especially since he himself was still married, but he was forced to admit that he couldn't stand it. He loved her. He felt excited every time he saw her. But if they were to continue, she would have to stop dating.

Delphine exploded. In the process of making a Greek soup with lemons and eggs, she began to slam eggs on the kitchen counter to emphasize each point she made. "No!" Crunch. She would not stop seeing other men! "Yes!" Crunch. "You are insecure, and you are a coward," she announced, and with that she washed her hands, tore off her apron, and stormed out of her apartment. Hailing a cab, she headed for her weekly appointment at the beauty salon. Forty-five minutes later, handsome, white-haired Kermit burst into the salon, strode to the back of the shop where Delphine sat under a dryer, dropped to his knees, and grasped her hand. Fishing a small box from his pocket, he slipped a ring on her finger—a wedding ring.

"You are mine," he declared defiantly, as he gripped her hand so hard her fingers turned white. With a gracious smile, she stood, shrugged off the smock that covered her clothes, and walked out of the salon in curlers to the waiting cab. Eventually, the two agreed that she could to go out whenever she chose but as part of a foursome or a larger group, and wearing the ring. They were in this relationship forever.

When Kermit left the city late that afternoon, he drove to the Jersey shore and there, dressed as usual in a suit, walked for an hour at the water's edge. Wave after wave ran up toward his feet, and wave after wave of relief ran through his body. To his astonishment, he realized he was in love—helplessly, joyously, jealously, and lastingly in love.

"My secret fear had been that nothing could move me."

Kermit must have made a funny sight as he picked up a piece of drift-wood as tall as himself and, heedless of the sand that sifted onto his dark suit, carefully drew his initials and Delphine's in very large letters on the deserted beach. He was lining the letters with shells as it grew dark. The tide would remove his testimony, he knew, and even worse, the mosquito-like men would continue to hover over Delphine and make him suffer, but nothing could take away the great mixed feelings of love and gratitude, happiness and relief.

He was right. Although he and Delphine were never married legally, they remained devoted to each other until his death some twenty years later. Afterwards, she returned to Greece to live with her sister.

Of course there is always another angle from which to view such a liaison, and the poignancy and surprising perseverance of secret rela-tionships can only be unambivalently appreciated if the lovers' spouses are left out of the equation. In Kermit's case, his wife Alice survived him by several years. During that time she reread, annually, each of the books that had been sitting on his nightstand when he died. Her favorite was a collection of love letters sent by Robert Browning to the future Elizabeth Barrett Browning, the same Miss Barrett who struggled so hard to leave home. Alice became so famil-iar with Browning's love letters, especially those that Kermit had marked as particularly meaningful to him, that she began writing her own responses.

"Always with you in spirit," Browning had written in one of the let-ters that Kermit had checked, "always yearning to be with you in body—always, when with you, praying, as for the happiest of fortunes, that I remain with you forever."

"My Darling, I feel that forever is at hand," Alice wrote back. "Although you have passed beyond the sight of my eyes and the touch of my dry hand, my spirit accepts your invitation with a joy the color of grass. The marks you have left behind, on this book, in the garden, throughout the house, mark the trail I follow."

In all likelihood, Alice misread the marks. Does this make her a fool? This woman who missed her husband so much that she sent him love letters after his death? Or does it make Kermit an evil man? The perversity with which love incorporates all that we despise into the stories we cherish most is unfathomable. Like a fragrant flowering vine that suffocates the crowns of trees, a great love does not adorn a life, it invades it.

~

Leah and Daniel Blackman, Dora, and Kermit, all defined the love of a lifetime as the person with whom they finally discovered the strength to stay connected. This quality of devotion had been missing or in doubt, and to feel like a loving person, they needed to prove to themselves that they could stay the course in spite of their fears and vulnerability. None of these people expected to have an easy time with love. They came from families where people dodged intimacy like bullets, and all faced the possibility that the years might pass without bringing them a real love. They could easily have been right. But they weren't, and when love held them in the ring, they were grateful.

Often lovers value most what they work hardest to learn. For the cautious, it is leaving home, for the fearful, staying in the ring. For still others—those with a strong need to maintain control over their own future—it is giving. For these men and women, giving everything to another person makes life far too uncertain. It robs them of their power to plan. Once they start, however, the person they give everything to be with becomes the love of their lives.

Chapter 5
Giving and Getting

ATTENTION IS
THE MOST BASIC
FORM OF LOVE.
—John Tarrant,
The Light Inside the Dark

Here is a generalization that's hard to believe because it is so simple: every person who talked to me about the love of a lifetime described some form of giving, but those with no experience of a great love imagined getting—always. This difference gradually became a kind of test so that when I wasn't sure what to make of a story, such as one where the teller couldn't decide which of his four wives had been the love of his life, I would listen for the part about giving. If all I heard was getting, I had my doubts.

"I am most alive when I'm being watched," a stunning pianist told me matter-of-factly. "I hunger for unconditional approval, and when the audience roars I feel fully alive…glowing, wonderful. I'm at my best then. It's like being in love, and the love of a lifetime would make me feel like that all the time. I want to find someone who is endlessly fascinated by me."

Or from a cocky young man: "It's the woman who would keep on taking you back when you mess up."

Or: "A great love ought to be dependable. I want a woman who is loyal and appreciates what I do. She should be good at taking care of things, but she should need me, too."

In stark contrast with these lists of requirements is the credo formulated by the famously difficult Katharine Hepburn after twenty-seven years with the famously difficult (and married, and alcoholic) Spencer Tracy who was, by everyone's account, the love of her life. "Love has nothing to do with what you are expecting to get," she stated, "only with what you are expecting to give—which is everything."

This chapter describes another one of the changes that, set in motion by the love of a lifetime, alters a person's outlook on life. Before falling in love all the way, we have given many things to many people, but always with a certain calculation. With the exception of our children, we usually do not seriously jeopardize our own well-being by what we give to others. After the love of a lifetime, however, "give" takes on a new meaning. Its essence is not the perfection of the gift, the magnitude of the effort, or even the size of the sacrifice. Instead, the new giving is characterized by a willingness to step from behind our protective separateness and join another person with no "ifs," "ands," or "buts." It is the big "Yes."

Earlier, we heard this kind of giving described as "an overwhelming willingness" by sixty-nine-year-old Nancy, who met the love of her life in Bermuda. The doors and windows of her heart blew open, and she wanted to give everything to her lover—her dreams, her energy, her caring, her memories, her plans, in fact her entire past, present, and future. This willingness seemed to pour from an open heart that had taken off its armor. It said, "Take me. I'm yours."

This kind of giving is the participation that Brahma was talking about when he told Kama that his job was to get every living thing to join the eternal dance. "Get them to throw away their separateness," I imagine him saying. "Get them to give themselves to the dance of life. They must be taken over by the music. The results will surprise them."

~

Although lovers don't give themselves to love in this radical way on a permanent basis, they never forget the moments when they do. It is the difference between flying in a plane and skydiving, between going underwater in a submarine or snorkeling on the Great Barrier Reef. To give ourselves over to love is to be fully and nakedly immersed in life. Everything touches us directly and has a personal meaning. Even stars a million lightyears away feel so close we can join them for a swim in the sky.

I remember how beautiful the world became the summer after I fell in love. Every day I ran along a narrow road that circles halfway around a pond before climbing a hill and dropping into a kettle hole. I would thread my way into those summer mornings, through patches of cool shade and hot sun, exquisitely aware of everything. Roses that scrambled the length of a low stone wall surrounded me with a dry and faded fragrance. Wild azaleas blooming in the marshy soil near the pond caught me with their sweet gardenia smell. Hot and dry followed cool and damp like phrases in music, and soon I found myself being carried along effortlessly. I ran up a steep, shadeless stretch of road, then dropped precipitously into the cool, green air of the kettle hole, into the twittering of birds. It reminded me of Sunday mornings when the sound of church bells drifts through the woods around my house and collects in the hollows like mist. The air was thick with accumulated blessings.

The giving that love engenders runs in mad circles. Finding such beauty when we hand ourselves over to love, we immediately want to give all of it to our beloved. We give treasures, we sacrifice, we write poetry, we take risks. We are wild to share the happiness we feel, and when we do, we join the dance, take our hands off the controls, and sway into an unpredictable future. The greatest gift we give our beloved is handing ourselves over to love.

As we saw in the last chapter, when love demands that we accept the possibility of grief—of losing the love of our lives—some lovers stay in the ring and some don't. In this chapter, we will see what happens when lovers realize that a great love also demands that they let go of their plans and follow their hearts. They are not giving up their agenda in order to follow another person's itinerary, although it is easy to get mixed up on this point. They are both joining *the* dance. How will this kind of giving change them? What does it have to do with getting? And does giving become more difficult with age and rising expectations of the good life?

~

One of the great love stories that revolves around passionate giving is the centuries-old account of Paolo and Francesca, which today is known primarily from the brief account included in Dante's *Inferno*. The romance took place in an Italy of viciously feuding land owners who raised their own armies and made their own laws. When Giovanni Malatesta, the aging tyrant of Rimini, gray and gimpy, decided to cement a political bargain, he arranged to marry the beautiful Francesca. He ordered the teenaged girl removed from a convent where she was preparing to enter the order. This was not an uncommon occurrence. Ever in need of alliances, men like Giovanni frequently married or gave their daughters in marriage to secure a pact. What was uncommon was the tyrant's tact. Rather than yanking the girl from the convent, throwing a three-day wedding feast, and raping her, he tried to ease the abrupt transition from the spiritual to the secular world and the shock of being coupled to an old man by sending his much younger brother, Paolo, to bring Francesca to the castle. The two were much closer in age, and Giovanni reasoned that if his loyal brother watched over Francesca while he, himself, fought a few more campaigns, everyone would profit. This was the plan. Oh, foolish Giovanni.

In due course, the lovely black-haired girl with skin the color of white roses was brought from the quiet convent and installed in her own rooms in the castle. Some days later, she and Giovanni were married, but even after the elaborate ceremony, she was allowed to retire to her own quarters every night. Giovanni did not immediately force himself on his child bride, whose innocence was so complete that she thought her new husband wanted her to pat his hand each night as he fell asleep.

Unfortunately for everyone, however, Paolo and Francesca were "fated" for each other, or as they said then, she had been born with his kiss on her lips. As he taught her to sing and play the mandolin, or as he read her courtly romances in the fragrant shade of the rose garden, he fell in love as if drugged. She, too, found in Paolo's company a pleasure she couldn't name, but given the level of her naïveté, she had no way of interpreting his sighs or her own accelerating heart. When Paolo was on the verge of losing control and pulling her into his arms, he announced that he must leave immediately and go to war. No undertaking was as dangerous as staying in the castle. Francesca was mystified. Was he tired of reading to her? Was her singing not pleasing to his ears? Paolo could not make her understand. "What do you know of grief?" he finally asked her. "The only tears I have shed," she replied, "were on the pages of a book."

Although Paolo managed to wrench himself free, his desire for Francesca was so great that within several days it pulled him back to the castle. His brother was still away when he returned. Trembling, Paolo walked through the great halls and out into the rose garden where Francesca was reading the story of Launcelot and Guinevere. Bending over her, he took her face in his hands and gave her her first real kiss. Their reactions were instantaneous but dissimilar. He, overcome by remorse, fled back to the stables. Jumping on his horse, he rode off to purchase poison with which to kill himself. It was his only chance at honor. If he remained alive another day, he would steal Francesca from his brother.

Francesca, too, was alarmed. Struggling to understand what had just happened, she sat immobile on the garden bench for a long time. Slowly, she began to read and reread the page she'd been looking at when Paolo kissed her. Sir Launcelot had escaped from a tower where he had been left to die, and, still weak, had traveled at last to Queen Guinevere. He was standing under her window. She heard his voice calling her name.

Suddenly Francesca's passion caught fire. The roses around her began to shimmer, and the sky poured its beautiful blue over the heads of the trees.

"Will you break all the rules for love?" asked Launcelot.

Francesca started to sob and could not stop. She read the phrase again through her tears. "These tears are mine," she realized in amazement.

As Francesca wept in the rose garden, Paolo purchased the poison he needed to end his life, and galloped back to the castle. Determined to see his love once more before he died, he stole into the garden. Coming up behind the weeping Francesca, he sat down beside her, and taking the book from her hand, turned the page. In a soft, sad voice, he read to her of Sir Launcelot's longing for the married queen—how his heart ached, how in his dreams they were together. Hearing the words coming from Paolo, Francesca suddenly understood everything. Turning, she looked at him through her tears. "I know what love is," she told him calmly, "and I know my destiny." To love Paolo was worth life itself. It was the only gift that could express the enormity of her love.

When Giovanni Malatesta returned that night to his castle, he found his beautiful young wife and his own brother together in her curtained bed. Struck by rage, he stabbed them both to death then ordered them carried through the castle on a bloody litter.

According to Dante, Paolo and Francesca were sent to hell for their betrayal of Giovanni. There, they circle endlessly among the damned, close enough to each other to feel the heat of their mutual desire, but not quite close enough to touch. Eternity spent on the verge of a passionate kiss. Dante tells the story with respect. The lovers were neither stupid nor weak. They knew that giving themselves over to love would cost them their lives. Not giving would mean an eternity of regret. Sometimes that is the choice we are given.

~

The love of a lifetime rearranges the definition of giving in ordinary lives, too. For one thing, lovers discover that the person who gives a great deal of love is the one who feels most "in love." For another, the person who gives everything for love often feels chosen by someone else. It is as if we can't believe we are deeply loved until we ourselves have finally embarked on the love of a lifetime.

In the Weinstein family, three generations lived by the maxim: "It's the person who *gives* who feels the love. Just give, give, give."

On a beautiful day in June when the trees in Gramercy park were still a tender, edible green and the smell of freshly cut grass ran like rivers through the city streets, Harold Weinstein heard an alarming "Bang!" and felt his Ford lurch toward the sidewalk. Pulling over, he unfolded his long frame from the small car, assessed the damage, and sighed. Not only was he going to be late for his date, but he was also going to get grease all over his white suit.

"You'll ruin your suit!" called a girlish voice, and Harold looked up to see three young women, arm in arm, come swinging toward him along the pavement. Smiling and thoroughly amused by his predicament, the cute, dark-haired woman in the center had all the answers. Still linked to her girlfriends, Miriam stood on the sidewalk in a light-blue summer dress and open-toed shoes and deftly surveyed the situation.

"Why don't you take off your coat and roll up your sleeves?" she suggested, and as Harold complied, she stepped forward and took his coat.

Harold never got to his date. Instead, after changing the tire, the tall, slightly awkward young man drove the three women to the park and treated them all to lemonade. The next afternoon he stood on Miriam's porch, hat in hand. "More lemonade?" he asked. He had the sweetest smile Miriam had ever seen on man or angel, and as soon as she agreed, he took her arm, stepped on her toe, and escorted her to his waiting car. Exactly one year later they were married.

"He chose *me!*" Miriam said to her girlfriends, and it became a refrain that lasted throughout her life.

Although the industrious Miriam considered herself a natural homemaker, when Harold arrived on her doorstep, she had lost hope of making a home. She loved to cook and sew. She had a knack for turning every room she entered into a homey, welcoming place. It was her gift. She even had the well-endowed figure that her mother and aunts said was perfect for having babies. But she was much too old. Miriam was a dreaded thirty-two when she met thirty-year-old Harold—a fact she successfully hid from him his entire life. She was so grateful that the future she wanted might still be hers that she started giving the moment he knocked on her door. No obstacle was going to get in the way of her love, and she was more than willing to give this relationship everything she had. Luckily, the match was perfect. Awkward Harold wanted exactly what organized Miriam had been yearning to give, and now she gave it with a willingness that surprised even herself.

Over the next twelve years, the Weinsteins started a family, and Miriam, who worked tirelessly, was not surprised to find that her greatest pleasure came from giving to those she loved. A boy, a girl, and another boy were born in quick succession and, after a pause of eight years, a final girl arrived. The father worked and the children went to school while Miriam ran the house. She cooked, she cleaned, she shopped, she complimented, she encouraged, and the more she gave, the luckier she felt. Although she was immensely proud of her children, Harold remained the focus of this wonderful life, and it was his photo that she showed to everyone first. Each time she took the picture of a tall young man in a white linen suit out of her purse, she would say, "and this is the love of my life."

As often happens, however, the love between the Weinsteins was somewhat asymmetrical. Harold was a faithful husband and good provider, but his sweetest smiles and deepest laughs were increasingly lavished on his youngest daughter, Pat. She was so cute, he used to say, so willing to please. Besides, she needed his protection from the older kids. "Harold just adores Pat," Miriam would say, "but he babies her," and indeed even after Pat was married, her father continued to invite her back home. Every conversation they had on the phone ended with him saying: "Anytime you want to come home, sweetie, we'll take care of you."

But Pat stayed married as did her brothers and sister.

"It's the person who *gives* who feels the love," their mother had told them many times. "Just give, give, give."

When Harold died, Miriam began carrying a love letter he had written to her when their first child was born. The letter and the photograph resided together in a plastic envelope in her purse, and years later when she died at the age of ninety (or ninety-two), her children knew she would not depart this earth without her treasured mementos. Into the casket they went, and as a final tribute to their mother, the children had her fake age engraved on the family stone.

Her motto is written on their hearts as well. "Everyone has a special gift," she loved to tell her children, smiling at them with undisguised devotion. "Find the person who wants your gift and just give, give, give."

And for at least two generations they all did. When Pat had to postpone college and career for twenty-five years in order to marry her great love, she did it willingly, and when her daughter had to arrange to raise her children in both the Jewish and Catholic faiths in order to marry her great love, she agreed. Nor was it only the Weinstein women who made sacrifices for love. Miriam's sons did, too. All the Weinstein descendants lived by Miriam's maxim even as giving became more complicated in two-career and two-religion families.

"Is the Weinstein legend true?" I asked Pat as she finished telling me her family's stories. "I mean does give, give, give work every time?"

"It doesn't matter whether it's true," she replied with a sweet smile that I imagined was much like her father's. "What matters is whether or not you believe it. In our family we do. It moves us in the right direction."

"What do you mean?"

"I think if you care for others generously, you actually 'make' love. Your home is filled with it. The more you give, the more everyone around you gives. Mother taught us that feelings are contagious. She also believed that the loving life is better than any other kind, so love always gets top priority. It's become a habit.

"Giving is odd," she continued. "Mother said the person who gives feels the love, but I think people who give feel more of every emotion. They get the life."

~

A brief example makes exactly this point.

While I was having my eyes checked, I asked the technician what she thought the term "the love of a lifetime" meant, and I found she was sitting on the fence between giving and getting. She had been married for thirty-five years, she told me, when her husband ran off and divorced her. For years she had nothing good to say about love. Now, however, she was in a relationship with a man who claimed that he had fallen for her at first sight. "He says he adores me," she said bluntly. "He calls me the love of his life. I guess this time, I'm the lucky one."

"Why is that?"

"It's lucky to be the one who's adored," she answered rather grimly. "It's a much safer position."

"True," I agreed, "but I just talked with a whole family who believes that the person who gives love is the one who feels most *in* love. Your new man is the one who daydreams and buys flowers. He's the one, not you, who gets a charge out of listening to love songs. He's doing the work and having the fun. Do you think he'd trade places with you?"

She stood and thought for a minute. "Maybe not. He smiles more than I do. I think he's happier than I am...right now."

"But even if he knew that eventually you'd leave him," I countered, "do you think he'd give up all the happy excitement he feels for the safety you have?"

The techie smiled for the first time. "He'd better not," she said, "because I'm beginning to think I'll stick around."

And stick around she did. Two annual checkups later, I learned they had married.

~

Although receiving love from another person, either in the sense of getting our needs met or getting a measure of safety, doesn't play much of a role in the love of a lifetime, being chosen as the perfect partner by someone who understands us and adores us does. Like the ability to let go and to give, the capacity to believe that we are chosen without qualification is an essential step in a great love. Like so much else in love, it is a paradoxical step as well. Until we start pouring out all our love as Miriam Weinstein did the instant Harold showed up at her house, or until we have had the experience of giving ourselves to another person, we don't seem able to receive wholeheartedly from another. The gifts we can give and accept keep pace with each other.

A woman of unusual intelligence and charm went through her twenties, thirties, and forties having several serious love affairs but never being swept away. She had come close with her first lover, but he was a wild, creative man, and the risk was too great. At fifty, this woman finally fell deeply in love with a widower. They walked, they talked, and their interests were perfectly matched. She could not believe her good fortune. When the man refused to let the relationship become intimate, however, she was heartbroken. After months of waiting, arguing, and pleading, she gave up. Although she had finally loved a man wholeheartedly, all she got was rejection.

Over the course of the next two years, this woman thought a great deal about her one-sided affection, and slowly began to take pride in the way she had risked her heart and changed her life. "Before, I lived in my mind. Now I live in my heart as well." The words were simple, the change profound.

As she realized she had finally let herself be swept away, memories of her first love returned. He had used certain phrases to describe her, and without knowing why, she had stored them in her memory like secret passwords. Now these phrases returned and made her realize that he had seen right into her and had chosen her above all other women as the perfect match for him.

Who does she now think of as the love of her life? Both men, she told me, but the widower, or rather her love for the widower, had to come first. Until she gave herself away, she was not able to believe that anyone could love her without qualification. People don't prove to themselves they are lovable by hearing the words coming out of someone's mouth, she realized. They prove it to themselves by loving.

The Dutch theologian Henry Nouwen maintained that the importance of feeling chosen could not be overestimated. It marks a shift in the way we see things as startling as those that mark the maturation of a child's mind. For a baby up to one year old, for example, a toy put behind her mother's back is simply gone. It no longer exists, and the child's attention turns to something else. But by age two, a shift has occurred. Now the child understands that out of sight does not mean gone, it means hidden. She remains focused on what she can't see and tries to get it back. Her understanding of the world has shifted in an important way and it will never shift back. Nouwen believed that feeling chosen is such a shift and that it too comes from the inside, not the outside.

Although we hope to be loved unconditionally by parents and later by a great love, Nouwen believed that all the signs of love we receive, even in a happy family, are not sufficient to convince us that we are fundamentally welcome in the world. We still have the nagging sense that we have to earn the love we receive or that we are loved because we are helpful, generous, or beautiful. Even Nouwen himself, who came from a loving home, felt he could never stop working for the love he received. Until...

One day, he heard the words, "You are the Beloved. My favor rests on you." And he believed them. Filled with unexpected joy, he felt as if a pact had been made between him and life. He was welcome on the planet. He was an essential member of the eternal dance. Many situations can trigger this realization, Nouwen understood. Opening our heart to the one we adore is one of them.

Nouwen maintained that from the moment a person has the sense that he or she is *the* chosen one, *the* beloved, such an individual begins life's most important journey and will not rest until the full meaning of this belief is discovered. The certainty of being welcome is the cornerstone of life, he said, and nothing of importance happens in our lives until this pact is made. Before, we are so beset by self-doubt that we always watch our own actions as if we were being evaluated. After the shift, we are spontaneously who we're supposed to be. We embark upon the authentic life.

The relationship between giving and feeling chosen is one of those "Which came first, the chicken or the egg?" type of conundrums. Although Nouwen maintained that no amount of love from others can convince us of our self-worth, psychologists argue that early love from a parent or from some other person is crucial. Without it, they say, we aren't likely to be trusting enough to open our hearts, give freely, and feel welcome in the world.

"Sometimes when I think about that phrase, 'the love of a lifetime,' and what it really means," Pat Weinstein had said uncomfortably, "I think maybe my father was the man I loved most in all my life. I know it's not supposed to be that way, but..."

Here was another father, I thought, but one who seemed to have made falling in love easy for his daughter. Was he singled out because he was the one who gave Pat the confidence to be the loving person that she so obviously is?

"No one paid such close attention to me," she continued. "He didn't simply adore me, he saw me. I was a funny little child, and he noticed and loved every bit of me. That's a powerful combination."

Perhaps when a child of high spirits or widely scattered dreams is born to a parent of similar temperament, the two resonate to each other in a way that is not likely to occur again in either life. Staunch allies in a land of common dreams, they feel a natural affinity and a deep devotion for each other, which is difficult to duplicate. Their bond may not guarantee a lifetime of love for either one, but it provides a model and makes a great love seem possible. I agree with Nouwen that being told we are wonderful is never enough to convince us we are welcome in the world, but I also believe that we cannot take the frightening step of giving our hearts away without deep memories of early love.

If giving ourselves over to love can lead to feeling chosen, which in turn starts a new phase in our lives, what happens to lovers who aren't willing or able to risk their separateness and join the dance? I heard quite a number of love-of-a-lifetime stories that started well but ran into trouble when lovers were asked to give up their plans. There were Easterners who wouldn't live in the West, Americans who wouldn't move abroad, and women who were unwilling to be with the man who said, "I adore you, but no kids." Of all the stumbling blocks that lie in the way of giving ourselves to love, a disagreement concerning children is, I think, the biggest, most common, and most painful. This puts any love to the test.

When Jim met Myra Louise, he was one week short of thirty-nine. A professor in a small New England college, he had never married or lived with a woman, yet the dream of having a wife and family had remained fresh in his mind. As a birthday present to himself, he'd purchased a membership in the Appalachian Mountain Club, and thus he found himself in North Conway, New Hampshire waiting to meet hikers bound for the summit of Mount Washington.

"Girl Scout alert!" said a man who had joined him, and nodding, he indicated three women dressed in canvas climbing shorts and flannel shirts, carrying backpacks and canteens and striding toward them across the grass. All three were in their late thirties, Jim estimated, and obviously fit. With a light brown ponytail swinging in and out of the sun with every step, one in particular caught his eye.

"Nice," he thought to himself. "Determined."

By the time the hikers had been bussed to the base of the mountain, Jim had fallen in step with Myra Louise.

"We're both built like pears," she had said by way of introduction, and indeed they were. Short, slightly round, and supported inexhaustibly on heavily muscled legs, the two of them were regular little engines. At five feet six, Jim was about two inches taller, he noted with satisfaction, and he was glad he'd used the Nordic Track in his living room all winter long. He was in the best shape of his usually sedentary life, and with a full head of brown hair and a dimpled smile his sister envied, he figured he looked pretty good. So did his new acquaintance.

"Unusual to find a woman who can keep up," Jim thought, as the two trudged up the steep, rocky trail. Later Myra had told him that it was nice to find a man who talked about books. Like the sun that moved in and out of wispy clouds overhead, the two drifted in and out of each other's company that cool spring weekend, and before they parted, it dawned on Jim that this might be his lucky year. He had her phone number, they had a date to climb Mount Monadnock, and for no particular reason, he was feeling ridiculously happy. Over the summer as the two hiked, gardened, cooked, and planned, they fell in love. It was a first for Jim in many respects, and he felt stronger, younger, slightly taller, smarter, and sexier every time he met Myra. He thought they had an unusually tender relationship, too, which he chalked up to age. He'd been wise to wait.

"I think the love of a lifetime is the first love or, if not the very first, then one that comes soon after," he said tentatively. "I doubt these loves often last," he added, "or rather they don't thrive. They sit like an orchid on a New England windowsill. "

On the anniversary of their meeting, the couple returned to North Conway to buy a tent. Dressed as usual in their hiking shorts and flannel shirts, the two stood shoulder to shoulder in the showroom of Eastern Mountain Sports amid what looked like a room full of butterflies. The orange, blue, and silver tents looked so vibrant, Jim thought, so beautifully made, that he was sure they would see their owners through a lifetime of weather, good and bad. Feeling a great surge of confidence, he put his arm around Myra Louise and proposed. To his astonishment, she bolted from the store in tears. When he caught up with her in the parking lot, she told him in no uncertain terms that he had not been listening.

The problem was that Jim wanted children and Myra Louise did not. Once before she had been in a serious relationship that had broken up over this issue. It was a very sore point.

"Do you love me or the child I might give you?" she asked as she stood by their car, arms crossed angrily over her chest. "I'm forty, you know. I might not be able to have a child."

Her light brown hair already streaked with gray swung off her face as she lifted her chin defiantly. "Would you divorce me then? After how many years? And what if *it* was retarded? What then?"

"Not *it*, honey, a baby," Jim said helplessly. They had had this same fight so many times, they both knew the words by heart. Myra always cried, and Jim was always drawn even more strongly to her when he saw how vulnerable she was. She didn't want to live alone for the rest of her life any more than he did. They were such a comfort to each other.

"Nevertheless, we had incompatible agendas," he said with a sigh. "Legitimate agendas," he added quickly. "Myra felt she didn't have the patience to be a good mother, for one thing, and for another, nervous troubles ran in her family. She didn't want to saddle a child with that. For my part, having a family is part of being Catholic. We were both right, and neither would budge."

For over a year, Jim and Myra Louise remained at an impasse. They had moved in together, made many small compromises, and were still in love. They were also increasingly frustrated and disappointed. One evening when they were fighting over who had the right to decide, Myra burst into tears but refused to let Jim comfort her.

"Why aren't I enough for you?" she asked between sobs. "Why isn't my love and my caring good enough for anybody?"

"Because love is never enough!" Jim shouted. "You're in love for a year, but you're married for the rest of your life. I want a *life*, too!"

Abruptly, Myra Louise stopped crying and dried her tears.

"I'm afraid I agree with you," she said coldly, and within a week she was gone.

Falling in love at forty, Jim and Myra seem to have found themselves in the grip of gratitude more than ecstasy. Both reasonable people, they tried to argue their way toward a workable compromise without the help of an overpowering passion. Although they certainly started falling in love and felt the excitement, they never gave themselves over to love. When they felt the pull of passion's undertow urging them to reverse the ordinary order of things and care more for love than for the business of life, they were afraid. No diving into a dangerous world for them, and no returning from that world with an altered perspective. They heard the music, but they didn't join the dance. Years later, both looked back on their romance with regret. "It had great promise, but we were stuck," as Jim put it. "Something had to give."

I talked with seven people who fell deeply in love with someone whose view on children was opposed to their own. After great struggle, some married and remain married, others tried and divorced, others walked away. All remember this romance as the love of their lives. Obviously, I shouldn't generalize on the basis of seven examples, but I can't help noticing that in five of the couples, it was the man who said, "No," to children, and in six instances, the woman eventually got her way either with the love of her life or with someone else. I conclude that in these romances, passionate love was up against another form of passionate love. Asking a woman who is helplessly in love with a man to give up the idea of having a child with him must be like asking her both to join and not join the eternal dance at the same time. It doesn't often work.

∽

At the beginning of the chapter, I asked if giving becomes more difficult with age and accomplishment. Not surprisingly the answer is yes—and no. When young men and women are experimenting with where to live, what to do, and what kind of family to build, they can change the direction of their lives without too much upheaval. Once set-tled on a track that leads to a specific career, however, giving themselves to a great love almost always involves more sacrifice. This situation is becoming increasingly common as we saw in the article about romance by the Harvard graduate. Men and women form serious plans very early now, and when love hits them, they may already have a career estab-lished, a business underway, or a year abroad all planned. The more stuff they've acquired, the harder it gets to give. The more options they've exercised, the harder it gets.

"Love is like the measles;" runs an old aphorism, "we can't have it bad but once, and the later in life we have it, the tougher it goes."

It is also true that the common obstacles to a late love of a lifetime can promote what they impede. In other words, when late bloomers invest themselves wholeheartedly in whatever they do, their personal confidence is likely to rise with their expertise. As they approach fifty, I have seen quite a few of them begin to lose interest in the world of things and turn, or return, to thoughts of love. Have they missed something? Have they ever given themselves heart and soul to another person? As in the Persian story of the pearl, these men and women find themselves longing for something of rare beauty that they were not strong enough to grasp when they were young. Kermit, who didn't dare pursue love past the stage of flirtation until he was sixty years old, is a good example, and we will see others. Age and accomplishment seem to enable these lovers to give them-selves to love. Although the resulting romance is likely to be complicated by all that the lovers have and have done, and although it leads to mar-riage less often than among the young, the middle-aged find that giving their hearts away leads nonetheless to a new life.

Love-of-a-lifetime stories suggest that how wholeheartedly we give ourselves to another person and how well we love them determine in large part how we will look at ourselves as well as our romance. "I have loved with all my heart," is not just a good memory to have; it seems essential for a full life. The stories I heard also suggest that feeling chosen by someone who pays attention, sees right into us, and adores us is part of the same process and closely linked to giving. "I am beloved," is another memory essential to a life lived at full capacity. Reclaiming the energy once spent on wondering if we are lovable enough, attractive enough, worthy, and so on, we are now free to get on with our lives.

When it comes to handing love a list of requirements and getting specifically what we want, this form of receiving is neither important nor likely in the love of a lifetime. Although getting respectful, loving attention from a partner with the right qualifications is an important consideration in establishing a lifelong relationship, in a grand passion it is of little concern. No one in my sample fell for a résumé.

It is easy to see that in a great love, the willingness to give everything for love goes hand in hand with a break from our old ways of doing things. Giving also strengthens our resolve to be and stay connected. Although less obvious, a willingness to give also goes hand in hand with questions of destiny, coincidence, and mystery. Just what are we handing our lives over to when we join the dance? Something "out there"? Or "in here"? In the next chapter, we will look at the unknown something that, named or unnamed, seems to do more than a little pushing and pulling in every love-of-a-lifetime experience.

CHAPTER 6
Dealing with Mystery

WE THINK WE KNOW THE LAWS THAT GOVERN OUR EXISTENCE. WE GET GLIMPSES, PERHAPS ONLY ONCE OR TWICE IN A LIFETIME, OF A TOTALLY DIFFERENT SYSTEM AT WORK BEHIND THEM.
—Novalis, Romantic poet (1772–1801)

What does it mean when an urbane gentleman says he felt pushed forward by an unknown force? And what is a woman talking about when she says, "In this lifetime I think I've gotten all I'm going to get, but I feel sure I'll be with him after death"? Is this simply a way of talking about love's power and endurance? Or do some people believe that a supernatural force guides them to and through the love of a lifetime? In the last chapter, we met lovers who realized they could not dive into a powerful romance and also maintain their separateness. They needed to let go of the notion that they were in control of their future or destiny. Setting aside their personal agenda, they handed themselves over to—what? In this chapter, we'll ask lovers what gave them the idea that there's a mysterious force behind love. What do they think it is? And whatever they call it, have they been able to incorporate their understanding of mystery into the rest of their lives?

For most of history, questions like these would have struck people as ludicrous. Of course love is governed by a mysterious force. Take a look around. Everything is. In all cultures, there are myths that tell of lovers who have been destined for each other before birth either by the gods or fate. The pairs are connected at birth by a thread, a sign, a kiss. These stories reflect the feeling that the love of a lifetime started long ago and will last forever. They also reflect the belief that although the accidents of life may separate true lovers for a long time, fate will eventually unite them. "I have been versed in the reasonings of men; but Fate is stronger than anything I have known," wrote Euripides.

Some 2,500 years ago, the Greek comic playwright Aristophanes made the wry suggestion that the feeling that there is one everlasting partner for each of us came from the time when we were all two-headed, eight-limbed, male-and-female creatures who enjoyed complete self-sufficiency. He told this story not as fact, but as an illustration of how people feel about love. These creatures, he said, "walked upright, as we do now, in whatever direction they wanted. Whenever they set out to run fast, they thrust out all their eight limbs, the ones they had then, and spun rapidly, the way gymnasts do cartwheels..."

Although lacking nothing, these creatures were inconsiderate. They ran riot over the land, taking whatever they wanted and rarely pausing to give thanks to each other or the gods. They also made a lot of noise. Finally, the gods became so irate that they persuaded Zeus to cut them all in half, like apples. Apollo, the god of healing, was called in to seal them up by drawing extra skin from the back over what was now their stomachs. He pulled the skin together like a pouch with a drawstring, which he fastened at the navel and turned their heads around to face front.

The results were disastrous. The halves were so upset that each threw itself on its recently severed partner, tangled its arms and legs together, and refused to let go. No work got done, no new people were made, and soon the unhappy creatures were dying of starvation. Forced to modify his plan, Zeus finally figured out a way to make them feel better. He had Apollo move their genitals around to the front and tuck the woman's inside her body so that instead of broadcasting their seed on the ground like grasshoppers as they had before, they now reproduced internally. This turned their embraces into an experience of perfect oneness. Thus intermittently consoled, they returned to work. Now they made more sacrifices to the gods and a lot less noise.

"This, then, is the source of our desire to love each other," proclaimed Aristophanes. Love calls the halves back together and tries to heal the wound by making one being out of two incomplete individuals. While apart, their separated souls had been like oracles, he said, sensing a great truth but unable to say, except in riddles, what it was. Once reunited, these couples "are struck from their senses by love, by a sense of belonging to one another, and by desire, and they don't want to be separate from one another, not even for a moment. These are the people who finish out their lives together and still cannot say what it is they want from one another."

This was the way love felt to those who found the person destined to be their mate, claimed the playwright. They could take little credit for their good fortune. It was fate that decreed their unspeakably mysterious union.

Needless to say, such a heavy reliance on the gods is less common today. A handful of people I talked with denied the existence of all forms of mystery. They claimed that ideas like God and destiny are invoked to explain occurrences not yet understood by science, or to give a name to the dark workings of the unconscious. Although they couldn't explain certain unexpected events in their own romance, they weren't going to invoke a supernatural power to do so.

A sizable minority held the opposite belief. Mostly Christians, they believed the mystery of love is a clear manifestation of God's involvement, and that He brings pairs of individuals together like a lock and key. For these people, mystery and love are evidence of an intelligent higher power.

The majority of the people I talked to had ideas that lay between these two extremes. Many initially told me they did not believe in destiny or fate. Then, reflecting on the love of their lives, most turned around and contradicted themselves. Coincidences occurred that they couldn't explain, they admitted. One impulsive change of plans permanently affected their lives. Yet they remained tentative, and it seemed to me that unless they were comfortable using religious terms, they did not have the words to discuss spiritual matters. Afraid of exposing their most important romance to ridicule by invoking unidentified forces, they said only that a great love seems to involve more than the wills of two individuals and seems to last longer than a lifetime. There was no intelligent being arranging their relationships, they insisted, and they made it clear that the idea of love being influenced by a source outside ourselves was difficult to talk about.

An example of a common, conflicted view of destiny was given to me by a thirty-something British woman named Lizzie, who currently lives in London and works as a speechwriter for a political organization. A tiny, elfin woman with a ski-jump nose, brown eyes, and straight blonde hair, she was dressed in tight jeans, a tie-dye halter, and platform sandals. "Vintage Hippie," she explained with a wink. It was easy to imagine her whirling into a great love affair in fine style.

"I do and I don't believe in destiny," Lizzie began, kicking off her shoes and folding herself like a Yogi into one corner of her couch. "I certainly don't feel the need to invoke a supernatural power to explain why the people around me feel and behave as they do, but when I think of my relationship with Martin…"

When Lizzie and Martin were six years old, they attended the same small, suburban primary school. There were four sections for each year, or grade, as we would say, and annually each child was moved to a different section to assure a thorough mix of personalities and talents. Every September, several hundred students would come pounding into the school yard, their class assignment in hand, to see which of their friends would be in their section. Yet right up until the last year of primary school, Lizzie and Martin were never assigned to the same class. "He must have been one of a tiny handful of people I hadn't shared a class with by the age of ten," she said.

After the age of ten, students were divided on the basis of ability, and both Lizzie and Martin were considered "clever." Finally, the two were assigned to the same section. Just before school opened, however, Martin came down with tuberculosis, which kept him out of school for the entire year. Over the next several years, he was either tutored privately or was sick again.

"Our paths never crossed, and we never said one word to each other," continued Lizzie, who had seen Martin only in the schoolyard or at assemblies. "All I could vaguely recollect was that he wore horrible cardigans with zips."

Then, at eighteen, the two enrolled at the same university. Although they didn't know it, they were assigned to the same residence, and had signed up for different sections of the same class. One afternoon, Lizzie started up a flight of stairs with her girlfriend deep in a conversation about a play her class was studying. Without warning, a thin young man in front of her turned around, blocked traffic on the stairs, and in a single sentence straightened out her question about the play.

"It was Martin. I can't describe my reaction as instant physical attraction," she recalled slowly. "He has one of those mismatched English faces—big forehead, long nose, not much chin, a little like Prince Charles—and I was surprised by what a bookish bloke he'd remained. But as soon as I heard him talking about the play, something gave a very loud 'ping' in my mind. I had never come across a mind like this—not among my classmates or professors. He didn't think like me or anyone I knew, but I liked it. His ideas were strong. No 'bullshit' as you would say. I wanted to talk to him."

Lizzie and Martin began to notice each other. She would wave when she saw his tall, slightly bent figure coming down the hall. Once, when she dyed her hair blue for a lark, he said with approval, "Good on you, Liz." She treasured the remark.

"Martin doesn't stand out in a crowd," she confided. "He's not the laddy type, but I found I could instantly pick him out in a crowd. There's something dear about him and oddly familiar. When I'd spot him trudging out of Main Hall with his fellows, it was a bit like finding my own glove in the lost and found."

One evening, Lizzie found Martin sitting alone at The Pig and Parrot, and slipped into the chair next to him. Never at a loss for words, the two dove into a conversation. A plate of chips and a couple of pints later, she found herself hoping that Martin would walk her back to the residence. He wasn't wearing a jacket, she noticed. It would be easy to slip her arm around his waist as they ambled through the misty streets. However, at that moment, in walked his girlfriend. She was a striking young woman with hair bluer than Lizzie's. Martin smoothly stood up and introduced Lizzie as an old childhood chum.

For several months, Lizzie felt the fool for having indulged in such fantasies about a man who obviously wasn't interested in her. Eventually, she started going with someone else. On their fourth or fifth date, they agreed to meet at the pub. This time it was she who was sitting alone in The Pig and Parrot when Martin walked in and sat down.

"He'd just broken off with his girl and wanted to know if I'd have a bite to eat with him at a Thai place. So many thoughts raced into my head. I just sat there and stared. Right away, he looked around and asked if I was expecting someone. I said I was, and he left."

For four years, Lizzie and Martin played seesaw. One was always in a relationship when the other was free. With uncanny regularity, they crossed paths at The Pig and Parrot every time one—but not the other—was available.

"It was like one of those awful dreams where I keep coming onstage ready to say my lines, but I'm in the wrong play," Lizzie said with a frown. "It's painful to remember how we mistimed all our exits and entrances. I wanted to be with Martin in a deep, basic way, but he had other ideas."

Without telling anyone, Lizzie finally went to an Indian psychic. She slipped through narrow lanes in the Soho district of London until she came to the woman's flat, rang, and was escorted along a dark hall to a tiny room full of deep-red rugs and pillows. The woman, who never stopped smoking, took Lizzie's hand and saw problems in love.

"That was easy," Lizzie laughed. "I was determined not to tell her a thing, but soon I was pouring out my heart about Martin and how confused I felt.

"She told me that Martin and I had been joined in another life, which rather disappointed me. It seemed too pat an answer. I was after something startling—and hopeful. But here's the interesting part. I got the best sleep of my life that night. I'd been a terrible insomniac, and staying asleep was always a chore. But from that day on, I began to sleep. When I'd wake in the night, I'd whisper, 'Martin and I were together a long, long time ago, and we didn't quite finish our conversation.' And then I'd have a kind of drowsy sensation of 'going back'—going back in time and going back to sleep. It was stupid, but comforting.

"None of this got me on Martin's dance card. He had a reputation as hard to pin down. In spite of his ordinary looks, he could talk any girl into bed, but soon he'd break off. He told me several times he would never marry. Commitment of any kind was too close to ownership for him."

Lizzie and Martin settled into a friendship. From her point of view, it was better than nothing.

"Things remained platonic after University," Lizzie remembered. "I wasn't dating much because I wasn't interested in casual relationships. I always felt like a swan—sure that there could be only one person for me. Was Martin the one? It seemed doubtful. We'd had so many years of friendship that we were probably past the place where sexual sparks would be ignited. I conditioned myself to accept things on those terms. 'Don't wait for Martin!' I told myself, but I was dating less and less."

When a room became available in the flat Lizzie was sharing with several recent graduates, she invited Martin to move in. Now the two passed more frequently. In the mornings, they stepped over each other's clothes and newspapers. In the evenings, they traded leftovers from take-out meals. They had great conversations, especially late at night when Martin would come in from a date and find Lizzie's blonde or blue head bent over a news magazine at the kitchen table.

"Coffee?" she'd ask simply.

"Lovely!" he'd reply. Cups in hand, the two would immediately take off on one of their marathon discussions.

One night, Martin didn't return from his date, and Lizzie had a meltdown. Sure he'd spent the night with a new conquest, she could not stop her tears, her anger, or her sadness. She had no right to complain of his habits, she knew, but she couldn't stand it any longer. Sharing a flat was not working. As she got out of bed the next morning and made tea, she eyed Martin's empty bedroom. Although she sensed it was the wrong thing to do, she called in sick and waited for Martin to come home.

"I knew I was going to cry the instant I saw him, and say some very stupid things."

Martin returned looking subdued. Before Lizzie could open her mouth, he confessed that he had, indeed, gone to bed with a new woman. But, he said, he was unable to have sex with her because of the profound loyalty he felt to Lizzie.

"I was so shocked I can't remember what I did, but Martin tells me I said, 'Well, now can we finish our conversation?' He thought I was batty, but we stumbled into my bedroom, and we've been together ever since."

Now, twelve years later, the couple has two daughters. Martin still refuses to get married. By Lizzie's account, they lead an exciting life—a mixture of passionate politics, rough-and-tumble home life, and increasingly tender sex. Coffee granules litter the kitchen every time Martin makes coffee. Dirty socks, wadded into tiny footballs, fly through the flat. Books are everywhere, and in the middle of everything is Martin's supple, idiosyncratic thinking.

"I feel that Martin and I were kept apart until it was the right time for us," she said. "It's uncanny that our paths never crossed at primary school in all those years—uncanny. It's very strange that whenever one of us was free at University, the other had just started in with someone else. But if we'd gotten together earlier, maybe everything would have been spoilt. We wouldn't have been 'cooked' properly. Martin believes this. He says he was horrible and arrogant in school because his teachers told him he was the cleverest boy. His personality changed during his bouts with tuberculosis, but it took time. He said if I'd known him at school, I would have loathed him. Everybody did."

~

Although Lizzie does not want to believe that a supernatural force controls important aspects of her life, she cannot deny that a series of improbable coincidences held her and Martin apart for more than fifteen years. It was as if there were a traffic light that let other women through to Martin but turned red every time Lizzie approached. Something very strong and cagey held them apart, she feels, until just the right time.

Lizzie's love-of-a-lifetime story was by no means the only one I heard that involved what sounded like a conspiracy of unlikely events. Coincidences are the most common evidence given for the presence of a mysterious force in love. A friend of mine met her great love four days before she was to be married to someone else. They talked all night long, and she postponed her wedding. But soon they broke up. Both married other people. Twenty years later, he called. By the time he had finished saying, "Hello, this is . . ." she knew this was the true beginning of the love of a lifetime. And it was.

When I recently inherited cartons of correspondence, I found a box in which my mother had saved all the letters I'd written home from college and vacations. Among them was a postcard in which I casually mentioned that I had changed plans at the last minute and decided to take a boat trip on a Sunday, rather than a Saturday. Reading the card,

I had no recollection at all of changing plans, but I certainly remember meeting the love of my life on that boat. How could I have come that close to *not* meeting him? There are other oddities in my story, like a phone number that didn't work for two years and then suddenly did. For all of us, strange coincidences seem to hold us apart for just the right amount of time and then bring us together. How does this happen? Either the most important events of our lives are at the mercy of trivial minutiae or they are helped along by "something" out there. For me, both ideas are difficult to swallow. And add another odd sensation to the list. Along with improbable coincidence goes a sense of inevitable outcome; our chances of meeting the one, perfectly matched person for us seem simultaneously remote and assured.

The second-most-common occurrence that makes lovers suspect they are dealing with a world that is organized on different principles than the ones they are used to is an uncanny feeling of recognition. Lizzie felt Martin was as familiar as her own glove. Aristophanes's lovers recognized their missing halves as readily as they recognized themselves. Even Dr. Niemeyer, who did not consider himself a superstitious man, remarked several times that Leslie's brain was just like his own and her way of thinking was instantly recognizable. True lovers recognize each other the way exiles recognize the land of their birth. I have been told that homesick sailors from the States can smell America more than fifty miles out at sea. They can even tell what part of their country lies over the horizon.

Feelings of unexpected strength and support are also given as evidence of the mystery. Kermit, who, at sixty, finally stopped flirting and found the courage to dive into love, insisted that he could literally feel a pressure between his shoulder blades push him back into his relationship with Delphine every time he tried to back out. Many others reported feeling the heavy hand. Finally, a surprising number of people used the metaphor of floating to describe what felt to them like a miracle. Overwhelmed by the tension, uncertainty, and demands of their first passionate love, they felt themselves going down in a flood of emotions. When they finally gave up the struggle to keep their head above water and surrendered, they thought they would drown. But they didn't drown, they floated.

Altogether, a sizable majority of the men and women I talked with had experienced something mysterious in conjunction with the love of their lives. I was surprised, although perhaps I shouldn't have been. Some twenty years ago, a group of researchers became interested in near-death experiences and set about surveying a large number of people. They were amazed at how common these experiences apparently are yet how little they are discussed. Outside religion, it is difficult to talk about mystery.

"What name do you give to the coincidences that choreographed your relationship?" I asked Lizzie as she unfolded herself from the couch, slipped on her clunky sandals, and walked me to the door.

She shrugged. "I admit there's a mystery," she said, "and I guess I'd call it destiny, but honestly, I don't think much about it. I don't see this power operating in my life every day."

"So it hovers in the background and comes out…when you need it?"

Lizzie threw back her head and laughed. "That's terribly inconsistent of me. Martin would be appalled. But you're right. I have a private idea of mystery and I keep it in a box."

~

Tucking mystery into one corner of the mind where it is forgotten, but not gone, is a thoroughly modern way of handling an inexplicable force. According to lovers who believe in a higher power, however, it is not a good way. They believe it is only the first baby step toward a spiritual life. Tess, who spent her high-school and university years on the frozen waterways of Toronto with Bobby Walsh, agreed.

"I don't think mystery is optional," she said. "It belongs at the center of romantic love.

"I was raised a Catholic and educated by nuns," she told me, "so I have a strong faith in God and His mysterious ways. Everyone around me took it for granted that things happen that can't be explained except as miracle or mystery. Every day during the mass, for instance, the wafer turns into the Host—it becomes the body of Christ. The sisters didn't try to explain to us how it happened. They simply pointed to transubstantiation as an example of the mysterious power of God. He does things like that.

"Looking back, I can see that it was wonderful to grow up in a world infused by God's mercy. I didn't have any comparison as a child, but now I know people—kids, grown-ups—who live in a complicated, scientific world with no sustaining power behind it. They can never relax. They can't have a bad day and simply slump into God's arms."

When Tess was twenty-two, still small enough to fit under Bobby's arm like a gym bag and still wearing her red hair in a curly mop, she graduated from her university and returned home. Naturally, she assumed she and Bob would start looking for jobs and talking seriously about marriage. She has a clear memory of going to her parent's house just long enough to kiss the dog before begging for the family car and heading for Bobby's.

"Shouldn't you call first?" her mother asked.

Although Bob has no memory of this, Tess says she will never forget racing into his backyard and finding him spraying a blonde with a garden hose. The two were laughing. The blonde was gorgeous.

"In one instant Bobby was completely changed," she said, hurt coming back into her voice. "He turned into a life-size photograph of my boyfriend. I could recognize him, in fact he'd slimmed down and looked more attractive than ever, but there was nothing to connect to. I couldn't get away fast enough."

She paused, gazing into space. "That was the beginning."

Tess described heartbreak the way I have heard others describe the descent into clinical depression. It was not only that she shut down and couldn't move or think, but that color leached out of the world leaving an empty shell. People moved around the house. They ate. They drove cars and went to work. But everything was unreal. All the juice was gone. Tess found herself isolated with no way or will to make contact with anything. The only thing that "happened" in those dark days, she said, was the constant replay of Bobby and the blonde. That painful picture came back to her in full color.

"But I didn't complain," she remembered, "because I didn't have the strength to communicate anything, least of all the feeling I got when I thought of Bobby looking so happy with someone else." She gave a shudder. "After that, nothing mattered at all, and that's my definition of hell.

"I didn't realize it right away," she continued, "but I was losing my faith. As the meaning and light left, God disappeared, too. The vitality I longed for *is* God. He was gone. And so was Bobby."

At the end of summer, Tess moved to Boston, and for several years she saddened her family by staying away from church. It was too painful to go to mass and find that the mystery she had grown up with had disappeared. The wafers remained bits of bread.

Tess put one foot in front of the other, worked at a bookstore where she had plenty of time to think, and began exploring the New England countryside.

"Gradually, I got the idea that although I'd lost Bob, I didn't have to lose what we'd had together. I mean, we'd really been in love, and as long as I didn't let my mind get stuck on the watered blonde—which, of course, it often did—I could remember the rest. We'd had years full of love before she came on the scene. We'd given each other a wonderful start in that part of life. I began to think that maybe that's what young love was supposed to do. Maybe it could be wonderful *and* not last forever, kind of like the scene that inspires a painter for the rest of his life or the book that turns someone into a doctor. If it was like that, then I could take this good start and build on it.

"After I started thinking that way, I remember driving down to Cape Cod one Saturday morning. I went over a bridge that fed into a rotary. In the middle was a big sign, written out in bushes. 'Welcome to Cape Cod.' The thought flashed through my mind that it was the most beautiful sign in the world because it was so green and the sky was so blue. Color was coming back into my life. I think I went back to church soon after that, and the next year I met my husband not two miles from that sign.

"What I learned with Bobby," Tess concluded, "is that God's love is in romance, no matter what happens, just as He is in the rest of life...no matter what happens. This force or vitality gives meaning to everything in a way that science or money can't do. Without it, you're in the dark watching a pointless film. With it, even disappointment contains evidence of His presence, and that's a gift. In my opinion, if you're lucky enough to find great love, you're in the presence of mystery. They're the same thing."

~

I am a newcomer to the discussion of spirituality and mystery. As I said before, I am not ready to say that the love of a lifetime is wholly explicable in terms of hormones and selfish genes or that it is orchestrated by a supernatural power. I agree with Tess that a life force, whatever name you give it, animates both life in general and love in particular, but I'm not convinced that this power is an intelligence that actively prompts people to change their boat reservations or cross the street to bump into the love of a lifetime. What I do believe is that in today's world, it is difficult to fit an understanding of coincidence, a sense of inevitability, or the pressure of a guiding hand into daily lives that are run almost exclusively on other terms. We may acknowledge the existence of destiny in moments of reverie and nostalgia, but when it comes to actually living with mystery, it is tough not to put what we glimpsed in the grip of ecstasy into a box the way Lizzie did. However, I am beginning to believe that waffling in this way has its consequences.

I am reminded of a charming story told by the French theologian Teilhard de Chardin. One day, a large group of tourists started off from their chalet in the Alps with picnic baskets and binoculars. Some had walking sticks and began vigorously poling themselves up a narrow dirt road. For an hour or so, the hikers stayed within sight of each other, but soon they drifted quite naturally into three groups. The slowest group soon regretted having left the inn. The fatigue and risk seemed all out of proportion to the value of the climb. They decided to turn back, and as gravity tugged them gently down the mountainside, they were already looking forward to eating an early lunch on the terrace. Rest and safety was their idea of happiness.

The second group climbed farther. They trudged above small farms where cows grazed on steep green hillsides, their bells sending up musical clinks and clanks. They toiled through pine forests. When they reached the first high meadow, they spread out their blankets, sat down, and admired the beautiful view. There was no point going all the way up the mountain, they agreed, they could see the top from where they sat. But perhaps the picnic baskets could be opened now. Pleasure was their goal, and they had found it.

The third group pressed on, not because the views became more dramatic or because they were determined to reach the summit, but because they wanted to know what lay ahead. They were drawn upward by inexhaustible curiosity. The tiny, unfamiliar flower, the waterfall, narrow as a child's arm, that fell fifty meters and broke into segments every time the wind blew, the emerald-green lake—this group found happiness in amazement.

In terms of mystery, it is clear. The first group turned away in fear, the second sat where they could observe from a distance, and the third climbed as far as they could into the unknown. Although Teilhard de Chardin was quick to say that all of us seek rest, safety, and pleasure as well as discovery and amazement, he maintained that lasting happiness, lasting vitality, only comes from tracking the mystery as far as possible.

Form "a collaboration with the universe," he liked to say. Discover "the explosive joy of a life that has at last found a boundless area in which to expand." In other words, live with mystery all the time. "Attach your life to the universe." *Be* it and *do* it as well as feel it.

But let's not rely on a theologian to tell us what the right relationship to mystery should be. What would a theoretical mathematician like Bertrand Russell, who described passion so eloquently and who sampled it so frequently both in and out of his many marriages, say?

In his autobiography, Russell admitted that as hard as he tried to believe in God, he had never been altogether successful. It remained an appealing intellectual idea, but not a reality. He certainly connected to a great and mysterious force each time he was overcome by ecstasy. As soon as he came to, however, his mind went to work and explained the mystery—and the connection—away.

"I have loved a ghost," he wrote, "and in loving a ghost my inmost self has become spectral...my most profound feelings have remained always solitary and have found in human things no companionship."

In other words, Russell found to his surprise that if he couldn't bring himself to believe in God, he couldn't connect with other people or with himself, at least not consistently. He went on to say that he had hounded passion as a way of throwing himself in the path of mystery, but it hadn't worked. The night wind in empty places blew through his heart. Ruled by reason, he said he lost every ecstatic connection he made.

Years after completing his autobiography, Russell, in his nineties, fell in love in an altogether different way. Looking back on what he had written about his inability to believe and connect, he said, "This is no longer true." Apparently when he finally handed himself over to love, he was able to believe he was the chosen one.

~

A more modern example of a strong, creative mind grappling with destiny in the Age of Science comes from *The Soul's Code: In Search of Character and Calling* by Jungian analyst James Hillman. He seeks to reintroduce into current conversation what he understands to be the real but unprovable force of destiny. He wants to rouse the group sitting in the high meadow to get up and continue their climb. He argues that to explain what happens to us, we need more than nature and nurture, genes and environment.

Calling this guiding force by several names—fate, destiny, vision, character, a personal calling—Hillman claims there is a force in the world working to shape each life in particular ways. Appearing as odd and accidental happenings, as well as feelings of love, delight, instant recognition, or antipathy, this force tries to keep each of us on track so we will unfold into the most perfect possible expression of ourselves. This is not predestination, Hillman insists, not a map with all the roads and major attractions already drawn in. A calling is flexible. It is an urging that can be postponed or avoided. It is a sixth sense that tells you when seemingly trivial events are worth paying attention to and when apparently important events are not your business. It makes certain people, landscapes, and activities seem "fitting" and immensely appealing. It prompts you but does not force you to change your mind about a boat trip, run off with a gangster to Africa, drop out of a third-floor window, or pick up the phone after thirty years.

It is important to understand that scientific explanations neither supplant nor invalidate beliefs based on altogether different explanatory systems such as faith. Fate, for example, cannot be proved or disproved by scientific methods because it deals with forces that are not observable and measurable. It belongs to the mystical world, not the physical. Hillman argues that we will not be able to come up with a plausible account of how experiences like the love of a lifetime work without acknowledging *all* the forces that run the world. From the beginning of recorded history, great lovers have agreed. They have relied on the mystical realm to explain the unbreakable bonds that connect them to each other. Examples extend into our own time. Katharine Hepburn dashed off a four-page letter to Spencer Tracy eleven years after he died, asking him questions about his drinking and telling him what a remarkable man he was. When Richard Burton was on a plane lost in clouds among mountain peaks, he silently recited a poem and tried to "beam" it to

Elizabeth Taylor. He wanted her to know that he would not forget her when he died, as he fully expected to, that afternoon. "Forever you abide," he wanted her to know, "A singing rib within my dreaming side."

~

The love of a lifetime is about a relationship with another person, and it is also an intense encounter with a realm that has long been considered the province of mystics. There is in every great love a shower of surprises that demand our attention. Glimpses of breathtaking beauty, music that suddenly tightens our throat, coincidence, support, morning stars that sing—so many things "move us" when we are in love. For a time we don't know how to make sense of this sudden radiance, and there is no one to ask. No one else felt what we felt or saw what we saw. The sun rose only for us on that glorious morning.

Many of the men and women I talked to found it difficult to hold onto this unique experience. They did not cultivate an understanding of what it meant, or immediately rearrange their personal philosophies to accommodate the music of the spheres. Instead, they let the mystery sink into the ground. As the modern Indian poet and Nobel Laureate Rabindrath Tagore put it:

When the lotus opened, I didn't notice and went away empty handed.
Only now and again do I suddenly sit up from my dreams
to smell a strange fragrance. It comes on the south wind
a vague hint that makes me ache with longing, like
the eager breath of summer wanting to be completed.
I didn't know what was so near or that it was mine.

~

Like the poet, many lovers catch repeated glimpses of something wonderful or hear a sound they want to follow. It is as if an underground stream has begun to carve its way through their lives, perhaps to emerge at some other place or places. In later chapters, we will see how mystery repeatedly surfaces and disappears during the course of our lives.

~

"When my mother was dying at home," a friend of mine said, "the hospice worker came out of her room one afternoon and asked, 'Who's Jimmy? Your mother's been talking about him for hours.'

"When I went in, Mother talked about me, which I liked because she said some very nice things, but later that evening I heard it, too. As she lay drifting in and out of consciousness, poor thing, she said she was in a hurry because she had to meet Jimmy at the real-estate office. She was excited and eager in a feeble sort of way. I got the impression they were going to buy a house.

"When my sister flew in, I asked her if she knew Jimmy. No one did, but Mother kept talking about him until...well, until she died. We read her will then and learned that the one thing she insisted on was to be buried wearing the diamond and garnet ring that she had always worn. It wasn't worth much, so no one minded. We thought it was her engagement ring, but one of our relatives said it wasn't. She told us it was given to Mother years ago by her best friend's mother-in-law. Her best friend's husband was Jimmy."

"So your mother and Jimmy . . ?"

"Nobody knows; it's a mystery. He died many years before Mother." My friend paused. "All these years, and she never said a word...Yet a romance with all its ups and downs was going on inside her. My definition of the love of a lifetime is the person you get ready to meet when you're dying."

The mystery always reappears.

CHAPTER 7

Imagination

Where I live, Native Americans belong to the Wampanoag tribe, and one man I know goes from powwow to powwow telling stories to willing listeners. His best stories are about the mythical Uncle, a Wampanoag who was five feet high and five feet wide. The man was ugly as a toad, but he seemed to have an extra eye in his head. He saw what others didn't even think to look for.

One day Uncle was driving through Mashpee, Massachusetts, in his old pickup truck when he spotted a young girl trudging alongside the road. She was limping, and her face was averted.

"Young Girl!" shouted Uncle, "What happened to you?"

She stopped. "My Daddy beat me," she mumbled.

"Look at me," commanded Uncle, and as she straightened painfully and met his gaze, he sized her up with his extra eye.

"Take me to your Daddy," he said, waving her toward his truck.

The two drove in silence along the back roads until they came to a shack guarded by a snarling dog chained to the bumper of an old car. Uncle got out and beat on the door.

"You this girl's Daddy?" he demanded, as a man a head taller yanked open the door.

The man squinted past Uncle and saw his daughter in the truck.

"Get in here!" he bellowed. "That's my daughter and I'll do what I want," he started to say, but Uncle pulled a pistol from his pocket and shot out his knees so fast that the second one was gone before the man hit the floor.

Uncle got back in the truck. He and the young girl drove back to his place where he scooped her up like a sack of clams and carried her into his house.

"Stay with me," he said.

That was many years ago, and as far as anyone knows the two remained together their whole lives.

Uncle's third eye was his imagination, and with it he could see things that weren't there. Like all imaginations, it played with whatever he turned his mind to. It mixed things up and tried out possibilities and explanations. Eventually, what he saw with his imagination got him thinking so hard that the pictures in his head actually had an influence on what he did. Like his ancestor, Granny Squanit, a mythological crone who lived in a sea cave and thus saw what lay beneath the surface, Uncle's imagination saw the underlying connections and the "could be" of all things. He knew at a glance that Young Girl had a good heart, and he could imagine her as his wife. In love, we all become visionaries. We picture what lies beneath the surface and what might lie ahead. And what we can picture, we can do.

~

In this chapter, we see lovers trying on new possibilities. With their imaginations fired by love, they write poetry, make shapes out of clay, dance, turn themselves into someone quite wonderful, and imagine their beloved in a dozen different ways. In their new role as the King or Queen of Limitless Possibility, there is nothing they can't see themselves doing. Of course, there are two ways to look at their inventiveness. Either they are besotted and will soon return from the land of illusions, or they are experimenting with an important new way of seeing.

British analyst Adam Phillips points out that psychoanalysis, like many other forms of conventional thinking, "endorses the view that falling in love is not a good way of getting to know someone." Why? Because what is learned in love will always be invalidated by the more reliable knowledge gained when passion has departed. However, Phillips thinks there's more to the story than that. He suggests that seeing through the glasses of love is not wrong, just different—and difficult. Because love invariably triggers imagination, it involves the constant reinvention of oneself, the beloved, and the future. Anything is possible. Actually living for any length of time in the constantly shifting landscape of possibility is difficult, however. Thus we fall *out* of love, Phillips suggests, with a certain sigh of relief. Ahh, back to the more predictable world of diminished possibility and familiar routine. Although there is truth in both ways of looking, it is as difficult to combine them as it is to hold onto the fragrance of the lotus as we commute to work. Nevertheless, if the love of a lifetime is to do its work and transform us from innocent bystanders to experienced participants, we need our imagination, for it is the catalyst of all change. If we can't picture it, it won't happen. If we can, we have a chance.

~

When we fall in love, the imagination works in many ways to get at the "underness" and "could be" of our love and our life. Perhaps its simplest pleasure is embroidering our romance with fantasies and dreams. While driving, jogging, eating, or working, we dance through the streets of our imagination pulling our beloved behind us. We imagine passionate lovemaking and tender conversation. We picture how happy we will be together and how miserable apart. Our daydreams heighten the pleasures of being in love. And they do more—they also exaggerate our feelings to the point where some of the hidden and contradictory emotions that pass between lovers become discernible.

"Whatever you invent is true," stated the French novelist Gustave Flaubert, "even though you may not understand what the truth of it is." My sister gave me a convincing example. As part of her work as an outplacement counselor, she attended a workshop to learn a technique for getting groups of strangers to open up to each other quickly. To demonstrate the technique, the leader went around the circle asking each person to make up an outrageous story—a whopper. Then they had to present it to the group as solemn truth. "Use your imagination," she encouraged.

"What did you say?" I asked my sister.

"I said that my parents were both linguists and had taught their children as many languages as they could fit inside their heads. I myself had learned twenty-seven, and now one of my pleasures is to stroll through international airports listening in on all the conversations. There is not one I cannot understand."

"Perfect!" I practically shouted, realizing that the story expressed our family's chronically frustrated attempts to figure out what was being said beneath polite exchanges. "What a wonderful lie," I said. "It's exactly right!"

Along the same lines, a woman told me she became obsessed with fantasies of being lifted into her lover's arms by someone she couldn't see. Sometimes she imagined herself swimming when, without warning, she was lifted out of the water and into his arms. After a dozen such fantasies, she set her mind to picture something else, but couldn't. She was unable to redirect her imagination. Suddenly it came to her that the lifting fantasies expressed an unacknowledged fear that her family was handing her over to the first man who would take her. Like the developing solution used in the darkroom to turn a blank piece of paper into a photograph, the imaginative fantasies in which we immerse our love affairs bring out what we did not know we knew.

Imagination does more. When we repeatedly picture what concerns us and pour energy into imagining our involvement, we are actually creating possibilities for ourselves: good ones and bad ones. We are saying, "This could happen. I can imagine it." Serious athletes are taught to see themselves winning. The anxious are taught to visualize themselves relaxing. Left to themselves, worriers rehearse disaster. Lovers daydream in the same ways. The imagination takes ideas that are merely words or intellectualizations and, by visualizing them, moves them to the heart. There they become what we call "real possibilities."

Because imagination heightens, explains, and finally shapes our view of love, it influences the outcome of each romance. The possibilities we tirelessly imagine in love, both the hopeful ones and the fears of failure, become part of a story that might be called "What Could Happen in This Relationship." These possibilities actively pull our behavior toward the envisioned goals. Daydreams of marriage pull a couple toward the altar. Fantasies of being left or lied to make lovers wary and hold them apart.

Before meeting Elizabeth Barrett, Robert Browning had already imagined what might occur when a talented woman in distress met a man who saw her hidden gifts. In "Flight of the Duchess," a fiery woman is held back by her mean-spirited husband until her eyes are opened to her own worth by a Gypsy. The Duchess then flees to a better life. When Browning met Barrett, he was reminded of the heroine he'd created in his imagination. The ensuing courtship was much easier for him to conduct than it was for Barrett because he had already imagined his role as admirer and rescuer, and she had never imagined being an adored woman. Initially, she fought with him over who should play the role of admirer. Already at the time of their meeting, she was the more famous poet, yet she wanted to be Browning's admirer because it was a more conventional role and thus easier for her to imagine. In her day, women put their husbands on a pedestal. However, Browning's imagination prevailed. This love affair would be about a man who worshiped a talented woman and enthusiastically promoted her freedom. The history of love has evolved as people with powerful imaginations like Browning envisioned what new forms love could take and then made them a reality.

~

When choreographer George Balanchine fell in love with the much younger Suzanne Farrell, their intense love affair was molded not only by their own visions of love but also by the imaginations of Shakespeare, Cervantes, and the other writers whose stories formed the plots of the ballets they danced together. No wonder actors and actresses fall in love with each other, especially during a stage production. Their feelings are fanned into flames six days a week and twice on Saturdays by the most powerful imaginations in history.

Balanchine first began taking an interest in Farrell when she was eighteen and he was sixty. She had joined his company, The New York City Ballet, when she was a snub-nosed seventeen-year-old. With her small, regular features and luminous eyes, she looked so young that when she smiled no one would have been surprised to see braces on her teeth. She was a slender, underweight, high-school kid. Before moving to New York from the Midwest, she had practiced dancing around her living room and falling dramatically into an armchair she'd named Balanchine.

She thought of him as a god. In spite of her awe, and her extraordinary talents, the real Balanchine initially took no notice.

Then one day, as dozens of leggy dancers in leotards crossed and recrossed the studio to the rhythmic banging of the piano, Farrell caught his eye. The gray-haired Russian with the hatchet-shaped face was standing to one side as usual, scrutinizing the dancers. In his rumpled slacks and polo shirt, he looked like a stevedore, and indeed, he could still leap, lift, fall, and spin with the best of his dancers. His sharp eyes fastened on Farrell. There was something about the way this girl held her body or moved that intrigued him. From then on, whenever he dropped in on a class, he would stare at her. When he wanted to demonstrate a *pas de deux*, he'd ask her to do it with him. To her astonishment, Balanchine then wrote her a love poem in red ink. She was so embarrassed that she never spoke to him about it. Next, he choreographed a dance especially for her that set her apart from the other dancers, who quickly realized she had become his new favorite. And most surprising of all, he began asking her advice. Even as she painstakingly followed his instructions, he was asking her, "Can this be done?" "Why are you moving like that?" Balanchine's imagination soared when he looked at the supple, reed-thin girl with the flying hair, and both on stage and off, he insisted she play the role of the elusive muse who would inspire him to glimpse and then realize possibilities he had not been aware of before.

This was not an altogether new kind of relationship for Balanchine, who had admired and then married at least two previous ballerinas. He was currently married to his fifth wife. His favorite dancer before Farrell had been Diana Adams, and everyone in the company had realized that Balanchine could not watch Adams rehearse a love scene without becoming unbearably jealous. So vivid was his imagination that he "saw" her falling in love with another dancer and was forced to leave the studio. It was said that he lived every one of his productions.

About a year into this intense and, for Farrell, dangerous relationship, Balanchine decided to put on a production of Cervantes' *Don Quixote*. To no one's surprise, he cast Farrell as Dulcinea, and as rehearsals proceeded, it became clear that the aging but still powerful choreographer was getting more and more into the role of Don Quixote himself. When he demonstrated how the man from LaMancha was supposed to look at Dulcinea or touch her face, dance with her, dream of her, he seemed to be expressing his own yearning for the young ballerina. On opening night, Balanchine elected to dance the part of Don Quixote himself. Emerging from his dressing room in a suit of armor with gray hair flying around his head and makeup accentuating his craggy face, he looked like an Old Testament prophet about to hand down the word of God. Farrell knew something incredible was about to happen. The curtain went up on an indomitable warrior entranced by the dream of a beautiful girl, and in front of a packed house, the two dancers released all the feelings they had for one another—the love, yearning, tenderness, and fire that they would not or could not express offstage. On stage, as in the land of love and windmills, the obstacles of age and position dissolved and the two were free to express their mutual adoration.

"We lived that love affair...Our whole life was in *Don Quixote*," Farrell later recalled. Especially as she danced the dream solo, her simple night dress glowing in the moonlight, she seemed to move into another state of being where she was transformed into some elemental force. Watching from the wings, her fellow dancers said they could feel her pulling power right out of the air. As the curtain came down, the house sprang to its feet roaring its approval and astonishment. "My God, what happened?" people asked each other. "What did we just see?"

Decades later, Farrell, with tears in her eyes and a broad smile, insisted that, "There will just never be another night like that!"

After touring Europe with *Don Quixote*, Farrell and Balanchine, who in all likelihood never consummated their relationship, danced *Meditation* together and later *A Midsummer Night's Dream*. Every production involved the pair in yet another kind of love story. Balanchine said he choreographed *Meditation* as a love poem for Farrell who was supposed to embody the transformation of physical love into ethereal love. In *A Midsummer Night's Dream*, she was the Queen of the fairies tricked into loving the mortal Balanchine, who had been turned into an ass. Farrell said that she and Balanchine lived their own lives, each other's lives, and all the lives they played on stage. Because they inhabited every romance they danced together, their love for each other was continually changing and expanding. Unlike most lovers who have been together for several years, they went on leaping and spinning far above the land of diminished possibilities.

Eventually, however, Farrell found it difficult to live in her imagination full-time, even if it was full of fascinating dreams. She had been enjoying a thoroughly ordinary friendship with fellow dancer Paul Mejia, and the two, both lonely, began dating each other. Once Balanchine spotted them together on a city bus, and Farrell felt as if she'd been caught having an illicit affair. When she asked other members of the company what Balanchine's reaction was likely to be to her new relationship, they were quick to answer. If she wanted to dance, get rid of Paul. Instead, she married him. Although Balanchine said nothing, he snubbed Farrell and wouldn't let her husband dance. The couple was essentially kicked out of the company. Brokenhearted, Farrell and her husband joined a company in Belgium. Balanchine fell into despair.

Four years after Farrell's defection, as Balanchine called it, Farrell asked to return to the company, and Balanchine let her. She began dancing again, but rarely, if at all, with Balanchine. Both were careful not to let their hearts get actively involved again.

Balanchine and Farrell never spoke directly to each other about either the love they felt for each other or their heartbreak—except once.

"I shouldn't have thought of you *that* way," Farrell remembered him saying to her after her return.

"I had wanted to hear those words," she said, "but now I didn't."

When the choreographer died in 1983, Farrell felt like an orphan. She realized that she would never be as understood, cherished, or loved again by anyone, nor would her imagination be as inspired. The curtain had come down on the realm of dreams. For months she missed Balanchine so much that she tried to will his familiar form to appear at the bus stop on Broadway where she was in the habit of meeting him every morning. Unsure whether or not she wanted to dance again, she eventually continued. Later she taught, as Balanchine had predicted she would.

"I could not have *not* loved him," she said. "He made me who I am."

～

The great romance that Farrell shared with Balanchine was inspired by a large number of powerfully imagined love scenes, and until about a century ago lovers commonly used great literature to enrich their own feelings of affection. Robert Browning read Elizabeth Barrett "The Flight of the Duchess" to introduce her to his vision of what their love could be. Paolo read the story of Launcelot and Guinevere to the innocent Francesca. Thousands of lovers read out loud to each other through long winter evenings. For weeks at a time, they inhabited classic tales of love from ancient to present times, and each long and convoluted story prompted them to imagine different ways of loving each other. Even now, lovers commonly exchange tapes or compact discs of their favorite songs, and urge each other to see their favorite films. Although a song is less powerful than a full-length classic, each tale of love says, "Imagine loving like this."

~

Sometimes the full force of a person's imagination is not released while he or she is with the beloved, but only when they part. For example, pre-Islamic odes in Arabic begin with a convention called "standing by the relics." A wanderer arrives too late at the camp of his one true love and sees only the traces of her departure. He looks at the cold fire, the scraps left from meals, tufts of goat hair on a thorn bush, and he feels a surge of longing and loneliness as vast as the desert and as overarching as the sky. What will he do with his feelings of love? Where will he put them? He begins to sing. The greatest love stories in the world are told by the sorrowing imagination.

~

Twenty-three-year-old Rick told me he didn't know he had either an imagination or a soul until he fell in love with a heartbreaker. I had known Rick since he was in high school, a powerfully built, yet surprisingly sensitive young man who hoped that good people were always rewarded for their efforts. He was the kind of honest, good-hearted kid that mothers want for their daughters but fathers can't figure out. Why was a dark-haired, dark-eyed hunk who wore sunglasses and could pass for an Italian movie star acting so shy? Why wasn't he running around with a harem? I'd wondered myself.

Now here he was again, older, leaner, still sporting the designer shades that were his trademark. He had his working clothes on—snug jeans, a blood-red polo shirt, and construction boots—and he seemed to have grown a couple of inches since I'd last seen him. We were catching up on four years of news. Walking to his truck, he flipped down the sun visor on the driver's side revealing a small photo of a dark-haired girl with a perfect, heart-shaped face. She was the news.

"Every time I catch sight of Andrea I feel like a guy in a truck on a summer day who pulls off the road for a fifteen-year-old, you know, for the kind of girl who climbs in and just stares at you like, 'You are the one guy in the world for me.'" Rick shifted his muscular frame and slung an arm over the rearview mirror of his freshly waxed pickup. "Picture this girl," he continued earnestly, "ready for her first love, looking right into you. Everything stops. 'This is it,' you say to yourself and you can hardly breathe. That's how it is with me and Andrea, not just when we were going together, but every time I think of her."

Rick pulled himself back from his vision of Andrea reluctantly. He was talking about the young woman who first ignited his imagination and transported him, for better or worse, into the realm of his wildest dreams. But Andrea was not Rick's first girlfriend. He had paired up with a petite blonde in high school and the two had gone out together so long and so faithfully that everyone assumed they would marry.

"Don't you want some variety?" his twice-divorced father once asked when Rick came to visit. "You're so young."

But Rick shook off the question. No musical-chair partners for him. He was anxious to give what he most wanted to receive—loyalty. Unlike his parents, he envisioned love as a solemn, once-in-a-lifetime pledge, and he had already made that promise to his girl.

A month after graduation, however, the steady girlfriend decided to pursue a career in a distant city, and over the next year, the two broke up by degrees. Eventually, Rick sensed that his dreams of happiness were over.

"I was heartbroken," he recalled. "I knew I'd never get over her because I had pledged my love and I would never go back on my word."

So Rick stopped socializing. As the months passed, he took an extra job to fill up his time and eventually made enough money to buy his own home. On weekends, he helped his mother cut grass or stack wood, and occasionally he watched sports with the guys. There were two possibilities, he thought. Either his girlfriend would eventually discover that there was no one out there as loyal as he and come back, or he would live alone for the rest of his life.

Then one Sunday afternoon when he was in a bar with friends watching football, in walked a dark-haired, full-lipped girl he hadn't seen before. She came up to Rick's table, leaned so far forward that the cross she wore around her neck swung off her dark skin, and stared straight into his eyes. Instantly, he got that guy-in-a-truck-on-a-summer-day feeling. Who was this beautiful girl with hair that swung heavily around her shoulders who obviously wanted his love? By the end of the afternoon, Rick had asked Andrea for her phone number and had gotten it. Only when she left the bar did a friend clue him in. She was engaged. Rick called anyway, and the two started seeing each other "as friends." Rick was amazed at how different this experience was from his first relationship.

"It was like the biggest high in the world all the time," he began, blushing slightly. "My feelings for her were intense. She was beautiful, sexy, great to talk to—all the usual stuff—but there was more. I know it sounds corny, but when I drove home at night, I felt like I'd swallowed the sun. I was invincible, totally turned on, alive. Andrea told me it was my soul coming to life. I didn't know I had a soul until I met her. We talked a lot about being soulmates."

Rick paused, apparently still bemused by the concept of "soul." "It was like we recognized each other instantly after being separated at birth, or sometimes we wondered if we'd been lovers in another life who'd been torn apart. At last we'd made it back together, and something clicked 'on' that had been 'off' my whole life."

After several months, Andrea gave her engagement ring back to her fiancé, which caused less of a storm than Rick had expected. It seemed her family was used to her impulsive changes of heart and felt sure she'd return to her original plan. She apparently jumped into and out of everything with considerable speed.

"But not this relationship," Rick had said to himself. "This is destiny."

Two months later, Rick received a ten-page letter from his first girlfriend.

"I've made a mistake. *You* are the one. Take me back."

Rick groaned at the memory.

"You have to understand, this was the letter I'd been waiting for every day for three years," he explained, his hand moving involuntarily to his heart. "Until I met Andrea, that is. It was the letter I'd written in my head every night as I went to sleep."

Rick didn't know what to do. He still wanted to believe that life was pretty simple. You do the right thing, and everyone is OK. Somewhat naively, he told each of the women about the other, and announced that he would date both until he made up his mind. Andrea went up in smoke. She had publicly broken her engagement for Rick and now he was dating another woman in order to decide who was right? Wrong! She called Rick incessantly. She screamed. She cried. Quickly she delivered an ultimatum.

"She told me that she was willing to defy her family and move out, but only if I would catch her as she jumped. 'You have to promise me *right now* that you'll catch me,' she said...and I couldn't. I didn't know which love was right—the old one built on loyalty? Or this new thing I'd found with Andrea.

"I blinked," he said softly, "and Andrea split. She was married by the end of summer. My old girlfriend was at my house when Andrea called from Bermuda on her honeymoon. It was six o'clock in the morning, and when the call came through Andrea and I both started crying. Before I was off the phone, my old girlfriend had walked out for good."

A week later, Andrea returned, heartbroken, confused, and scared. What had she done?

"I know this was wrong," Rick said, grasping the door handle of his truck to anchor himself. "But we started seeing each other again. Not only had I broken my pledge to my first girlfriend, now I was breaking a pledge to myself. I became the kind of person who cheats, and I never thought I would do that—not ever. Of course it didn't work. It couldn't, because she was married. I got little bits of her, but I was having a slow heartbreak and the pain was bad. I'd blown the chance to be with the love of my life. I'd run off the road I was supposed to travel, and it was my own fault."

Finally, Rick stopped answering his phone and stopped seeing Andrea.

He averted his eyes. "I wish I had words to describe that time," he said simply. "It was pain like a hammer in the hands of an angry man. I'd never imagined pain like that."

Rick had never imagined a lot of things, but swept away by love, he was unceremoniously introduced to a much broader spectrum of feelings, possibilities, and actions. For months, he could not fit this shocking jumble into a picture of himself that made sense, and he suffered continual doubts and confusion. If Rick had been an actor or a dancer like Suzanne Farrell, he might have had an easier time expanding his identity so that it could accommodate all he had learned about himself and the ways of the world. Each role he played would let him try on a new personality. But he wasn't an actor, and so like the rest of us he had to use his own imagination to construct an explanation of who he had become. This is not a simple task. He was asking his imagination to sort through the stored treasures of his brain and pull out all images and explanations relevant to Andrea. Then he had to put them back together in a new way that both felt right and fit the facts.

Initially, Rick imagined himself as a broken engine that could not be repaired, but that story couldn't accommodate more than a few of his saddest feelings. Some months later, he imagined that Andrea was responsible for the ultimate breakup. She was the one who couldn't decide whether or not to get her marriage annulled. But that wasn't right either. He was no blameless victim. His imagination kept searching for new ways to look at his love affair, and to his surprise all this daydreaming and obsessing was hard work.

A year later, as Rick was putting together still another account of the love of his life, he hit on a way of looking at it that gave him some relief. Going with Andrea, he decided, was like taking apart an engine for the first time.

"It was jumping into life and getting dirty, and that's the way I've always learned things," he said. "I don't get stuff from books. I have to get in there. Fix things, break things, that's how I get it. Maybe," he added quietly, "that's how a lot of guys operate, even my Dad.

"I think I trust myself more," he continued. "I gave Andrea everything I had, made mistakes, learned, and now I'm much clearer about the kind of person I want to be and the kind of woman I want to be with. When I look in the mirror every morning, I don't see a perfectly loyal man anymore, but I see a person I like."

Rick went on to say that he has started a huge vegetable garden in his backyard and now, instead of working all the time, he comes home to water the garden or pick tomatoes. He has even started freezing his extra produce in empty tennis-ball containers, and realizes that he will soon need to learn more about cooking. He is making himself a home.

"I expect to get on with life," he concluded, "but I don't think she will—not right away. But I don't want to say too much because with love, you never know."

He's learned that, too.

Swiss analyst Carl Gustav Jung was a great believer in the kind of imaginative tinkering that Rick used to adjust and readjust the story of the the love of his life.

"Without this playing with fantasy no creative work has ever yet come to birth," Jung wrote. "The debt we owe to the play of imagination is incalculable."

~

In love, we all become visionaries like Uncle and Granny Squanit. Playing with our imagination, we see things that could be true or that could happen, and these become new possibilities for us. The process continues even if our beloved departs. Our imaginations rework memories just as they rework experience. In both cases, imagination expands our understanding of what happened, which in turn changes the story just a little. Whether it was Farrell and Balanchine dancing *Don Quixote* or Rick comparing himself to an inexperienced auto mechanic, living inside the daydream for a while showed these people something about themselves they hadn't understood before. Gradually, their accumulating insights modified their relationships as well as their view of themselves. It is a continuous cycle; imagination alters and enriches the very explanations it preserves. In doing so, it alters and enriches us.

CHAPTER 8
Believing

I AM ALWAYS AT A LOSS TO KNOW HOW MUCH TO BELIEVE OF MY OWN STORIES.
—Washington Irving

One of the most immediately recognizable characteristics of individuals who have had and appreciated the love of a lifetime is their conviction. They believe their own stories. "I know *exactly* what you mean," many stated emphatically when I asked what the term "love of a lifetime" meant, and although they didn't know what I had in mind, they certainly knew what they themselves meant. They knew who the love of their life was, they knew that their romance was a perfect example of love in its own way, and they felt an unshakeable allegiance to the experience. All this they asserted quite fiercely, and their conviction was itself a pleasure and a wonder. Whether it had taken twenty seconds or twenty years to figure out what love had done to them, everyone who spoke confidently of the love of a lifetime told a story that was in large part about coming to believe in themselves. How did these people develop a faith in entities as shifty and elusive as self and love? And why did their new certainty matter so much to them?

In this chapter, we will listen to people who struggled to believe they experienced a great love in spite of considerable evidence to the contrary. Often lacking support from friends and from a culture quick to tell us which kinds of romances do *not* count, how did these people decide they could trust their own judgment? Although the lovers described here had a harder time than most, all lovers who experience the love of a lifetime come to a crossroad where they must find the strength to believe in themselves and their version of the romance. No unshakeable trust in ourselves; no love of a lifetime.

~

A brief but unusual example of conviction involved an eighty-six-year-old man who, when he was fifteen, fell in love with a girl named Hannah that he saw in trade school. That was seventy-one years ago. So shy was Walter then that he never spoke to the girl, whom he saw when he and the boys hung around the home economics class hoping for cookies. But so strong was his conviction that she was the perfect girl for him that he followed the course of her life through the wedding, birth, and death announcements in her local paper—a paper he subscribed to from his home a hundred miles away. Both Walter and Hannah married other people and raised children. Walter's wife died, and later, when he saw in the paper that Hannah's husband had died also, he discreetly waited a year, then made his move. He called, introduced himself, and suggested dinner.

"He's a pervert!" Hannah's younger brother shouted when she told him of the call. "Change your phone number!"

"Dennis, he's been married himself most of these years. He's eighty-six—like me. A widower with great-grandchildren."

"It's an obsession," her brother insisted. "He's been obsessed with you all these years. Leave him alone."

And Hannah did—until Walter called a second, third, and fourth time. Finally, she agreed to have dinner with him, and then another. When they met—a white-haired old lady shaking hands formally with a hundred-thirty-pound scarecrow wearing suspenders—she had no recollection of the man before her. Walter, however, had carried an image of a happy fifteen-year-old in his heart for seventy-one years. He recognized her instantly. He could not tell her how he knew she was the one for him or what had kept him hoping over the course of so many years. But he knew. "There was never a time," he told her, "that I did not believe you were the one."

And now, four years after their first date? They are still having dinner with each other, perhaps once a month, and he tells her that the wait was worth it.

~

Although Walter immediately believed in his love for Hannah, he is the exception, not the rule. It usually takes months, even years to form an unshakable conviction. In fact, I found that it wasn't until middle age that most men and women sounded as if they really knew they could trust their own opinion of love. The late-blooming Emily is an example.

When Emily was nineteen and a junior at McGill University in Montreal, she signed up for a field trip to Boston. She could no longer remember what the trip was supposed to teach her, but every girl who participated hoped to meet a boy from Harvard. Because hanging out in "the yard" was the agenda, Emily was somewhat annoyed to find herself paired with a young foreign student from Germany before the group even crossed the American border. Richard slipped into the seat next to her as the bus loaded in Montreal, and never left her side. Emily's uninvited companion with the heavy accent was short, witty, and ferociously energetic. For some reason, she still remembers that he wore blue jeans that seemed cut wrong and too dark. It was the first time she realized that only Americans know how to wear jeans. On everyone else, they look phony, and that included Richard. With his wire-rimmed glasses, beaky nose, and accent, he was unmistakably foreign. Emily surmised that she and Richard must have fallen into easy conversation, and must have covered the usual topics that students discuss. But in addition to "Do you know…" and "Have you seen…"—information that was quickly forgotten over the years—there was a great deal of flirtatious teasing that her memory held on to. By the time the bus pulled into Cambridge, Massachusetts, it was obvious that the two were interested in each other, and four days later when they spent their last night together walking through a misty drizzle, it was clear that Richard wanted to have sex with her more than anything in the world. He teased, he cajoled, he flattered, he promised.

"I looked like a farm girl in my teens," she recalled, "not fat, but what my father called 'strapping.' I had beautiful dark brown hair then, the true color of chestnuts, and I considered it my finest feature. I wore it in a long, thick braid down my back and Richard could not take his eyes or his hands off it."

Finally, the ardent young man in the rolled-up blue jeans and black leather shoes leapt onto the stone railing of the Harvard Bridge and declared he would walk all the way across the Charles River with his eyes shut.

"I think that's when I made a dash for the river bank below, supposedly to catch him," the now gray-haired Emily remembered with a chuckle.

Richard was off the bridge and down on the grassy bank in a flash, she recalled, and there in the black, wet shadow of the bridge the two became lovers.

"Big deal," she said with a warm smile, "I'd done that before, but I was Richard's first, and *Eureka!* was he happy."

Richard apparently approached sex the same way he approached his beloved studies in international law—with obsession. Back at McGill, he bought a contraband copy of the *Kama Sutra* (that same Kama who drove the gods crazy), and wanted to try every position for lovemaking described in the book, including one that required ropes and pulleys.

"You are *not* going to suspend me from the ceiling of your dorm room," Emily had yelped as Richard, book in hand, stood naked on his bed bouncing like a gymnast.

"That's Richard in a nutshell," she told me with a laugh. "And you know what you find in nutshells, don't you?"

Emily and Richard dated throughout their junior year, and when he returned to Germany that summer, she was able to visit him and his family in August. Their reunion was glorious. He showed her all his favorite places and fed her all her favorite foods, namely chocolate and more chocolate. He had inspired ideas of how to make love among the huge feather pillows that smothered his bed. The two romped through their days together like puppies. But in September, an unexpected financial reversal prevented Richard from returning to McGill. At first, ten- and twenty-page letters flowed back and forth. Richard suggested that she learn German and transfer to his university, or at least spend the summers with him.

"And then I simply stopped writing." Emily frowned. "It was a terrible thing to do, and I don't know why I did it. I suppose I couldn't picture a future for our relationship, or rather I couldn't *feel* any future with Richard. He was a great date, but we weren't ready to get engaged. I wasn't going to learn German and leave my country on the off chance that our relationship might get serious. Besides, Canadians are more patriotic than you think, and I couldn't imagine living in Germany, not forever. But I'm guessing at my reasons. All I know for sure is that I stopped writing."

Several years later, Emily and Richard met once more at McGill, although curiously, Emily had no recollection of the encounter. She had already been married briefly and divorced, and had turned her attention to a career in medical research. As far as she was concerned, all the good things in life lay not behind, but ahead of her, including the man of her dreams.

By the time Emily was forty, her idea of what life would give her had changed. Indeed she had married again, had two children, and worked in a laboratory where she studied the structure of the eye, but none of these accomplishments had cured her restlessness. She had an affair with the lab's sixty-year-old director, and more disturbing still, she had begun thinking again of Richard.

"I thought of him when I rode my bicycle," she said in surprise. "Whether I was toiling up a mountain or spinning along through a park, the soothing monotony of pedaling let my mind wander. I found myself wondering where Richard was and what he was doing. Pretty soon, I was looking forward to those rides specifically because I could make up fantasies about meeting him again. Over the years, Richard had sort of outlasted the competition—or rather my fantasies of him had. Although I wasn't conscious of it then and I can't explain it now, he was gradually becoming important to me.

"When I think about what was going on in my mind," she continued, "I'm amazed, or as my daughter would say, 'weirded out.' It seems now as if some seed had been planted in my brain and had been growing on its own for decades. Even when I finally noticed that my mind was 'inhabited,' I didn't know why. I mean I didn't know why I had singled out Richard from the other men I had dated, and I didn't know what all this daydreaming was going to get me. I remember thinking back to my childhood in the country, where forest fires were a problem every autumn. Once I was taken to the edge of a smoking, half-burned swamp, and someone, probably my father, explained that fire could travel underground through the roots of the clump grass. It was a shocking revelation, and it gave me nightmares. If threads of fire could run underground, then no one was safe. My daydreams of Richard gave me something of the same feeling. It wasn't only that I was after something, but also that something was after me."

Emily divorced again at forty-five and gradually found a state of mind that "resembled peacefulness." With both children in college, she was living alone, doing well at her career, and occasionally wondering about a man she could only sketchily remember. If anyone mentioned the love of a lifetime, Richard came to mind, but she said nothing. She had created an imaginary consolation for herself, she surmised. Her fantasies were those of a woman who didn't know much about love.

One evening, as Emily sat in the narrow living room of her row house writing a letter, the phone rang, and, pen still in hand, she answered it. A deep, heavily accented voice shook her like an earthquake. "Hello, Em," said Richard with a barely suppressed laugh, "How's the girl?"

"'Richard!' I screamed. 'Richard, Richard, Richard! Is it? I mean where? I mean, Richard! Where are you?' He laughed then, or we laughed, and I thought I'd lose my balance and fall on the floor. Thirty years later. Thirty years. Oh my God, I was shocked. 'Where are you?' I asked again, and true to form—that's Richard—he told me he was standing on the railing of the Harvard Bridge using a cell phone. Well he wasn't, but I think I fell over anyway."

Emily smiled from ear to ear. "I will never forget that moment—that call, that sound, that feeling. I knew for certain then that fire travels underground. It had reached me, and I was instantly ready to meet him."

Richard apparently felt the same way, and even though he was married and had children in Germany, he invited Emily to meet him in Boston—naturally—at the end of September.

"I won't recognize you unless you're teetering on a bridge," she told him.

"Of course you will," he shot back. "I look exactly the same, only fat and bald."

More excited than she had been in her whole life, Emily prepared for their reunion by thumbing through her old college diaries and yearbook, reading love poetry, and buying outrageous lingerie. She took out her first passport and compared its photo to a recent one. Would Richard recognize her? Would he be shocked?

"The two pictures looked like a mother-daughter pair," she recalled. "Now my hair was short and going gray, but it was still close to my head the way it was when I wore a braid. I weighed less now and my face was thinner, but the 'look' was remarkably similar—level gaze, big smile, interested in everything. I figured he'd recognize me once I smiled. I'd have to rely on his 'look' too. But what was it? 'My God,' I thought, 'I can't remember. All that's left is his voice.'"

By the time Emily boarded a plane for Boston, she didn't know who she was or how old, and upon landing, she was even more confused. Striding into the international arrivals area wearing her smartest suit and smoothest stockings, Emily tried not to look as if she was searching blindly for a middle-aged stranger who might or might not remind her of a boyfriend she had casually dumped thirty years before. She moved past drivers holding placards, families waiting for returning fathers, and young travelers sitting on backpacks. "He's not here," she thought as she reached the end of the room and a wave of panic started up from her stomach toward her head. Retracing her steps with far less panache, she suddenly spotted a bald-headed, bespectacled man sitting on a suitcase engrossed in a book. Without a word, she walked up and stood before him. A fifty-year-old German looked up in surprise. "Emily," he breathed, and still looking like a middle-aged stranger, he got up, took her in his arms, and held her tight.

For five days, Emily felt like an atheist who has just been trumpeted into heaven. She laughed, she cried, she danced, she swooned—she couldn't believe what was happening. Neither could Richard. They made love several times a day, and when they staggered out of bed it was to shower together, go off to a restaurant, and eat with one another's fork. At one point, Richard pulled an enormous hunk of rope out of his suitcase along with his old copy of the *Kama Sutra,* and Emily laughed so hard she had trouble catching her breath. "I didn't know," she kept saying. "I never imagined. Oh, Richard!"

As the initial excitement subsided, Emily wondered if Richard's marriage would at least be acknowledged. Was he unhappy? Had he had other affairs? Did he think of separating now or when the children were grown? But the topic was apparently off limits, and it was not until the night before she returned to Montreal that she finally asked him outright where this reunion was heading. To her surprise, he became annoyed. Watching his jaw set and hearing his voice harden as they sat across from each other in a dimly lit restaurant, Emily tried to recall if she had ever seen Richard angry before.

"I couldn't remember Richard getting angry," she told me, "but I did recall his parents saying that he had the worst temper in the family. They told a story about his being so angry that...I forget the German expression, but something to the effect that he'd fly up to the ceiling without provocation. As angry as a stone sinking through water is more like it."

Emily left Boston the next morning with glowing memories, a box of German chocolate, and no idea of whether or not she'd ever hear from Richard again. All he had been willing to say as he pressed the large gold box into her hands was, "Keep this memory, Emily. And don't cry."

"And that was that...basically," Emily reiterated. "Over the next year I cried a great deal. I wrote to his office in Germany. He never replied. I called several times. He cut me off. Then he changed jobs and was gone. The end.

"I found myself in a fix," she continued. "I had never been so in love before. I hadn't experienced the sense of giving everything and having everything received. We were—will always be—so well matched that nothing fell on the floor as it passed between us. Everything we exchanged found a home. I didn't know two people could fit like that." She looked away for a moment and sighed. "For me, the love of a lifetime is the person you recognize as your emotional homeland.

"It's funny," she went on, "my feelings for Richard kept on building after he cut me off, but so did my anger and confusion. At fifty, I could easily imagine living in Germany, traveling with him, watching him tie his shoes in the methodical way he has, and at the same time I wondered if he'd set up the reunion to pay me back for leaving him when we were twenty. Back then, I'd flown home from a great time in Germany and stopped writing. Now, he'd flown back from a wonderful time in Boston and cut the connection. So had I finally discovered love, or payback? Could the experience be both? For the first time in my life, I could actually imagine how people stay married and also how they have nervous breakdowns. I could not get my mind around the contradictions.

"You know," she continued seriously, "before getting mixed up in this crazy situation, I had thought that happiness lay in one direction and sadness in another. I worked hard to stay in the happy zone. But now it seemed that extreme happiness and sadness might lie up against each other like two sides of a steep mountain. I seemed to be teetering on the ridge where the two came together in their most intense forms."

With no idea of what she was doing, Emily began writing Richard a letter every week or so and filing it away in a drawer. Week after week and month after month, she vented her anger and expressed her affection. Soon she was describing every walk and bicycle ride to him with unexpected tenderness. However, the tenderness was not for Richard, she explained, but for all that she saw around her. As if seeing her homeland for the last time, or perhaps the first time, she was struck by the beauty of everything. Dry leaves hopped across snow-packed roads like brown toads that winter, and in spring, hawks hung on the air like kites. The wind made cat's-paws on wheat fields in summer that were so beautiful tears came to her eyes, and as fall approached, she saw silver-skinned beech trees standing in slanting showers of golden leaves.

"I was so painfully alive," Emily said, speaking without realizing it for all broken-hearted lovers. "I never noticed as much and loved as much as I did the year Richard left me. Never in my life. That's the experience that surprised me most."

Emily came down on the side of love. When September rolled around again, she took out the letters, read them from start to finish, and was not particularly surprised to realize that she was in love with the whole world—including Richard. She might never know what he had in mind when he planned the reunion or what he felt about her now, but she no longer doubted what they had shared. Having finally allowed herself to fall in love with the man who had fallen for her so long ago, the two briefly realized the love of a lifetime. Although some would not consider a romance that started with a year of adolescent blundering followed decades later by five days of passion to be a good example of the love of a lifetime, Emily felt it was perfect in its own way. The experience taught her that joy and sorrow don't alternate but burn together like logs in a fire. She had handed herself over to the extremes of all emotions. "Here. Take me. I'm in. Let everything run through me—the best and the absolute worst." She also believed that her first, unqualified love was reciprocated at least briefly by one odd and unpredictable person. Even after Richard disappeared, she found that her love for him continued to generate a bittersweet confusion that stirred life up from the bottom. Yet none of these changes would have occurred had she not first formed the apparently ridiculous idea over the course of several decades that Richard was the love of her life, and then consolidated and held on to this belief after he disappeared.

"And now?"

She smiled her big smile. "I'll hear from him again. I'm not waiting, mind you, but a hidden fire that burns for thirty years then bursts into flame isn't about to go out."

Love led Emily to a crossroad where she either would or would not believe that what she experienced was the real thing, and all the love-of-a-lifetime stories I heard passed through this same intersection. For many different reasons, every relationship came to a point where each lover had to answer the question: "Is this love or something else?" Along with this question came another: "Can you trust your own judgment?"

When Richard disappeared, Emily had two options. She could argue herself out of love, or she could let her heart break. If she focused on his abrupt departure and angry silence, she could unravel their love story and eventually "prove" to herself either that theirs had been something other than love, or that it had been love, but they had blown it. She might have put together a story of Richard paying her back for leaving him thirty years before, or she might have told a story about making yet another mistake with a man. In either case, the story would become one of betrayal—his or hers. Her other option was to take all the joy and the grief to heart, call the passionate turmoil love, and let her heart break open. Emily wavered at the intersection for well over a year. Follow her doubts and retreat? Or believe it was love, and advance on a flood of tears? A lot of people spend their whole lives at this intersection—here where the vote is taken, here where faith is or is not received.

~

Here is another example of the role that believing plays in the love of a lifetime...and what an example. Nowhere and in no place has the ability to remain true to oneself played a larger role in a love affair than in Paris in the twelfth century. There, the young, headstrong, and immensely talented Héloïse, "the woman who invented love," met the brilliant, well-established, neurotic Abelard.

Héloïse was a teenager when she met the famous scholastic Peter Abelard. Well-born, brilliant, ambitious, and twenty years older than she, Abelard had been going from triumph to triumph within the Catholic Church. Upon meeting Héloïse, this difficult and sexually inexperienced man was quite unexpectedly overcome by passion. Charming his way into her household, he became the young woman's tutor, and to their mutual delight, her secret lover. When Héloïse's uncle and guardian told Abelard that he could beat her if she were lazy, the tutor gleefully added paddling to his expanding repertoire of erotic calisthenics. They both loved it "deliriously," he wrote.

The intoxicating lessons did not last long, however. Héloïse became pregnant, and soon after the two were discovered together in bed. Héloïse's guardian was furious, and he remained furious even after Abelard privately married his niece. The lovers fled to Brittany where their son was born and given to relatives. Still hounded by Héloïse's uncle, the two separated and sought shelter in convents. Nonetheless, they met and made love every chance they got. When this too was discovered, Héloïse's guardian hired henchmen who broke into Abelard's room and "cut off those parts of my body with which I had committed the offense they deplored."

Abelard was ruined. Humiliated, bitter, and finished as a public speaker, he committed himself to a monastery for life, pausing only to tell his nineteen-year-old wife to do the same. Although still passionately in love with Abelard and yearning for a life in society, she obeyed him and renounced the world. Taking the veil and making her vows, she waited for a word, a letter, a visit—some sign from the love of her life. None came. For ten years, Héloïse heard not one word from Abelard, yet for all this time she remained certain that they had shared a great love. Greater trials lay ahead. When Abelard, now an abbot, finally visited Héloïse, he announced that she was his sister in Christ and no longer his wife. In fact, he had so thoroughly repented of his old ways that he wrote *The Story of My Calamity*, in which carnal passion—his and hers in particular—was depicted as the worst mistake he had made in his life. Héloïse was furious. She wrote letters to Abelard reminding him of the sexual ecstasies they had shared and declaring that she still loved him above everything, even Christ and the Church. An abbess herself now, she still felt his arms around her as she prayed, and she still swooned at the thought of his touch. "I am the sinner," she proclaimed. "I long for your arms."

Abelard was appalled, and the battle over the meaning of their relationship was joined in earnest. It was a mistake, he hammered. It was
love, she insisted. A long time later, Héloïse finally agreed to stop telling
him how much she loved him, and Abelard wrote a prayer that spoke of
being united with her forever in heaven.

In his early sixties, Abelard was excommunicated, and on the way to
Rome to contest the verdict, he died. In a rash move, Héloïse had his
"unholy" body exhumed and brought north to her abbey, where he had
wanted to be buried. She lived for another twenty years and, like
Abelard, died at the age of sixty-three. She was laid to rest in the same
tomb. Legend has it that at the moment she was lowered into the sep-
ulcher, Abelard's arms opened to receive her. Nonsense, said the practi-
cal French, *her* arms opened to receive *him*. She was the "the woman who
invented love" because she was the one who believed.

Every love-of-a-lifetime story is about believers. It is not that a miracle made them believe. It is their belief that is the miracle.

It is a sobering thought to acknowledge how difficult it is to believe.
It's easy to be swept away in a passionate romance, but difficult to
believe year in and year out that this one unsettling experience was the
love that finally penetrated the heart and changed us forever. If we live
for the rest our lives with our beloved, we are not spared the need to
decide what we believe. Daily contact will eventually challenge the idea
that this relationship is a great love. There will be plenty of times when
it will seem like an ordinary, if not restrictive, partnership. If we don't
remain with the love of our lives, then the passage of time will increasingly suggest that the romance was a fantasy. In either case, there is no
one to turn to for proof of this love's unique importance, because the

ecstasy that distinguished it from all others was experienced by us alone. No one can substantiate how we feel or felt; it is a private experience. Thus, like all lovers past and present, Héloïse was on her own when she claimed that what she felt for Abelard was the greatest passion a human being is capable of. It was her word against his. How did she gain such conviction and find such faith in herself?

No one comes into the world trusting his or her own feelings. We rely on our parents' interpretations for years. A toddler falls down and looks at his mother. Should he cry and wait to be picked up? Should he get up by himself? How important is a fall? He feels rattled and sore, but his mother's reaction will override or at least strongly modify his idea of what has just happened. She's smiling. Falls of this magnitude are not important.

Of course, at some point this useful process must change, and the adolescent must become the expert on his or her own feelings. This takes a long time and is never easy. Strange as it may sound, "I know what happened to me," is a bold statement. Quite a few people told me that they first said, "I know what happened to me" with utter conviction when the love of a lifetime hit them. Before this time, they had not been paying much attention to their feelings or had been letting others have a hand in defining them, but this romance was too important. They would decide on their own. It was a declaration of independence and the true beginning of their ability to trust themselves.

~

In the spring of 1997, I traveled to Israel to meet the psychiatrist Alan Flashman to talk about love and danger. What kind of confidence—or recklessness—does a person have to have to embrace the emotional dangers of a love of a lifetime? Israel seemed the perfect place to hold this discussion. There had been several suicide bombings that month, and when I arrived, I asked Alan how to determine which places were especially dangerous. Simple, he told me, I could judge the probability of violence by looking to see where the soldiers carried their ammunition. If the clips were stuck through their belts at the small of their backs, the danger was no greater than usual, but if the clips were in the machine guns themselves, get away fast. Thus, as I entered Jerusalem to talk of love, I took a look around. At the crowded bus station, along the swarming streets, under the dusty walls of David—everywhere the clips were in the guns. And everyone I talked to that day—in the old town, in front of mosques, seated in cafés, standing on buses—everyone had an urgent story to tell about something they called love. Jerusalem was the love-hungriest, most love-obsessed city I have ever been in. But as I learned the next day, living on familiar terms with physical danger does not guarantee the self-confidence needed to confront the hazards of love.

Rudi Tarnoff, a travel writer who moved to Israel with his wife when their children left home and who now resides on the outskirts of Old Jerusalem, believed he found the love of his life the year he turned fifty. His wife and twin brother laughed at the idea. They called his experience "an unfortunate entanglement," a garden-variety midlife crisis. They predicted it would pass and that he would eventually see it as they did.

"My brother likes to tell me that I made three mistakes," Rudi began as we sat down in a tiny sweet shop just inside the Gates of David. "I listened to my hormones, I hurt my wife, and I mistook some poor, mixed-up teenager for the goddess of love. My brother says I'm as disconnected from reality myself as a sixteen-year-old."

Now fifty-three, Rudi was a slim man of average height who, like everyone else I saw around me, had dark hair and eyes and was dressed in a white shirt, khakis, and sandals. He certainly had the look. He had rather mismatched features—soft, brown eyes with a thin, straight mouth—and it looked to me as if his face wanted to settle into an expression of sadness or perhaps confusion if only he would let it. But he wouldn't. Tucking his feelings behind a worried frown and pursing his lips, he glanced restlessly around him. He had agreed to meet me at the shop where he and his young lover had spent much of their time together, and now he was probably sorry he had. Twenty or so students sat at small wooden tables chatting in Hebrew, English, and French, and Rudi looked them over as if making sure there was no one who knew him. Along one side of the room was a counter where coffee and sweets that looked like glazed birds' nests were served, but Rudi's glance was increasingly pulled in the opposite direction, where a few shadowy alcoves opened off the main room. There was a table in each. One had a curtain of red and black beads drawn across the entrance, and I guessed that many of Rudi's memories sat at one or the other of those secluded tables.

"I hate remembering, and I love remembering," he said, as small brass cups of coffee were set on our well-worn table.

Over the course of the next several hours, Rudi gave me the outline of the romance that he alternately called his folly or great love. Until he met a young Palestinian schoolteacher named Shuraia, he had been, he said, somewhat of a stranger to passion. He had grown up in New Jersey, started a career, found a wife, fathered two children, and at forty-five moved to Israel. He thought he had felt the usual amount of passion for each of these people and experiences—"the way we all get excited by something new"—but looking back, he wondered if the color hadn't drained more quickly from his own enterprises than from other people's adventures. In his thirties, he blamed the insecurity of his job for this lack of vitality. Later he chalked it up to age. Everyone runs out of steam sooner or later.

Then, at fifty, Rudi received an unusual assignment. He was asked to do a magazine piece on Jewish and Palestinian school children who were being bussed back and forth to each other's schools in order to complete a project on their families' political opinions. The goal was to build trust and respect among the young Palestinians and Israelis, and also to teach them an important lesson about political positions. In collecting and comparing opinions, they learned firsthand that Israeli and Palestinian families did not hold just two opposing positions, but a wide range of beliefs on both sides. Although their convictions often conflicted, the students could see that there were areas of agreement as well. They further realized that children on both sides of the Arab-Israeli struggle were up against the same confusing mixture of fears and hopes.

Rudi was fascinated. For several months, he visited a Palestinian school where he talked with a young teacher's assistant whose enthusiasm matched his own. Shuraia was a lovely young woman, he told me, whose wide-eyed expression of innocent trust gave to her smooth, brown face a self-possessed appearance he had never encountered to the same degree and certainly did not possess himself. She simply was who she was. Her utter lack of guile never ceased to amaze him. She was small, he continued, indicating with his hand how high she stood, and like many but not all young women her age, she covered her hair with a light scarf. He was entranced by her and the program equally. Soon he was giving small amounts of money to the project and meeting regularly with Shuraia. One afternoon, he fell in love. As they say in his part of the world, "Heavily falls he who has never fallen before."

"We had been sitting at our table in the corner," he said, nodding toward the furthest alcove. "I had gone to get tea and when I returned..." his voice trailed off, and I sensed he was being bombarded by memories, like what kind of tea she liked and how she took it, what she wore and how her hands rested on the table. "When I returned," he continued, "she had closed her eyes and let her head fall back against the wall. She always dressed modestly—longish cotton skirts, a scarf— but with her head back, I could see the curve of her brown throat. It was the most beautiful, delicate thing I'd ever seen. It was like coming upon a flower that you'd been told since childhood was marvelous but extinct. I felt such an urge to protect her. It was astonishing. I remember look- ing down at her and being certain of only one thing: my life would never be the same again. And happy?"

Rudi's frown relaxed for a moment and his face took on a boyish quality. He opened his arms as if feeling the sun. "I was happy with everything."

From that moment on, Rudi considered that he and Shuraia were lovers, and although they were physically intimate only a few times, Rudi was ecstatic. His life had unexpectedly lit up like the desert at sunset. The high stone ramparts that surrounded the old city, the mats of fragrant rose- mary that grew everywhere in the powdery dirt, the bells, the call to prayer, the hustling crowds in their colorful scarves and robes—all were suffused with a rosy, golden glow that he recognized as love.

At first, Rudi resolved to enjoy this miracle without laying claim to it. His affair with Shuraia was as impermanent as Indian summer, he told himself. He would just bask in the miracle for as long as it lasted.

"I did a lot of walking in those early days," he said, enthusiasm return- ing to his voice, "and everywhere I looked—I saw. I saw perfect blue skies. I saw intricate patterns of footprints in the dust. I saw light soaking into stone walls as if it was water. You know the bazaars here are covered, but narrow slices of light come through the awnings. They look just like ribbons of light scattered through the gloom. Once I saw a long strip of light lying across a table of pomegranates. It was so dark the fruits were gray except for this thin red ribbon of light that ran up and down the bumpy fruit. I could have stood there all day."

Although Rudi told himself to just look, his fantasies led him in the opposite direction. By the time he had known Shuraia for the better part of a year, he was wondering if she would marry him. Would her parents hire someone to kill him if they ran off together? he wondered. Could he bring himself to tell his wife and brother? Could he afford to divorce? He became obsessed with holding onto the golden year.

"She really was the light of my world," he said with a flicker of a smile. "I had never had such a pure relationship—so open and easy, like her face. She was instantly my helpmate. Once we spent an afternoon at a park along the Dead Sea. We bobbed around for a bit—I'm sure she was taken for my daughter—then we rinsed off and sat in the shade. She had a hand-woven, black-and-white sack filled with oranges, and without saying a word, she peeled one for me and fed me the sections. I'd seen Palestinian women do that for their men, and I'd thought it was ridiculous." He laughed shortly at the memory. "But no one had done it for me."

During that year of light and kindness, Shuraia said very little, and Rudi assumed that she was as deeply in love as he was and as troubled by the barriers that kept them apart. It was an understandable assumption. The twenty-year-old risked terrible consequences if their affair were discovered, and the risks she took seemed proof of her devotion. He further interpreted her silence as contentment, for he himself was enjoying a silent happiness he had never experienced.

"One of the greatest things about this love affair," he said with surprise, "was the feeling it gave me that I was no longer missing out. I hadn't realized how much I resented getting older, life passing me by, but once I had Shuraia, I could smile at whatever came my way. It was a delight not to feel cheated anymore by a difficult job or a critical wife. I stopped being a malcontent. I relaxed, and what a relief that was for everyone."

Rudi told me that for the last month or so of his golden year, he had agonized over whether or not to leave his wife. Then Shuraia began talking of moving to another city and joining a full-time project devoted to peace. Move? Join a houseful of young people? Rudi was shocked. The very next day he asked her if she would be happy if he divorced. He had been leaving home gradually, he explained, shifting his perspective and priorities little by little, and now, at last, he had made up his mind.

Remembering the conversation, Rudi began to deflate. Slumping slightly in his chair, his frown returned and he began shaking his head.

"She thought it was a bad idea," he said in disbelief, "a bad idea. I had finally summoned the courage to abandon my entire past only to discover that her answer was 'No.' She told me she had made a commitment to the project, and I know she hated the idea of hurting my wife. But then why...? I mean, what did she think we'd been doing for thirteen months?"

Rudi was so upset he threw his back out and couldn't move for a week. When he was finally able to call Shuraia, she was sweet, loving, and decisive. Her move out of the city, she said, was best for everyone. Besides, it wouldn't happen for another several months, and she was sure they could continue to be friends until she left.

"Friends!" Rudi groaned, setting his cup down with a sharp clink. "What was she talking about? Suddenly we spoke different languages, and we couldn't understand each other. My back was so bad I could hardly walk. I still had a magazine assignment to finish, which meant I had to go to her school. And here she was walking out of my life with a stupid little smile. I had a really awful feeling that the important, happy portion of my life was over...and I only had myself to blame."

With cautious civility, Rudi and Shuraia talked past each other until she moved. He went to her new home a few times, but the trip was too long and Shuraia emotionally unavailable. When his wife became suspicious at the additional miles on the car, Rudi didn't bother to make excuses. He confessed everything. The affair was over.

Rudi fell into a deep depression. Should he have acted sooner and more decisively? Or had he been a jerk not to see from the beginning that the match was impossible? Every morning he awoke to find that a further batch of questions, along with sexual fantasies, grinding regrets, and innumerable replays, had accumulated in his head like emails after a long vacation. Some mornings his head was so heavy he couldn't get it off the pillow. As the weeks went by, there was more and more to sort out and grieve for, and soon he felt as if he were being buried alive. But he found a certain perverse pleasure in all this pain, he admitted. As the expression goes, "Heartbreak is the second best feeling in the world." For Rudi, obsessing became his way of being loyal to Shuraia, and he preferred grief to forgetting. This simple pattern of being either preoccupied or fitfully asleep eventually splintered into more complex forms of torture. He felt abandoned and betrayed by Shuraia, then warm and protective toward her. He felt sad and then numb. He felt guilty for the pain he was causing his wife and furious at her for trivializing his affair by calling it a midlife crisis. No crisis could cause the kind of agony he was experiencing, he reasoned, yet his wife's accusations of living in fantasyland and being self-centered sounded true enough to make him miserably uncertain. She desperately wanted her old Rudi back. But was he worth reviving?

"It occurred to me that I had never known what I was doing," he said candidly. "Amazing that I hadn't noticed before. My whole life had been random zigs and zags—unannounced halts, sudden accelerations. I was a drunk operating a car with a dirty windshield. What a wasted effort."

As Rudi's family hammered home the idea that he must return to his cautious, predictable ways, Jerusalem itself began to change.

"My own house seemed foreign, and the street I lived on was unfamiliar. I associated Old Jerusalem with Shuraia so completely that this beautiful, troubled pile of a city with its dark alleyways and bright vistas became hers. I no longer belonged in it. Even after five years of constant exploration and enjoyment, I was a tourist again, someone who needed a native guide to justify my presence. I felt rejected by thousands of years of history. Expelled. Why hadn't I noticed that it was love that kept me interested in all these places and things? What would I do when the light went out of Jerusalem?"

A year after Shuraia moved south and after Rudi had "let the guillotine fall on all communication so I could get on with whatever a headless life was like," Shuraia unexpectedly returned to Jerusalem. Rudi no longer hoped to rekindle their romance, but he leapt at the expectation of comfort, at finding a companion in misery. In his mind, they would meet once a year at the small café, and there they would tell each other how wonderful their love had been and how lonely they were without it. They would shore up each other's belief. He wept in anticipation.

The meeting was a disaster. Changed in some ineffable way, Shuraia smiled blandly and told Rudi that her work was wonderful; it was God's will that he was still married; and she would remain his "forever friend." After a few minutes of silence, she would play the tape again.

"'Where are you?' I kept asking her. 'Where is the Shuraia I knew?'

"Had I misjudged her all this time?" he wondered now. "Had I made up a lovely young woman who was simple, passionate, and devoted, and then superimposed this dream woman on a person who in reality wanted nothing more than to be a follower in some peace project?"

Rudi absentmindedly took my empty brass cup in one hand and his in the other and started clinking them together slowly and softly. Together. Apart. Together. Apart. Abruptly, I found myself holding my breath for the next sentence for I sensed he was about to tell me whether or not he was a believer. Had he managed to hold onto the golden year despite Shuraia's departure?

"As we drank tea together," he said slowly, "it occurred to me that she was a sheep. I had fallen in love with a sheep. I was so wrapped up in myself as the great shepherd or rescuer, that I'd...well, you see what I mean. I felt stupid. I had fallen in love with my own dream of being a protector—and of course a great lover—and it was all a fantasy.

"Shuraia and I have not met since that afternoon," he concluded glumly.

Frowning, he started tapping the cups gently on the table. "But...but a year later I suffered a heart attack," he continued in pinched voice, "and what crossed my mind as the ambulance carried me through the streets, its siren blaring, was that some force in the universe was *angry* with my passionless, wasted life." He leaned forward abruptly and slammed both cups down on the table. "I was dying in the back of a red and white truck," he said between clenched teeth, "and all I knew about life was the one year I'd spent in love!"

~

Several years after talking with Rudi in Jerusalem, I decided to write to him and find out how he was doing. He had been so honest in explaining what love was like for him and so willing to describe the sorrowful lessons he'd learned, that he had won me over with his candor. Don Quixote courts Dulcinea, then agrees to talk of love. Although he'd been discouraged when I talked with him, Rudi had given me a perfect example of what the love of a lifetime can accomplish. In all likelihood, he and Shuraia would not get together, but love had opened his eyes to a new and beautiful Jerusalem. Of course, the rest of his life counted, too—his marriage, children, job. He had exaggerated when he said that the only year that mattered was the one he spent in love. I think he meant that the only time he had taken living to the limit and had been aware of the vitality that can infuse the world was during the golden year. It seemed shameful to him that he'd stumbled around like a sleepwalker the rest of the time. Perhaps his brush with death had stepped in to reawaken him again and finish the transformation that love had begun.

"How do you think of Shuraia now?" I wrote. "Are you glad you met?"

Rudi wrote back from the middle of the crossroad where belief is or is not received. He was still stuck. Yes, he was glad he had met Shuraia, *but*...But their romance wasn't real because it didn't last. But he hadn't proved worthy because he had wavered and let her get away. But she didn't love him because she ultimately rejected him. Stitch by stitch, Rudi appeared to be unraveling what he had learned in the grip of an unexpected ecstasy, and I admit his long letter was painful to read. Although still shaken occasionally by disturbing dreams, he wasn't ready to let the music of life with its joyous ups and heartbreaking downs take him over. If love didn't give him what he wanted, it wasn't love. If he couldn't get a guarantee, it wasn't worth the risk. Armed with the memory of all that went wrong, Rudi had apparently marched back into his old life.

A story like Rudi's is not over until the lovers are dead, as Bertrand Russell's ambivalent tango with love and mystery makes clear. Russell didn't surrender to love until he was in his nineties. More than once, I have seen love gain a toehold in a person's life and then, taking advantage of the next available calamity, complete the transformation. Naturally, I don't wish Rudi ill, but I do wish him more than one year of what he himself once recognized as "the *real* real life."

Rudi's story reminded me of a dream told to me by a woman who, like him, was vacillating between admitting and denying a great love. Her charismatic husband had walked out, asked for a divorce, and then died. In her mind, rage and sadness fought with each other, and she was always on the brink of tears or fury. Then a starling appeared to her in a dream and she knew immediately that the bird—an unwelcome import like her foreign-born husband—had come with a message. The bird lit on a branch close to her face and ruffled its little wings.

"Mack wants you to know that he is sorry," twittered the bird.

"He damn well oughta be sorry!" shouted the widow, feeling the familiar anger rise in her chest.

"*Well he is!*" roared the bird.

The woman was so shocked that she woke up.

"That was the end of the recriminations. I got the message. The part to hold on to is the love."

Someday, I believe Rudi will learn the same.

The ability to believe that our great romance was a perfect example of love says several things about us. First, it is evidence that we can trust ourselves. We can say, "I know what happened to me." Second, it is evidence that we can trust what we don't understand, which is a form of faith. No one can explain why we are sandbagged by ecstasy by one particular person out of the thousands who have crossed our path. We have no control over this experience, but when it comes, it asks to be acknowledged and given meaning. At some point, we move from feeling the unexpected passion to thinking about it, and we go about deciding whether or not it is real and important. Do I believe this is love? Do I believe stars sing in Jerusalem? Belief in the love of a lifetime is belief in mystery. Even the relentless realist who believes love will eventually be fully explained by science has to proceed on faith until the clarifications he feels are possible are actually proved.

In claiming a love of a lifetime, we take a brave stand. It is an act of self-trust and an act of faith. No wonder people are proud of the certainty they feel when they say, "Love of a lifetime? I know *exactly* what you mean."

Part Three

The Reward

CHAPTER 9
Transformation

To find an answer
is in a sense to
become the answer.
—Stephen Mitchell,
Meetings with the Archangel

In the Zen tradition, there is a series of drawings called the Ox Herding Pictures that, in either five, six, or nine frames, shows the progression of a profound transformation. In the East the process is often called enlightenment, in the West conversion. It could also be called being changed by the love of a lifetime.

In the five-picture version of the Ox Herding series, the initial frame shows a young person catching sight of the ox for the first time. In terms of love, this is the first experience of being transported by joy. It is the invitation. Although this glimpse may or may not lead any further, it is an altogether new and electrifying experience. There is something in the world—out there—that I must have. Walter, the man who waited over seventy years to make contact with the girl who had captured his heart in trade school, merely glimpsed the ox in tenth grade. If he had taken no action, his memory of the perfect girl would have seemed to many people just a fantasy. In fact, it was a beginning.

The second picture, capturing the ox, is analogous to accepting the invitation and falling passionately in love. Wanting more of this wonderful, vital sensation, the lover leaps on the back of the ox and hangs on for dear life. No other experience will do. No other ox will do. Her passion is focused entirely on this being, and she embraces love with all the strength at her command. Life itself seems to reside in this romance. I talked with a man from Georgia who went to school in Massachusetts and dated a Northern girl who was wild and willful compared to the girls he knew at home. His "most promising memories," as he calls them, are of becoming wild and willful with her. They swam naked at night. They cut class to climb mountains. This was love as he'd envisioned it. But his mother constantly warned against bringing a "stranger" into the family, and he himself couldn't imagine his girlfriend adjusting to the South. He left her on graduation day. To his surprise, he never found love again. Nor did he forget her. He had captured the ox for a year then let it get away.

If this is as far as the story goes, it will most likely be remembered in one of two ways. It will either be viewed as a star-crossed love affair that could not continue, or as something less than love—puppy love, a fling, a midlife crisis. Rudi, the journalist in Israel who fell so hard for a Palestinian girl that he seemed to get a new pair of eyes, seems to be leaning toward the idea that what he experienced was a botched attempt at love—better to pretend it had never happened, he sometimes thinks, and resume his old life. In contrast, those who thought they did a good job loving and valued the insights they received cherish the memory of the short-lived love of their lives. Dr. Niemeyer spent very little time with his colleague, Leslie, but she is, nevertheless, the love of his life because he believed the relationship was love and he let it change his thinking. Perhaps she has done so as well.

The third picture, putting a ring in the ox's nose, seems oddly out of place. I have been saying all along that love is the uncontrollable force that runs the show. Yet it looks as if the person is subduing the ox. I am told that this picture shows the lover learning to use love to do whatever work he or she undertakes in the world just as a farmer learns to use an ox to plow a field or pump water from a well. It is a cooperative effort. Leaving behind the roller coaster that was falling in love, lovers enter the work stage and learn that the passion they have shared has given them a new perspective. Sometimes the first job that their insights prompt is a break from home or from the old way of doing business. As the not-so-young computer fanatic discovered, the day he realized he loved his girlfriend was the day he knew he'd break his parents' hearts by moving out. Or perhaps passion makes a man so crazy for a woman that he finally manages to tolerate the frightening vulnerability he feels in love and stay in the ring. Lovers also learn to give themselves over to love. Miriam Weinstein and her family discovered that letting go of the controls and adopting love's agenda got the ox to come along with them and help with whatever they were doing. But Leah and Daniel Blackman, who lived on the grounds of a mental hospital and fought constantly, had a terrible time learning to work with each other in a loving way. Only when Dr. Daniel agreed to take ballroom-dancing lessons and his wife finally stopped badgering him did they figure out how to give themselves over to love. Some never do. Jim and Myra Louise, the couple who hiked through the mountains together but could not agree about children, held onto their personal agendas. They never got the ring in the ox's nose, and it soon wandered off.

A particularly tough lesson to figure out is how to incorporate the mystery that we glimpsed in the grip of ecstasy into the rest of our lives. Can we really trust a power that can't be proved? Perhaps it was easier in the old days. Nearly a hundred years ago, former British Prime Minister Herbert Henry Asquith repeatedly referred to "the love of his heart" as "something greater than a miracle," and this did not strike him as a silly way to describe a great love. Unexpected and unparalleled, the late gift of love that arrived as he led the British Empire into the Great War was simply one of life's miracles, a sustaining force that helped him with every aspect of his difficult life.

Learning to use the ox in daily life also includes exercising our imaginations and believing in ourselves. It is growing into or inhabiting our own lives rather than standing on the sidelines and watching ourselves operate. "Out of the control tower and into the plane!" my mentor loved to shout. However, this transformation from spectator to participant is as risky and difficult in love as it is in pro football. Many get trampled as they try to work with the ox. Often becoming cynical, people like Rudi in Jerusalem conclude that love tricks good men into becoming fools. Off to the glue factory with the ox, and back into the tightly circumscribed world of deals for the disappointed.

In brief love affairs, which many loves of a lifetime are, learning to work with the ox is a process that continues with other partners after the beloved has gone. Many of the men and women I spoke with—people like Dr. Niemeyer, whose married lover moved across the country, or Emily, whose crazy lover Richard lived in Germany—never set up housekeeping with their great love, yet found ways to work with other people to put into practice what they had learned. I heard dozens of stories in which the lovers, now on their own, continued to follow some version of the hero's code. With family, friends, and new partners, they showed up, paid attention, told the truth, and let go of the outcome. Rather than dropping the insights that being deeply in love had revealed, they held on to them.

In the fourth picture, the ox is following its master. The learning has been completed, and the master has the ox available to him wherever he goes. Whether or not the ox stays now becomes irrelevant (at least in theory) because the master has learned how to put love into practice so well and so automatically that it is no longer the partner who triggers the master's loving response. Although still fallible of course, and still temperamental at times, the master is a person for whom love makes as much sense as breathing. In her more serene moments, Leah Blackman felt that she had mastered the art of loving so well that she no longer needed the ox tagging along behind her or Daniel pouring compliments into her glass. The day came when she knew "for a fact" that she was a loving person.

Others never get to this point. Even after marrying and spending many years apprenticed to love, some people can't quite believe they are loved or that they are themselves loving partners unless the ox stays right at their shoulder. If it disappears, they lose their confidence and begin to doubt they were ever in love.

In the last picture, a stage according to Zen teachings that few reach, the ox has disappeared, and the person walks through the village alone. He is apparently carrying out the ordinary tasks of an ordinary life except that as he passes, trees burst into bloom. In terms of the love of a lifetime, this is the stage where love has spread out like water over an irrigated field. Every plant and every person is nourished because the enlightened, loving person sees everything as lovable in some way. His or her benign attention brings out the best. Although this degree of ease and contentedness is extremely rare, I think people who are being transformed by love catch glimpses of it. Perhaps at a school reunion decades after graduation, at a church picnic to welcome a refugee family, or at the end of a successful effort to roll a stranded seal back into the bay, there is a glimpse of what it would be like to love as sweetly as water.

This is the complex transformation that the love of a lifetime leads many people into and a few through. "All things excellent are as difficult as they are rare," said Spinoza. Although the momentary transport of a two-week affair is less likely to start a revolution than the first years of a solid marriage, the strength of the love is more important than the duration. The medieval Italian poet Dante Alighieri literally glimpsed the love of his life, Beatrice, when she was a girl of nine. He spoke with her only three or four times, but so profound was his reaction to her presence, and so powerful his imagination, that she became his life-long inspiration, or as he put it, his revelation. That Dante could let a glimpse of the ox permanently transform him from a man who had lost his way into the poet who composed *The Divine Comedy* is incredible, but with every additional stage that ardent lovers pass through—capturing the ox, putting a ring in its nose—the chances increase that the relationship will be remembered as the love that shook them up and changed their lives around.

There has been an "incredible revolution in my inner life..." wrote Herbert Henry Asquith to his lover. "...One I shouldn't have thought possible."

~

When former British Prime Minister Herbert Henry Asquith was in his late fifties and England was wavering on the brink of World War I, he was struck by a late-life love affair that, he said, transformed his life. Asquith was vacationing in Sicily with his young friend and junior member of his government, Edwin Montagu, when they were joined by Asquith's daughter, Violet, and her friend, Venetia Stanley. Both men fell in love with Venetia. As Asquith remembered:

> I was sitting with her in the dining room on Sunday morning—the others being out in the garden or walking—and we were talking and laughing just on our old accustomed terms. Suddenly, in a single instant, without

premonition on my part or any challenge on hers, the
scales dropped from my eyes; the familiar features and
smiles and gestures and words assumed an absolutely new
perspective; what had been completely hidden from me
was in a flash half-revealed, and I dimly felt, hardly knowing, not at all understanding it, that I had come to a turning point in my life.

It was the beginning of the "incredible revolution," as he documented
in his letters to Venetia. When Asquith's daughter, Violet, lost the man she
hoped to marry in a motoring accident, the naturally pliant and caring
Venetia had stepped in and offered comfort. She loved to listen sympathetically to Violet's accounts. She hated to see anyone in pain. With several other women in their twenties, Violet and Venetia made up what was
known as Asquith's "little harem." Swirling through his household in their
long summer dresses or laughing in the garden over tea, they added charm
and gaiety to the endless round of dinners and card games that, surprising as it sounds today, formed the setting for serious political discussions.

There was a Mrs. Asquith also. Although Asquith had been married to
someone else when he met her, the first Mrs. Asquith died of typhoid
fever, and he married again. The second Mrs. Asquith was a high-strung,
"challenging" woman, and was regarded by the whole family as a trial.

Asquith became Prime Minister in 1908, and inherited the chronic
tensions and troubles of a far-flung empire, plus several truly impossible situations. As he struggled with the question of Irish Home Rule,
for example, and misjudged the degree of animosity that existed
between Irish Catholics and Protestants, he increasingly felt the loneliness
that he knew was an inherent part of his job. Many Prime Ministers

before him had formed romantic or at least affectionate attachments to women who served as sympathetic confidantes. He could see why.

Although Asquith began writing letters to Venetia in 1912, when he suddenly saw her in a new light, he proceeded slowly, gauging both her discretion and ability to understand the business of government. He was nothing if not savvy. Gradually, however, the weekly letter became twice weekly, the chat at the country castle became the leisurely drive in his chauffeured motor car. By 1914, the two were exchanging letters daily.

Typically, Asquith would write to her at the end of the day as he sat alone in his drawing room. He would pull out the letter he had received from her earlier in the day and had carried into meetings sandwiched between official documents. Responding as if no time had elapsed, he would continue their ongoing conversation. "Strictly in private," he described the day's dealings, but what he really liked to write about was love. A regular fountain of quotations, he would embellish his thoughts of Venetia with poetry and occasionally a sonnet of his own. She was beautiful with her white skin and dark skeins of hair. He liked it when she wore her hair piled loosely on her head. She was intelligent. The perfect companion, she listened patiently, and counseled balance. She was loving, although here, the P.M. had to push and prompt a bit. "Don't ever drop the 'My' from 'My Darling,'" he instructed. Nor did he want her to forget to close with "certain endearments." (What they were we don't know as her letters have been lost.) As a couple, didn't she think they embodied what the classics called grand passion?

"Isn't it a wonderful thing that we—you & I—should be like that?" he asked in amazement. "I could never have...even dreamt of it... My darling...I shall see you Saturday—and am always and everywhere *Yours*."

When a Saturday rolled around, Asquith would send for his motor car, and with a cheery wave to the dozen or so others who were always at his home, he and Venetia would set off over the cobbled streets of London for the country. If anyone caught a glimpse of them, Asquith knew they would guess him to be her father. A man of medium build with sandy hair and fair skin, he was an average-looking, middle-aged man with a slightly worried look. But people rarely saw them. Even at fifteen miles an hour, it didn't take long to get into the country, and soon the empty green fields and hedgerows were passing by the slow-moving car. This was the best moment of the week for Asquith. The troubles of the world slipped away, and in the intimacy of his private car he was alone with the woman who brought out more strength, intelligence, and just plain joy than this world-weary man had dared imagine would ever be his. With the discreet chauffeur taking a long leisurely route through the green hills, Asquith took Venetia's lovely hand in his and was free at last to express his thoughts and feelings without censure.

Sometimes this curious May-December couple stopped at one or another of their favorite places—a little bridge, a secluded glade. Here, the stocky but still agile P.M. escorted his darling out of sight of the car. Just what happened next is not clear. Apparently, Asquith did not feel a great urgency to have sex with Venetia. In his letters, he loved to remind her of their "divine moments," but he knew she was saving his correspondence in a large box, and he was careful to fade off into an ellipses when describing what transpired after the embrace. They talked. They held hands. They kissed, "and. . . ." But someday he would no longer be in politics, he assured her repeatedly. Then he would disentangle himself from family obligations and start over with the love of his heart. Privately, he envisioned her as the mother of his child.

Then in the summer of 1914, as their romance heated up, it looked as if the P.M.'s career was over. Negotiations had broken down over Irish Home Rule, and if Asquith couldn't break the Ulster Impasse, he was finished.

"I'm not in the best of moods," he wrote Venetia glumly. He wasn't sleeping, he confided. He was depressed. Instead of eating, he was drinking. He was much "over-strained" and ready to snap. Then, on the very day that negotiators pushed back their chairs and left the table in Ulster without an agreement, Austria delivered an ultimatum to Serbia and everyone's attention turned to the possibility of war.

"Do keep close to me beloved in this most critical time of my life," Asquith wrote after reminding her of their "heavenly drive...You were never more wonderful. "

Three days later, Austria was more menacing still, and Asquith thanked Venetia for "two hours of respite and real companionship." Although he declined her dinner invitation for that evening—"I hate even the possibility of gossip about us"—he wanted her to know that, as the hymn put it, "I need thy presence every passing hour."

"Our lives and interests are so mingled together," he wrote to her as army recruits began flooding onto the parade grounds outside his office window, "that any *real* separation is to me an unthinkable tragedy. Every hour I think of you & refer things, big & little, to the unseen tribunal of your wise and loving judgment. I always think of you."

August 1914 was a terrible month. On the first, Germany declared war on Russia, and two days later on France. Neutral Belgium was next, and as Germany prepared to invade, Belgium swore to resist and asked for Britain's help. The guns of August might as well have been shelling Asquith's house. Night after night, he could not find his way to sleep.

Eventually, he discovered that if he reread Venetia's most recent letter and called up a vision of her lovely form bent over a writing desk or sitting with him in the car, he could slip into sleep before thoughts of war drove rest away.

"We are on the verge of terrible things," he wrote to her. "I wish you were nearer."

On August 4, Germany rolled into Belgium and Britain declared war on Germany. Eight days later, the Empire declared war on Austria-Hungary as well. Asquith became a political juggler. He reined in young Winston Churchill who, "with all his war paint on," pined for a sea battle. He prodded King George, who was reluctant to escalate the war. He was everywhere and knew everything. As thousands of rosy-cheeked lads stood on the parade grounds unable to imagine what lay in store for them, Asquith increasingly drew on the inner reserves of strength that he called his love for Venetia. He earned the reputation of a decisive politician with an admired sense of timing.

"The House met in large numbers, and we introduced another dozen Emergency War Bills. (I don't know whether you like this sort of hour-by-hour diary. But you say today that I am to give you *all* my news—'esp. personal.' If that means *my very own*, you know well my darling how every hour you are with me.)"

Then back he went to telling her about the war. In a second letter, he reported on munitions, the number of German prisoners flowing into the country, and how peevish the French were with anyone who didn't speak good French. Later still, "we saw a most interesting & even thrilling thing—an aeroplane...[It was] on a bomb-throwing expedition...It made a magnificent flight, 4000 or 5000 feet high, and circled up & down in every direction."

"I ought to stop now," he frequently closed, "for I have a lot to do...Talking with you in this way is the one alleviation of my days...Write to me my own darling a *dear* letter...I *love* you."

By the end of 1914, when Asquith sat alone at his desk at midnight, writing to Venetia, the world had changed in ways that seemed both ominous and permanent.

> ...This year has been in the fullest sense what the Ancients used to call 'annus mirabilis.' I am not as a rule very sensitive about anniversaries: the 'daily round' is more important to me. But this particular one is an exception. From the world-wide point of view it is impossible to exaggerate the difference wh. it has made in values & the things that matter. I won't enlarge on this. Nor do I think much of the effort wh. its unforeseen unrolling of events has had on my own personal position... But to you & me...it has been a succession of marvelous experiences. Looking back, I can hardly remember a day out of the 365 when I have not either written to you, or seen you, or often done both. And there have been very few when you have not either seen or written to me. We have interchanged everything—the greatest & the smallest; never has there been between man and woman fuller & franker confidence: & whatever may be the case with you, rarely, if ever, has a man gained or owed so much.
>
> I thank you my darling from the bottom of my heart, from the very source of my being, for what you have been to me. Without you I must often have failed, & more than once gone down. You have sustained & enriched every day of my life.

"No one," he had added to her birthday letter, "will ever love you more—or so much. *Never.*"

Asquith was immensely pleased with the volume of love that came rushing from the bottom of his heart each day. Although he loved to quote Pascal's "I know that, whatever happens, I shall die alone," he was sharing more of his inner thoughts with Venetia than he had thought possible. He had written to her "with more confidence & fullness & intimacy (a thousand times) than I ever have to any other human being." In these difficult times when every day brought news of the death of a friend or a friend's son, the men around him were aging quickly, but not Asquith. He was drinking less. He was more patient, more appreciative, more focused, and happier. In short, love had made him a new man.

"My beloved," Asquith boasted, "no one can say that *we* kept our lamps unlit, or allowed them to grow dim & flicker out."

There was one step in love's transformation, however, that gave Asquith trouble. It was faith. Did Venetia care for him even half as much as he loved her? Was their love mutual? Or was he dotty? He closed quite a few of his letters: "Think of me & *try* to love me & write." Although he wanted to believe that their relationship would last to the end of his life, he admitted that now and again he liked to have his "unshakeable & undying faith confirmed by outward sign & expression. If that is a weakness, I confess to it..."

Asquith had good reason to doubt Venetia's passion. Although unfailingly agreeable, she was a detached young woman who did not respond strongly to anything. "I'm no fun to be in love with..." she admitted to a friend, "my supply of emotion is a thin and meager one." Poor woman, her supply of self-definition was meager too, as was often the case among those raised to be helpmates. She drifted through life turning herself into whomever was needed. Not surprisingly, she had never fallen love, and found it hard to imagine what that state of mind was like.

In the spring of 1915, Venetia began to slip from Asquith's grasp. First she decided to become a nurse, which cut into her free time. Asquith thought it a terrible idea and could not abide the thought of her actually touching young soldiers to turn them over in bed. He could not overstate his opposition, he said, and if she was serious, he'd have to find "the speediest & most painless exit from the disappointments of life." Second, Venetia was writing to her "best of friends," Edwin Montagu, who was now in Asquith's cabinet and a kind of honorary member of his household. "But he is not a *man*," Asquith scolded her, "a bundle of moods & nerves & symptoms..." He too would cut into their time together, and "I *must* see you at least *twice* in every week: otherwise I shall starve." Third, Venetia seemed suddenly to realize at age twenty-eight that she needed to marry in the next year or the good life would be over for her.

Since economic security had more to do with her decision to marry than love did, Venetia made up her mind quickly. She would marry Montagu. But what about the Prime Minister? Montagu asked her. He had known for some time that more than one man was surreptitiously writing to Venetia during cabinet meetings. Wasn't the great man in love with her?

"If it hadn't been me," she wrote back nonchalantly, "it would have been someone else or a series of others who would have made him just as happy."

Yet when it came to telling Asquith that she was marrying Montagu, Venetia couldn't do it. The P.M. was now sending her letters by private messenger on Sundays addressed to the "Pulse of my Being, pivot of my days." He would be terribly hurt, she acknowledged, and she hated to hurt anyone. The very thought prompted her to write him such a "delicious letter" that Asquith swore to keep it in the pocket of his jacket forever. Montagu responded by withdrawing his proposal. Venetia countered by promising to tell Asquith she was going to France as a nurse and would marry "someone" when she returned. Although she had just received a letter from the Prime Minister reminding her that "you can (if you were so inclined) give me more pain than anyone else in the world," she knew he was a fair man and would understand her need to marry.

During their next outing, Venetia brought up the subjects of France and marriage. That night Asquith wrote:

> ...Whatever the future has in store for you in the way of companionship and intimacy (with some undisclosed person, whom in advance I loathe more than words can say) I shall be ready at the day of judgment to mention that I had the best of it...My conviction is unshaken & unshakeable.

May 1915 was not a good month for Asquith. The war was escalating, Venetia was waffling, and he was staggering. Several days after the *Lusitania* was torpedoed by a German U-boat, drowning over a thousand people and bringing America closer but not into the war, and two days before the British government collapsed, Asquith found out that Venetia had chosen his weak, nervous friend Montagu for a husband.

"Most Loved—As you know well, *this* breaks my heart."

Asquith was sore and humiliated. How long had they been carrying on a relationship behind his back? he demanded. Clearly Venetia had not cared for him nearly as much or for as long as he had imagined. As resignations poured in from the British government, and Asquith prepared to dissolve Parliament and start over as a coalition, if possible, he found himself without a confidante—a compass with no North Pole. What could he do? Rethink and reinterpret the relationship that had been at the center of his life for the past three years? Discard it? Replace it? Asquith wasted no time vacillating. He had poured far too much of himself into his relationship with Venetia to suddenly stop loving her. Love, he realized with something of a shock, had not only changed him, but also changed his idea of love.

On the eve of her wedding he wrote:

> My love for you has grown day by day and month by month and year by year 'till it absorbs and inspires all my life. I could not if I would, and I would not if I could, arrest its flow, or limit its extent, or lower by a single degree its intensity, or make it a less sovereign and dominating factor in my thoughts and purposes and hopes. It has rescued me (little as anyone but you knows it) from sterility, impotence, despair. It enables me in the daily stress of almost intolerable burdens and anxieties to see visions and dream dreams.

As gracefully as he could, Asquith bowed out of Venetia's life. For several years he wrote to her sister, and later became special friends with a Lady Scott, although he did not love her. Having stepped down as Prime Minister in 1916, he retired from politics altogether several years later.

Some twelve years after Venetia Stanley's marriage, she and Asquith got back together as friends. Montagu had died in the meantime, and Asquith himself was seriously ill. The last outing he took before he died was to call on Venetia. He did not tell her how sick he was or how much or little he had pondered their three-year love affair, but only how sweet it was to see her again. "So this then is the child," he said when he met her four-year-old daughter, and Venetia thought she saw a tear. Asquith hinted gently that what he had told her earlier was still true. Wherever life might lead them, he had said, he would always be grateful for this passion that alone among all he had experienced went so completely beyond his expectations and changed him so profoundly.

From over-strained and weary, indecisive and unsure, depressed and fearful, Asquith became a man revitalized and redeemed. Although constantly pushed by people and politics, he took an immovable stand on love. Like a climber slipping down the side of a mountain, he found a foothold that held. It was not, as he originally thought, the affection of Venetia that stopped his fall, but his own ability to love without wavering. That was the saving miracle. He no longer wondered whether he was mad or foolish or anything else. He knew with certainty he was a man in love. He had become a man who could trust himself.

When people finally take a stand on love, they find themselves feeling confident about all sorts of other things. Sometimes they gain moral certainty, sometimes personal, sometimes political, sometimes spiritual. They go from being people who can be pushed around to ones who have such strong inner convictions that they are like rocks in a stormy sea. Something else happens during this transformation. They are likely to lose their fears. A woman told me that in the middle of a tumultuous love affair, she suddenly lost her lifelong fear of spiders. "What could a little spider do to me that this roller coaster hasn't already done?" One of the sweetest stories of love I heard made the same point. When love invades, fear runs.

~

"Look at all the bees in your garden," I said to Nicholas as we climbed the final steps of a long stairway that leads from Provincetown Harbor at the tip of Cape Cod to a high, wooded bluff where a gangly gray-shingled inn stands like a layer cake on legs. Around and under this curious structure, a riotous garden punctuated by sculptures, urns, a fish pond, and ornate Victorian birdhouses winds its way along either side of a brick walkway. This was Nicholas's pride and joy, and it was full of bees.

"It's the asters," Nicholas confided as he slid his small frame into a wicker chair. "Bees go berserk over asters. *And*," he continued in a dramatic whisper, "they're making their last batch of honey right now. It's precious stuff. In fact, it's the best honey in the whole world."

"You're sure of that?" I asked.

"Trust me!"

Nicholas was clearly a character. A small, wiry man of indeterminate age, he sat in his gray sweatpants and string T-shirt looking like a monk from some exotic culture whose goal in life is to sow parables through the land the way Johnny Appleseed spread fruit trees. His big ears stuck out from his head like handles, his oversized hands were folded quietly in his lap, and his elastic face assumed an expression of contented patience. It seemed to me that like the gardens and the inn, Nicholas himself must have evolved in some rambling, eccentric way over the past forty or more years. It felt very natural to ask this inspired gardener about the love of a lifetime.

"It's when a bell rings in your soul," Nicholas said, warming immediately to the subject, "and you find yourself saying 'I get it! I finally get it!'"

Nicholas "got it," he said, after his best friend, his mother, his abusive father, and his sweetheart—the love of his life—all died within an eight-month period. Four deaths in eight months.

"I can't imagine that," I thought to myself as Nicholas described how each death had detonated memories that were as tightly packed with pain as a land mine is with shrapnel. An unusually small child, he had first been ridiculed then beaten and sexually abused since the age of four or five. His father had beaten him, his mother had not been able to protect him, his best friend comforted him, and one by one they all died. Still, he rated his sweetheart's death as the worst experience of his entire life. And the best.

"He had blond hair that smelled like grass," Nicholas said with a wistful smile, "and wide blue eyes—azure really. He looked like Lady Di if you can picture her as a man. Just beautiful. When I first met him more than twenty years ago, he was just a boy and I was eight years older…and not beautiful. In fact, when we first met, he laughed at me and said I looked like a troll. But I told him: I said, 'No one will ever love you the way I do. Today, tomorrow, when you need me, you come, and even if it's a cold, rainy night, you'll find me waiting for you. Linen will be on the table, silk on the bed, candles will be lit, and I'll have food to feed you.'"

Four years went by and Nicholas heard nothing from the laughing blond until one autumn he visited New York City, and there on Broadway in front of the old Shakespeare Bookstore, where the streetlight flashes "to be" or "not to be" instead of "walk" and "stop," he unexpectedly bumped into his love.

"'Call me in a couple months,' I said, expecting absolutely nothing. 'Here's my number.' He squeezed my hand real hard then, and I remember thinking, 'Well...what's this?' Sure enough, I got a call not a month but a week later, and he came out to my place. Right away he said, 'I'm HIV positive,' and I said, 'So?'"

For the next several years, Nicholas and his blond sweetheart were together—or at least mostly together. There were times when the younger man took off and Nicholas was not sure exactly when or if he would see him again. "I have to go," his beloved would say, and Nicholas would feel sick.

"Some people thought I was being used," he said slowly, "and sometimes I wondered just why I was caring so much for a person who didn't care as much for me. That's a hard question to answer. Eventually I realized that my love came more from my feelings than his reactions. I loved him because I wanted to love him and was able to love him, not because I could get something back."

So Nicholas would take a deep breath when his sweetheart stood at the door, ready to leave, and repeat, "When you need me, you come, and you'll find me waiting for you. Linen will be on the table, silk on the bed, candles will be lit, and I'll have food to feed you."

Finally, Nicholas's sweetheart returned for good.

"He had Kaposi's—all over," Nicholas said with a distant look in his eyes. "Open, bleeding sores all over his face and body except for his left eye. God left him that one eye.

"I thought to myself, 'The time will come when I won't be able to love him. Sores will cover his body, and he won't be the person I used to know. Of course I'll feed him and hold him, but...you know what I mean, I won't desire him.' *But*," Nicholas continued with an air of amazement, "that never happened. The cancer never won. The last month, the last week—" his voice caught, "the last day, all I had to do was hear his voice or smell his hair and I was electrified with desire. My love stayed exactly the way it had always been. And that was victory. My love, the love I had built and given to my sweetheart, was stronger than anything in the world. I haven't been afraid of anything since then. Nothing. I keep hearing a bell ring in my soul, and I keep saying to myself, 'I get it.'"

"Did you earn that understanding, that fearlessness?" I asked, as Nicholas leaned back in his wicker lawn chair and the asters seemed to rise in an arch above his head. He thought a long time.

"Many are called," he replied, "but few listen carefully enough or long enough to hear. I believe the call or the opportunity to love is a gift from God, but the listening...? The listening is the gift I give back." Nicholas closed his eyes and smiled such a sweet smile for me, for his departed love, for the garden and the bees that rampaged around us, that I watched to see if the asters would burst further into bloom.

~

Nicholas's transformation from a person terrorized by life to a man who now believes his love—the love he continues to exercise in many ways—is stronger than anything that can befall him, was the central theme of what struck me as the richest love-of-a-lifetime stories. In several important ways, each of these transformations involved similar changes. Before love took them in hand, people told me that they had worked very hard to take themselves in hand. They remained vigilant and somewhat self-conscious much of the time, and because it seemed to them that both good things and bad came from the outside, they reached for all the control they could get in order to maximize the good and minimize the bad.

In other words, they worked hard for whatever love and security they obtained, and they suspected they would have to keep on working all their lives. Even so, they were never safe enough for long, nor did they feel as if they belonged anywhere permanently. As the Dutch theologian Henry Nouwen would have said, they did not yet feel welcome in the world or chosen as a beloved. Some eventually realized that they would never fit in because in order to give themselves away to another person or cause they would have to relinquish control over the life they were bent on preserving singlehandedly. They were trapped, and the question they asked themselves most often was: "What will happen to me?"

However, after the love of a lifetime turned their lives inside out, it was a different story. Inadvertently discovering that something inside was, as Nicholas put it, stronger than what was outside, lovers found they were far less concerned with the ups and downs of life. They relaxed when they realized that nothing could stop them from loving, and that precisely this ability to love made them welcome in the world.

"I am filled with confidence," wrote a young Jewish woman named Etty Hillesum whose great love unfolded during the Holocaust, "not that I shall succeed in worldly things, but that even when things go badly for me I shall find life good and worth living." This same woman discovered that she no longer had to strong-arm her life to keep it on course because she was in touch with something that permeated the world and that she could trust. At times, this sustaining strength seemed to come from the center of her self, and at other times from the cosmos or God. Both secular and religious thinkers have pointed out that belief in a power that links all parts of the universe, be it a personal God or an impersonal force, makes people less submissive, less fearful, and less resentful. They feel safe enough to lose themselves in the moment and lose themselves in love. They give themselves freely to lovers, children, friends, causes, art, and work without fear of losing themselves. "What will happen?" no longer has power over them. "What do I believe?" becomes their guiding question.

In her book *Lost and Found Lovers*, Nancy Kalish includes the story of a woman who fell in love at nineteen with a boy of twenty-two, who was already engaged. Although the two felt deeply attracted to each other, the young man didn't feel he could break his word. He married, and soon afterwards, she did too. Although they stayed in touch off and on for years, they eventually lost track of each other. Some twenty years later, however, the woman started thinking about her first love. To her surprise, she was unable to put him out of her head. They had chosen each other in a way that had never happened again. Finally she decided to look him up. Tracking down his phone number, she called and discovered that he was dying. Miraculously, she said, the two families stepped aside and let the lovers spend as much time as they wanted together. Sixty-three days after their reunion, he died in her arms. "It was as if they [the families] knew that it was meant to be and just backed away and let us be in love for sixty-three magical days. It has changed my life."

At the beginning of the sixty-three days, this woman may have agonized over what would happen to her great love and, once he died, to herself as well, but she didn't end her time with him still wondering. Like Nicholas, she discovered that her love was stronger than death.

~

Although the transformations that the love of a lifetime trigger have much in common, they also differ. Many focused on a new spiritual understanding, and for them the life of the spirit became more important than anything else. For others, however, the love of a lifetime began a transformation that was more existential than spiritual. These men and women felt newly connected. They moved from a life of alienation to one of engagement. Before, they felt trapped inside their own restrictive worlds. Afterward, they fit in everywhere. Discovering that love was a way of understanding the world, they realized that the effort to wrestle with everything as if it really counted was more important than achieving a goal or protecting their own interests.

"The true purpose of art was not to create beautiful objects," the artist in Paul Austen's novel *Moon Palace* realizes. "It was a method of understanding, a way of penetrating the world and finding one's place in it, and whatever aesthetic qualities an individual canvas might have were almost an incidental by-product of the effort to engage oneself in this struggle, to enter into the thick of things..."

~

The third way I heard the transformation described was as a moral revolution. The selfish became selfless, the unfaithful became loyal, and the self-obsessed were at last set free. In short, they felt themselves improved. When the great actor Richard Burton, who seriously thought there was something wrong with him that made him "sublimely selfish," married the love of his life, Elizabeth Taylor, he claimed that she "turned me into a moral man but not a prig..."

As if suddenly taking the complete stairway of moral development at a single bound, one man told me that he went from habitual self-interest to a position of "generous morality." All the dodges and feints he had used to avoid responsibility and advance his own position seemed not just wrong, but irrelevant, he said. He found himself telling the truth, being punctual, and even stopping all the way at stop signs, because he no longer needed what he called "the sneaky advantage." Love leveled the playing field for this man or, rather, it gave him the confidence to play on such a field. He no longer needed to get a jump on other people by cutting to the front of the line.

He went on to say that his moral transformation had the odd ability to change his past as well as his present. It seemed that becoming more concerned for others made him more sympathetic toward himself, and this included his past self. Particularly when he looked back at the dissolution of his first marriage, it was now easier for him to see himself as a man who was naive as well as insensitive, beleaguered as well as willful. In reforming his present life, he had somewhat re-formed his past as well. Surely this is one of the processes that makes all well that ends well.

Regardless of whether men and women called the transformation spiritual, existential, personal, or moral, the love of a lifetime ushered in a simpler, more decisive, and less worried life. Lovers saw something in themselves that reduced the clamor. As Rudi, the journalist in Jerusalem discovered, the love of a lifetime erases the resentments that inevitably accompany a lifetime of halfhearted efforts. A great love does not guarantee happiness, but it does guarantee engagement. We get a life.

~

It is all well and good that love transforms us, I thought to myself as I climbed down the path that led from Nicholas's garden to the harbor. But why does the ox disappear at the end of the story? Are we not supposed to care if the love of a lifetime ends? I stopped a moment and looked out over Race Point, the spit of sand at the tip of Cape Cod that curves back on itself like the whorls of a yellow shell. It was a still, windless evening, the time of day when everyone goes inside for dinner. The time when oxen depart. I could practically see them wandering down Commercial Street past silver-shingled cottages with window-boxes of geraniums.

"No love, not even those that are most peaceful and happy, escapes the disasters and calamities of time..." wrote the South American poet Octavio Paz. "All loves are ill-starred because all are made of time, all are the fragile bond between two temporal creatures who know they are going to die."

That's one meaning of the ox departing, I thought. Love is always borrowed. But then I remembered a phrase C. S. Lewis had used when writing to a young friend who, like Lewis himself, had just buried the love of his life. "Perpetual springtime is not allowed." Not for anyone, Lewis declared, even couples who grow old together. Love continually changes, and the passionate relationship we think of as the love of a lifetime is only the first steps in the dance. Lewis believed this love always changed into something else. The ox left long before one of the lovers died.

The ox leaves when ecstasy has done its work, I decided. When passion and its insights have soaked into a person and become part of their habitual outlook, lovers like Asquith and Nicholas who lost their loves and those like Miriam and Harold Weinstein who lived out their lives together realize that love does not reside exclusively in the beloved. It resides in them. It is their own willingness to engage that will never depart. At last they are prepared for a lifetime of love.

"Listen to me," Nicholas had said as I left. "Never be afraid to give your love away again and again. Yes, you may get hurt. So what? Give your love. It's the only way to live outside of Eden."

CHAPTER 10
A Lifetime of Love

As tall, gray-haired Dr. Niemeyer and I stood in the empty hallway of the hospital annex waiting for the elevator, he told me one last thing he had learned from Leslie. It had come to him in a dream after she and her family had moved away.

"When the dream opened, I was dancing with a woman on a stone terrace that I had just wired with explosives," he began. "I was working for the C.I.A., and my job was to blow up Iranian terrorists. The gel, or whatever it was, was timed to go off seconds after the music ended, and I was going to make a run for it. The music played on, and gradually I realized that my partner was Leslie. My God! Did I really have her in my arms again? I drew her to me in ecstasy, and she became more and more solid. When I felt a shoulder holster as well as her breasts pressing into my chest, I was only mildly surprised. Of course, I thought, she's one of the terrorists. We have plans on each other's lives.

"We kept on dancing, and detail after detail returned—the heaviness of her hair, the almost invisible freckles under her eyes, the *feel* of her. I can't tell you how wonderful it was to feel her in my arms. Although we didn't speak, I could feel the love running back and forth between us. I also knew how the dance was going to end."

He paused thoughtfully. "I remember feeling blown apart when Leslie came into my life, and blown apart when she left. Initially, I wasn't sure that either one had much to do with love, more a question of chemistry. But in the dream, I found myself quietly content to hold her even if it cost me my life. No doubts. It's the second explosion that finally convinced me I could love."

The elevator arrived, and I shook the doctor's hand.

"Good job," I said vaguely, and the doors closed. What a challenging project the god of love undertook when he set out to topple Dr. Niemeyer, and what a good job the doctor himself had done with the experience. Perhaps, I thought, it was lovers like Dr. Niemeyer who were eventually best able to discern love's lasting rewards. Although everyone I spoke to had a story to tell me about what they got from the love of their lives—surprising rewards such as self-confidence or a new appreciation of nature—it was only after the second explosion that they were able to say with certainty what love had given them for keeps.

~

Talking about death or divorce may seem like a funny way to examine the rewards of the love of a lifetime, but as the Greeks were fond of pointing out, we can never say a person's life is happy or sad until it's over. The same is true of what we gain from the love of a lifetime. Until the romance is over, we can't judge its full effect. In this chapter, we will see what it is that lovers hold on to from the love of a lifetime once their partner is gone. Some live in their memories. Some embark upon a more modest relationship that poses no threat to their primary allegiance. Others find that the love of their lives has prepared them for a new love that in some respects is more satisfying than the first. All feel again the "something absolutely crucial" they first glimpsed when they fell passionately in love. Here it is again in the middle of their grief.

Immediately after losing the love of their lives, most of the men and women I spoke with had no idea where to put the love that burst from their hearts and went racing through their days and nights like a pack of hounds after a fox. They missed everything about their beloved so powerfully that they could not believe anything could still the turmoil and contain even the smallest amount of their longing. Desperate ideas tore through their heads. "He wasn't really dead, he was hiding in the garage, bleeding, waiting for me to find him." Surely she could find him or at least talk to him again. Maybe if she prayed in the right way or stepped into a closet filled with his clothes. And dreams! Would he give her a sign? Did he need her and she didn't even know it? So much love, so much pain, and nowhere to put them.

There are certain pairs of people who, when permanently separated, are struck for the first time by the full impact of their love. Alan Paton, the South African author of *Cry the Beloved Country*, was one of these. When he lost his wife of many years, he was so grief-stricken that he asked a nun to write a prayer for him to use in daily, even hourly, meditation. It reads in part:

> Tell her, O gracious Lord, if it may be, how much I love her and miss her, and long to see her again; and, if there be ways in which she may come, vouchsafe her to me as a guide and guard, and grant me a sense of her nearness as Thy laws permit.
>
> If in aught I can minister to her peace, be pleased of Thy love to let this be; and mercifully keep me from every act which may deprive me of the sight of her as soon as

our trial time is over, or mar the fullness of our joy when
the end of the days hath come.

Paton said that he prayed this prayer with all his being night and day,
and when it was not enough to stem the onslaught of his longing, he
began a double diary that chronicled both his days of grieving and the
earlier time of courtship and marriage, *For You Departed*. On retreat with
his memories, he passionately began to tell his story of love and loss as
all lovers must do. Paton never fell in love again. Memory, he learned,
was his way of loving.

~

Paton enshrined his love in a memoir, and as any writer knows, this
way of preserving affection takes years of reliving and thinking—a
bittersweet experience. Other people enshrine their great love more
simply and privately. The dying woman who talked of going to a real-
estate office to buy a house with her secret love had hidden her most
precious memories of love in her heart. Even her children didn't know
that Jimmy had been the love of her life. Former President Teddy
Roosevelt *never* spoke of his first wife after she died in childbirth, nor
did he allow anyone else to do so in his presence. George Washington
wrote to the married Sally Fairfax, who was the love of his life, on the
eve of his marriage to Martha, then sealed his feelings for her in his
heart. The poet Robert Browning said simply, "My heart lies buried
with my wife in Florence." Many great loves are enshrined in these private ways.

When I was in Rome several years ago, I came upon a small shop
crammed to overflowing with religious medals. Crucifixes poured down the
walls like sheets of rain, and on either side of a narrow aisle were boxes

glittering with Blessed Mothers, St. Christophers, and St. Anthonys. At the very back of the store, under a table, I came upon a plastic bucket filled with tiny gold hearts. Each was suspended from a miniature safety pin, and as I picked one up, I noticed that the heart swung open. On the inside was an indentation the size of a child's thumbnail in which, I supposed, a tiny photo or strand of hair could be placed.

"These are *spillos*, Madame," said the clerk as I dropped four or five of the hearts into his open hand. "They are..." He gazed at the lockets for a long moment. "They are for remembering something that is both private and important. Perhaps a secret." He shrugged. "They are worn here," he continued, opening the collar of his shirt to reveal the corner of a white undershirt. "Just over the heart. Never outside."

For the rest of my trip, I asked everyone I met about *spillos*. One woman told me that her mother had worn a *spillo* all her life, but until she died no one knew what was in it. When she and her sisters finally looked, they found a barely recognizable photo of their mother's cousin who was also, perhaps, her first love. Another woman kept a strand of hair from a child who had died two days after it was born. Others pinned a *spillo* on their babies' diapers as a talisman. A man kept a button from his mother's glove. There are experiences in life, I was told, that are so charged with joy and sorrow that they change you forever. Whether or not something from this crucial event is literally kept in a *spillo*, the memory takes up residence in your heart and goes about its business there for the rest of your life.

～

One of the strangest ways that a dead lover made his continued presence known was to periodically return for dinner. At nineteen, a woman fell head over heels in love with a man seven years older than herself, and over the objections of her parents, dropped out of school and moved in with the love of her life. For five years the couple was ecstatic, and both sets of parents eventually agreed that the match was a good one. It was said that the young couple never took each other for granted.

When the young woman was twenty-four, her lover had a heart attack and died suddenly. Naturally, she was devastated. She cried all the time and felt sure she could not carry on. Then one night as she drifted off to sleep, her great love knocked on her door and told her matter-of-factly that they were going out to eat. Astonished, she followed him and soon was sitting at a table in their favorite restaurant chatting away as if nothing had happened. The waiter took their order, their salads arrived, they buttered their rolls.

"I was so happy and so comforted to see him again. And surprised! There he was, leaning across the table, loving me again with his eyes. I was afraid to tell him he was dead for fear he'd leave."

"Look," he said at the end of the evening. "I'd like you to go back to work."

Since that evening, this woman has enjoyed a continuous series of what are called lucid dreams. Unlike ordinary dreams, these unfold in a much more natural way with fewer sudden shifts and bizarre recombinations. Another difference is that lucid dreams can be controlled to a considerable extent. For example, the young woman discovered she could delay her lover's departure by asking questions or requesting another cup of coffee. Research on lucid dreams suggests that auto-suggestion plays a major role. Telling ourselves night after night that we will remember our dreams and will have control over them gradually turns regular dreams into lucid dreams.

The young woman's lucid dreams, which she called her "long sleeps," have recurred whenever she confronts a serious problem. As she wonders what her first love would advise, he returns for a late-night dinner date and helps her figure out what to do.

"It's always so wonderful to see him."

I couldn't help wondering what they did after dinner.

"Do you just talk?" I asked.

"No..." she replied with a smile. "We do everything we did when we were together."

Although this woman is familiar with the scientific explanation of lucid dreams, she is not sure whether or not she believes the dreams are products of her own desires. It feels to her as if the love of her life insists on returning because he cannot bear to see her struggle without him. Who knows what goes on when a great love takes up residence in the heart and goes about its business there?

The woman with the lucid dreams is now married to a man who seems to be "a second version" of her first love and who has graciously made room for her dream companion. She considers herself to be doubly lucky in love.

~

When the love of a lifetime dies, it is by no means clear whether or not the survivor will live in the past, as Alan Paton did, or will replace the love of a lifetime with someone else. What can be said with some certainty, however, is that if the original relationship lasted for many years, subsequent loves are likely to be more modest.

Although Richard Burton remarried twice after his second divorce from Elizabeth Taylor, his diary suggests that he was not trying to replace the love of his life. When Burton and Taylor made the movie *Antony and Cleopatra* in Rome, which is how they met, there is a scene where he takes her in his arms and says "Everything that I want to hold or love or have or be is here with me now." That was what Taylor meant to Burton, and he never forgot it. References to her run through his diary, and in addition to memories, there are tender descriptions of the scenes they both appreciated—light dancing on water or the powerful heave of ocean swells. "Ocean" was one of his nicknames for her.

Toward the end of his life, Burton married Sally Hay. "I am so lucky to have her," he told his friends. "She can do everything—cook, type, nurse, organize—and she takes such good care of me." Burton died of a stroke several years later. Those closest to him said that although he turned to this more comfortable kind of love with genuine gratitude, no one replaced Elizabeth Taylor.

I heard many stories of comfortable companionship following on the heels of a great love. "I love him," my friend Jane maintained, referring to her new companion, "but we're not *in* love." When Jane's husband of forty-seven years died after a long illness, she thought she would die, too. In fact, she said that if Bob had died in the fall or winter, she wouldn't have made it. It was only because he left her in springtime that she managed to get out of bed. "How can I get this day to pass," she would ask herself, "so I can go to bed again?" She shook her head at the memory. Words could not begin to express how hard that time was. In fact, that was part of the problem. Without a way to say what she felt, she was adrift in confusion. What she had shared with her husband, what she was feeling now, and what she imagined the bleak future to hold all heaved together like an angry sea.

Jane found herself clinging to any phrase that might explain why she felt such pain every single morning. She read a verse by Emily Dickinson, for example, and repeated it to herself for months: "For each ecstatic instant/We must an anguish pay/In keen and quivering ratio/To the ecstasy."

The better the marriage, Jane told herself, the sharper the loss.

Sometime later, she skidded on a snowy road, and as her car careened down a steep bank, it rolled over several times. When it stopped, her husband's voice said very clearly, "Jane, turn off the ignition. Now lie down on the other seat." That too became part of the story as did memories of them dancing, golfing, and taking their coffee to the beach in the early mornings. There were unsettling memories to incorporate into the story too—his penchant for buying cars that the family couldn't afford and the poor communication that persisted between him and at least one of their children. Jane's emerging picture of her husband often disagreed with her children's picture. She acknowledged what they had to say, but realized that she was remembering Bob as a husband and only she knew that story.

Some two years after her husband died, Jane met a charming widower and the two began to date. How important would this new relationship become? she wondered, and for several years as her story of Bob took shape and her relationship with her new companion grew, she wasn't entirely sure of the answer. Would they eventually marry? Then one evening she and her new love were dancing to Cole Porter songs when a sudden longing for Bob hit her like the proverbial truck. Tears sprang to her eyes, her knees buckled, and she had to sit down. "This will never change," she realized. "I am still married to the love of my life."

Part of Jane was not available to dance with anyone else. She had retired a certain way of loving. In her mind, her marriage to Bob set the standard for intimacy, vitality, loyalty, and much more. At its best, their relationship was everything a true love should be. This will never come again, she understood, but this is partly her choice, her way of remaining loyal. Fortunately, her partner felt a similar allegiance to his deceased wife. Both he and Jane wore their original wedding bands and kept pictures of their original family. The intense love they felt for the love of their lives fanned out in a gentler form to embrace grandchildren, great-grandchildren, friends, and each other. When this man also died, Jane was not felled by grief. She hated thinking of him cold and alone in the ground wearing only a light suit, but what really hurt were the returning memories of Bob's death. In grief as well as joy, he set the standard.

~

Sometimes the love of a lifetime prepares a person for the best relationship of their lives. The subsequent love doesn't replace the original one as *the* great love anymore than a perfect swim replaces the first swim. I can recall the moment I learned to swim, in a three-foot deep, tea-colored stream. One minute I could only stay afloat by using my toes to push off the leafy bottom, and the next minute I was a boat. I could go anywhere in the world there was water. As with swimming, so with love: there is a privileged place in the memory for firsts. Thus Tess, who lost her faith in God when she lost Bobby Walsh many years ago in Canada, went on to marry a wonderful man and start a family—but Bobby is still the love of her life. Dora, too, thinks of her first husband as her great love even though alcoholism separated them and she went on to form the relationship of a lifetime with someone new. Emily wonders if she is going through the same process. "Not of marrying," she says quickly, but of building a better romance. She has learned a lot about life since the German exchange student she met first on a bus trip and again thirty years later disappeared after their passionate reunion.

~

Eighteen months after Richard had cut off their rekindled love affair and Emily had decided that in spite of his bad behavior he was the love of her life, she finally got the phone call that she both did and did not believe would ever come. Earlier Richard had told her not to think about him any more—it was *over*. But when he eventually called, he acted as if eighteen days rather than eighteen months had elapsed. Laughing and joking seductively, he asked if she would meet him again in Boston.

"I was furious!" she recalled. "Furious, relieved, excited. Here he was again, still dreaming of me. Half of me was thinking, 'I'm right! He cares!' and the other half was thinking, 'You bastard. Say you're sorry.' It was the same old Richard."

But Richard did not find the same old Emily on the other end of the line. She demanded an apology for his earlier refusal of her phone calls and his abrupt disappearance. When all he would say was, "C'mon, it wasn't that bad," she hung up. Another six or seven months went by and the drama was repeated. This time he tried harder to set up a meeting in Boston, and she admitted that it took her longer to hang up. On the third or fourth call, Richard finally agreed that their relationship possessed a mind of its own and regardless of the decisions he made, it continued of its own accord. That satisfied Emily, and for a couple of years they met irregularly in Boston. There was no contact between meetings.

"The time finally came when all we really wanted to say to each other was, 'I love you, I have loved you, I will always love you.' We weren't a couple. We didn't do nearly enough together to have anything to talk about, and it seemed we'd come to the end of the line.

"About this time Richard called me from Boston unexpectedly. He was in town for twenty-four hours. Could I fly down and spend four hours with him? I almost said 'no,' but at the last minute I did it. I flew down, raced to the hotel, knocked on his door, and this deep, sexy voice says in German, '*Hast du einen grossen Hunger?*' I opened the door, and there's Richard, lying stark naked on the bed covered from his hairy chest to his toes with chocolate bars. There must have been sixty or eighty of them—a big mountain of my favorite German chocolate. 'Start at my toes,' he commanded, 'and work up.'

"Later I flew back to Canada, and when he put me and fifteen pounds of chocolate in the cab for the airport, he did an odd thing. He held my hand through the window as the driver got into his seat, and because traffic was creeping so slowly, he walked alongside me to the corner."

Tears came to Emily's eyes.

"I have never felt such love in my life," she said, "and I don't think I ever will again. When the cab picked up speed, I watched him standing on the sidewalk, waving and smiling, and I knew that this was the moment to say good-bye. I was pretty sure he knew it too.

"Perhaps he'll call me occasionally, but I think that's all." She shook her head in amazement. "I didn't know it at the beginning, but I can say now that Richard was the most wonderful thing that ever happened to me."

Emily describes herself now as "between habits." A year or so after saying good-bye, she began dating a man she'd known for a long time. She finds that she treats him differently from others she's dated before. Her old habit was to keep a mental ledger. If there were enough entries on the plus side, she must be in love. Wasn't that the meaning of love, the consistent meeting of her needs? If the man disappointed her, however, and red ink became conspicuous in the ledger, she assumed love was on its way out. After Richard, however, a new habit began to develop and now, several years later, it is fairly well established. When she and her new partner disagree, she brings up the problem, but her basic feelings for him don't change. Whether or not this relationship goes anywhere, she has found a sounder way to care.

"Richard had to come first," she concluded, "and no matter what happens to me, his love will count as long as the dream it inspired counts. I had hoped the dream was about living happily ever after with him, but it wasn't. It was about living happily ever after, period."

~

The scenarios that follow the love of a lifetime are many and varied, but they all have one thing in common. The "something absolutely crucial" or the pearl of great beauty that the Persian tale describes is the prize that every lover tries to hold onto when a great love ends. Dr. Niemeyer after Leslie left, Suzanne Farrell after George Balanchine died, Emily, Alan Paton, and twelfth-century Héloïse—all of them want to keep the essence or kernel of what they felt when they first woke up in love. Perhaps only a poet can clearly describe the state of the awakened heart, and certainly only a poet who has been so deeply in love himself that his description of what lasts has been wrung out of him like water out of a cloth.

Jalal al-Din Rumi was born in Afghanistan in 1207. By the time he was thirty-seven, this unusually bright and thoughtful man had moved to what is now Turkey, started a family, and become a teacher and the head of a small religious community. Unbeknownst to him, a member of the Mevlevi sect of the Sufis—in other words, a whirling dervish—was looking for him. This was Shams of Tabriz. He had traveled all over the Middle East searching and praying for someone who could "endure my company." A voice had come to him and asked what he was willing to give in return. "My head!" shouted Shams. The voice then told him to "find Rumi." Thus a wild man appeared in town one day, ambled into the religious community, spotted Rumi, and whispered a question in his ear. Rumi sank to the ground in a faint. When he recovered, he looked at Shams and Shams at Rumi. Each had found his match.

Without plan or preparation, the two raced off together and talked nonstop for weeks, not pausing to eat, drink, or sleep. They were intoxicated with each other and with their mutual quest for understanding. They became each other's reed pipes and sounding boards. When together, their thoughts flowed like music. Apart, they were distracted, thinking of what they would say when reunited. Although passionate, nonsexual friendships between two men were fairly common in their day and had a long history behind them, the students in the religious community became jealous. They were being treated like women or children, they muttered, whom everyone assumed were incapable of intellectual rigor. Rumi failed to see trouble brewing, but Shams was aware of the unrest and saw it was getting out of hand. Without saying a word to his beloved Rumi, who he knew would try to stop him, he simply whirled out of town and disappeared.

Rumi was beside himself. What did Shams's departure mean? And how was he supposed to think without his friend? How could he be the person he wanted to be without him? Rumi's intense longing for his partner—his first heartbreak—opened his eyes to things he had not seen before, and it was only at this point in his life that he began to write the poetry he is still famous for.

Wandering through the countryside in search of Shams, Rumi was struck repeatedly by a longing that seemed to train a powerful light on everything he looked at. Lying on his back one morning as the rising sun turned the eastern sky the color of lemons, he noticed the stars beginning to fade. He had never seen a more beautiful sky.

"Shams," he thought as he gazed upward, "you are like the sun. You extinguish my light with your radiance."

Watching as one star after another winked out in the silence of early morning, Rumi began to feel Shams's presence. It was so easy to imagine that he was lying beside him on the green grass. As always, the longing in Rumi's heart expanded as he thought of Shams. Yearning for his perfectly matched soulmate, Rumi felt his heart go out to the whole world. Still lying on his back, he called to the morning, and the bright air settled over him like a lover. He whispered Shams's name to the ground, and the warm earth held him in its arms. He ached to be near his Shams, and as the love he sent in every direction rebounded off the farthest reaches of the sky, the beauty of the dawn was pulled into his heart. Rumi continued to shoot his longing upward into the sky, and again and again his thirsty heart drew into itself the heartbreaking beauty of the morning, which he now recognized contained the essence of love just as surely as he himself did. For a few moments, his love for Shams was the same as his love for the sunrise. When Rumi felt his presence, it was now inseparable from the beauty that surrounded him—inseparable from him.

Had he been intoxicated by love? he wondered later. Had he been breathing in rhythm with the universe? Whatever it was, in those brief moments he had been reunited with Shams and with everything else in the world. "A burning heart is what God seeks," he concluded.

Rumi began writing poems about his longing and the beauty it revealed. Sometimes he would become so enraptured that he would cling to a pole outside his house swinging back and forth as love poems blew out of his mouth like wind from the desert. As was the custom, his verses were memorized and passed from ear to ear around the country. Perhaps Shams would hear his verse about stars that went spinning across the black night like dervishes on fire and know that Rumi missed him.

Finally, word came back to the village that Shams was in Damascus. Rumi sent his son to persuade him to return, and when Shams walked back into town and the two finally caught sight of each other, they fell at each other's feet. No one could tell who was the lover and who the beloved. The mystical conversations resumed immediately, and Rumi again became the person he wanted to be—quick, inspired, profound. Locked in thought with Shams, the rest of the world retreated into a beautiful haze. Not surprisingly, the jealousies resumed.

All went well for some time until Shams disappeared again. Rumi assumed he had gone off as before. He waited patiently, he looked for signs, and finally a terrible message arrived. Shams had been murdered by Rumi's students. Late one night, he had stepped out of the back door of Rumi's house and been overpowered by a group of men. Dragged into the nearby woods, he had been killed. The proof of Shams's death was unequivocal, and Rumi sank into despair. Dropping his classes, he whirled in the dervishes' exhausting form of meditation. When he wasn't whirling, he was writing. Now his poetry sang with a sadness that could break a stone. He longed for Shams's words and the sound of his friend's voice. He felt like a field mouse in love with a frog who lived at the bottom of a pond. How could he get to him? How could he comfort and be comforted?

For many months, Rumi sang of loss and separation—"the absence of the Friend"—and even though he knew Shams was dead, he couldn't stop himself from searching for him in wider and wider circles. It simply wasn't possible for all that wisdom and caring to have left the world without a trace.

Arriving in Damascus long after Shams had been killed, Rumi ended his search. He realized he had not lost the treasure of incomparable value. He still held it in his heart. The treasure bestowed by every great love affair is not the beloved, he understood, but the expansive longing that makes everything under the sun precious. Love's gift was nothing less than the enchantment of the world.

"A lover's food is the love of bread," he wrote, "not the bread."

Rumi returned to his home and gathered together his poems, which he called *The Works of Shams of Tabriz*. He continued to have a special companion and confidant as long as he lived, and his poems were always addressed to this friend. The later poems were not as fiery or as full of longing as those written for Shams, but as he aged, Rumi's work became increasingly tender. It was said that his soul was traveling the path of return. On December 17, 1273, Rumi died, and this day is still referred to as Rumi's Wedding Night. It was the moment he finally merged with the force that animates all love and was reunited with his beloved Shams.

"God lives between a human being and the object of his or her desire," Rumi had written. "It's all a mystical journey to the Friend."

~

Sooner or later every lover must discover that the "something absolutely crucial" that both a passionate love and its loss give to us is the expansive longing that makes everything under the sun precious to us. There are a million ways to say this. It is the inexorable power of spring that drives every blade of grass upward and every root downward. It is the power of life that enables a mother dog to chew through a three-inch chain to save her puppies. It is the power of love that electrifies Nicholas with desire as he gazes at his gruesomely dying lover or that gives to Asquith such magnificent generosity when Venetia reveals how little she has cared for him. It is the power of God, the soul, the spirit. It is our willingness to feel the desire to be alive in its most intense and heartbreaking form. Perfect love, said Rumi, is perfect understanding.

~

"Last night when I cycled home from S.," wrote Etty Hillesum, a young Jewish girl in Nazi-occupied Amsterdam, "I poured out all my tenderness, all the tenderness one cannot express for a man even when one loves him very, very much, I poured it all out into the great all-embracing spring night. I stood on the little bridge and looked across the water; I melted into the landscape and offered all my tenderness up to the sky and the stars and the water and the little bridge. And that was the best moment of the day."

When this young woman's lover died some months later, she stood in his tiny apartment looking down at the first dead body she had ever seen.

> There you lie now in your two small rooms, you dear, great, good man. I once wrote to you, 'My heart will always fly to you like a bird, from any place on earth, and it will surely find you.' And this is what I wrote in Tide's [a friend's] diary, 'that you had become so much a part of the heaven that stretches above me that I had only to raise up my eyes to be by your side. And even if they flung me into a dungeon, that piece of heaven would still spread out within me and my heart would fly up to it like a bird…

Returning to a transit camp that transported Jews to the concentration camps in Poland, Etty carried the strength she still felt from her beloved into the crowded, unheated barracks of the camp. Although surrounded by despair, and always in danger of being shipped off to an extermination camp herself, which eventually happened, she considered it the richest period of her life. Like all great lovers throughout history, Etty Hillesum tapped into the power of life when she handed over herself over to love.

Conclusion

Toward the end of my project, I heard a love-of-a-lifetime story from a big woman in goddess clothing who wore twelve earrings in one ear and exaggerated everything so much that as she began to speak, I wondered why I had bothered to bring up the topic. She worked at a coffee shop I frequented, and every time I saw her, she referred to some heart-stopping calamity or remarkable accomplishment. As Samuel Johnson observed, she was one of those people "for whom nature is hourly working wonders invisible to every other eye, only to supply them with subjects of conversation."

On this particular visit to the cafe, there were few other people in the shop, and curious as to what she'd say about the love of a lifetime, I asked my standard question. "Have you heard the term? And if so, what do you think it means?"

"I know *exactly* what you mean," she said in her husky voice. Placing her ring-laden fingers on the counter, she leaned forward, eyes sparkling. "I mean...if you've *had* it, you *know* it."

Here we go, I thought.

Glancing around quickly to see if anyone was within earshot, she wasted no time getting into the story. "We met in the projects when I was...let's see, twenty-four, with two babies, and he was thirty-four. And bad. Oh my God, he was bad. He was an undercover cop who ran drugs as a cover, but he'd work for whatever side gave him the most money. Dangerous, dangerous business, but he was tough. And looks? To die for. He was a big man with a long, brown ponytail, real shiny, and he wore black leather pants the way this counter wears paint. He was a Harley man and big into tattoos…oooh, from his eyes to his ass." She smiled suddenly as if she had unexpectedly come upon a favorite recollection that had been lost. "Wonderful tattoos…" She gave the empty space above my head one of those smiles of pure delight that are so close to tears I could feel the emotion in my own throat.

"Rhymes was a bad apple," she continued, turning serious. "Everyone in my family and all my friends were opposed. Not just because he was a gangster, either. They were afraid for me. You see he never entirely disconnected from his wife. He'd go over there when the mood struck him. My girlfriends told me, 'Cut the sucker loose,' but I knew how much he loved me." She gave me a quick glance. "Our song was 'Against All Odds.'"

"It wasn't an easy relationship," she continued. "I didn't have much free time with two boys eleven months apart—Irish twins—and my mother wouldn't take them if she knew that I was, you know, blasting off with Rhymes."

She paused a moment, shaking her head in disbelief.

"I'd hear a tap-tap on my window at 2:30 in the morning, and there he'd be strumming his guitar and singing some silly song he'd made up about 'Gotta have coffee with you-oo,' and I'd yank on my jeans and we were outta there, roaring down the highway to New Jersey for God's sake—for coffee! It was summer."

"Who took care of the kids?"

She frowned for a split second, then brightened. "He brought his sister over on the back of his bike and she'd stay with them. And we were gone. 'Hold on!' he'd shout, and we'd tear into the city, across the George Washington Bridge—like a necklace of lights it was—and I knew I'd found a man who was big enough to make me feel safe. I mean he wasn't Mr. Reliable, but he was big enough so I knew I wasn't going to push him around like I do everyone else, and big enough so no one was going to push me around either. Next to him," she added with a hearty laugh, "I was practically petite. It was the only time in my life when I felt safe from all sides."

She hesitated as if deciding whether or not to tell me something. "I have to say he drank pretty bad," she admitted. "He'd disappear when he was drunk. Back home to his wife, ex-wife. I don't think he wanted me to see him so...so bad and out of control. He was gone a lot. It wasn't always booze. Sometimes he went underground for weeks or months at a time. It took a lot of faith and patience to be his girlfriend. He even said that himself."

For a moment she didn't seem to know where to go with this story that, to my surprise, was sounding both realistic and fabulous at the same time. With another shake of her head, she started off in a new direction.

"Wanna know how he got his name?" she asked brightly. "His real name is Buck—can you beat that?—and he got so tired of people screaming 'rhymes with —!' that he finally just changed his name to Rhymes."

"Amazing," I said.

"But you know," she continued, her voice dropping again, "when we did get time together, it was...well, like nothing I expected. I mean you may not believe this but when we were together—sober—I sometimes got the feeling that we became one heart. I can't explain it better than that. It just happens. This feeling comes over you that the same blood is going through both your bodies, and you know that you were joined in the beginning and now you're one heart again for a little while." She looked away briefly. "The first time I felt it, I thought it had never happened to a man and woman before. Honest to God, that's what I thought. Such a beautiful feeling. Every now and then, when I can't sleep, I try to pull it up around me like a blanket."

"So what finally happened?" I asked, but the story had no real ending. One day, Rhymes made one of his characteristically abrupt disappearances—and never came back.

"At first I thought he'd dumped me," she continued, "then I heard rumors that he'd turned state's evidence and had to move to a foreign country. Then people said he was dead. There's a grave out on Long Island, but I don't want to see it. That's not where he is for me.

"When God closes a door," she went on, "He always opens up another one. Not the same kind of door necessarily, but some other place to put your love. It matters to me in a big way that Rhymes is gone. I miss the things we did together, and Lord, I miss the loving. But in another way, I tell myself it doesn't matter. I've had the experience of becoming one heart, and I'll never forget that. I didn't think it was possible for me...not for me." She gazed off into space, her big eyes suddenly teary.

"You found love in spite of yourself?" I asked, "Against all odds?"

She blew her nose on a napkin.

"It was the surprise of a lifetime," she said. "If I never have it again, and I doubt I will, I've already taken first prize. Yeah, against all odds."

With a sigh, she came out of her reverie and looked around the coffee shop as if she'd just come on the job. "You know," she said, "there are days when I just don't feel like working."

~

Nodding, I asked for a refill and ambled over to a table in the far corner. How many stories I had heard over the past five or six years, I thought to myself. I had sat with young kids, ninety-year-olds, doctors, professors, hairdressers, gardeners, my own friends and family, their friends and families, and heard love-of-a-lifetime stories that chronicled just about everything. Thinking back, I remembered the pride in a man's face as he stood in my driveway describing his forty-year marriage. I remembered a nineteen-year-old in the Boston bus terminal making thumbnail prints on a styrofoam cup as he described his mother who died when he was three. He couldn't really remember her, he said, but no one else cared a great deal so he thought she was the love of his life. Parents, con men, combat buddies, loyal spouses, Jesus, lost and found high-school sweethearts, unavailable or inconstant men and women—who hadn't been named as a love of a lifetime? Yet it seemed to me as I sipped my coffee that I could now recognize, not the content or setting of a love of a lifetime—each was unique—but the feelings associated with these special romances. I also knew the general itinerary they follow. If I had heard the waitress's story five years ago, I might have dismissed it, but now I could see that although it was lavishly embroidered with the symbols of a great romance so that no one could miss its importance, it contained certain tell-tale characteristics that suggested that it was, at heart, the real thing.

$\sim$

From the lover's point of view, the real thing is an electrifying whirl of excitement and astonishment. It is so much more than anyone bargains for. Passion burns at the center of each story, and exhilaration, ecstasy, fear, sadness, and gratitude come spinning out of each romance like the arms of a galaxy. Dozens of emotions are present—whatever human beings are capable of feeling. So much concern with so little control intensifies every sensation. Lovers are amazed to discover that jumping into this fire does not immediately result in destruction. Instead, they are intoxicated with a vitality that runs through them and everything else. The world turns gold, and they are gods. Daily discovering abilities they did not know they possessed, they stride through their lives powered by a strength they can cannot name and will never forget.

I do not believe that there is one best word for this silent feeling of adequacy, this inner certainty that begins to grow once a person encounters the love of a lifetime. But within the huge confusion of feelings associated with the love of a lifetime, this strength is the prize.

~

The love of a lifetime is such a strange journey. No matter how it proceeds, certain experiences seem essential. Regardless of how we meet our great love and regardless of what we do together, the love of a lifetime doesn't begin until one or both is felled by an overwhelming passion and submits to the inevitables of destiny. Swept out of our ordinary world of planning and doing into a larger world that includes more than our minds can understand, we stand outside ourselves. This is the literal meaning of the word ecstasy—*ekstasis*, to put out of place. From this new vantage point we see more, and we see in a different way. Why this happens is a mystery, but not entirely. Finding ourselves 100 percent involved with another person over whom we have no control, we become so vulnerable that we pay attention as perhaps we have never paid attention before. We become as observant as a painter, noticing every detail of our beloved's face and body. We become as attentive as a poet, considering every facet of his or her personality. We develop the ear of a musician, the nose of a perfumer, the insight of a psychologist, the vision of a mystic. We look everywhere for signs that the universe approves of a love that is so perfect it has no equal and never will.

In the grip of ecstasy, we resonate to our beloved and to everything that reminds us of love or strikes us as beautiful. Everything has meaning.

Everything matters and is connected. Fully engaged, we are living at full strength. Of course, we notice ourselves, too. Passionately stirred by hopes and fears, the superficial image we had of ourselves gives way to a more ruthless and complex picture. The tidal forces that operate beneath conventional behavior are revealed.

If the love of our lives is to do more than leave an encapsulated memory in our hearts, the insights ecstasy gives us must be incorporated into our personal philosophy. This requires mixing oranges and apples. How can we fit quiverings of excitement or glimpses of radiance into the daily round? Our knowledge of passion is too private, too disruptive, too divorced from the social world. If we can't even say what happened to us, how can we use the knowledge? It reminds me of travelers returning from India or some remote place in the world that is so strange and wondrous that a journey there has the power to transform those who pass through even against their will. What do these travelers do with their visions when they return?

The itinerary of many promising romances bogs down when lovers return from the land of ecstasy. Holding on to the memory of passion is too painful, and letting it infiltrate and inform their lives is too much work. Although I think it is fair to say that the best measure of the love of a lifetime is the road it sets us on, "the road" is a tough one. Love is a demanding paradise.

One of the first things passion has revealed to us is that we are not children anymore. We cannot be defined by anyone who knows us only from the outside. We alone are the experts on ourselves now, and no matter what our age, it is time to break away and stand on our own two feet.

We have also discovered the relationship between loss and commitment: if we can't tolerate the risk of a broken heart, we won't be able to stay in the ring. All loves of a lifetime make this clear, because all provide experience of temporary loss, possible loss, and eventually permanent loss. We are given the choice of backing away and saying, "Never again," or telling ourselves over and over that we still have the strength we glimpsed at the height of our love. In important respects, we are still that reckless, beautiful spirit that ran along the beach under the moon and dove in.

In giving ourselves over to love and letting ourselves be swept away from our concern for personal security, we gained a new definition of participation. At least for a time, we were part of the eternal dance of life. Taken over by the forces that govern roses, eagles, glaciers, volcanoes, hopes, and prayers, we felt connected to everything and on a par with everything. We discovered that the essence of the self and the essence of the world is the same. And from this understanding came a sense of being approved of and connected. Although I don't believe that one person can give another the inner certainty of being welcome, the words, "I choose you," are powerful. Being clearly seen and forcefully chosen by *the* person we most adore is often the cap that fires the charge. In giving, we can finally hear that we are beloved.

Can we enjoy or lament a great love and ignore the mysterious coincidences that brought us together? We try. However, unless we find a way of trusting what cannot be explained, we are forced to plan endlessly for our own well-being. Without mystery, we are back behind the wheel of our car, and our reason is again solely responsible for guiding us to our destiny or destination. In love, we learned we could not rely on reasons and explanations alone. That lesson is meant to outlast ecstasy. The willingness to cooperate patiently with the forces that move heaven and earth cannot develop if we cannot consistently acknowledge their existence and trust the rightness of their operation.

Love, imagination, and transformation go together. In love, our imaginations presented us with a kaleidoscope of possibilities. We pictured ourselves living in a distant city creating a wonderful relationship with our formidable partner. We also pictured blowing our big chance and losing love forever. Whichever way we move, in love or out, imagination is the catalyst of transformation. If we can't picture it, it won't happen. If we can, we have a chance. Like the other lessons learned in the grip of ecstasy, this one can never be set aside as irrelevant. As long as love keeps changing, which is forever, we need imagination as our guide.

Holding onto our belief in the love of a lifetime is also a life-long undertaking. It is here that a romance crosses the bar, so to speak, and it is here that many loves run aground. There are always reasons to downgrade the story of our romance to lust, a midlife crisis, or a mediocre marriage. Because these are sometimes accurate evaluations, we must take our doubts seriously. It is hard to tell when we are being realistic and when we are letting ourselves be unduly discouraged by disappointments. But in our private appraisal of love, it is more important to consider our own behavior than the outcome of the romance. Were we paying attention? Did we do a good job? Can we now keep faith with what we saw and believed when we were in love? Every love-of-a-lifetime story is about believers. It is not that a miracle made them believe in love. It is their belief that is the miracle.

If what we have experienced in the grip of ecstasy is brought into the rest of our lives and integrated into our philosophy, we will find ourselves transformed. Whether we call the changes moral, existential, spiritual, or something else, all will strengthen our inner convictions and loosen the bonds that tie our well-being to outside events.

"My love, the love I had built and given to my sweetheart, was stronger than anything in the world," Nicholas discovered. "What is inside is stronger and more important than what is outside."

~

The love of a lifetime reveals, teaches, and transforms. When it hits:

- It blasts away the innocent picture we have of ourselves and reveals a passionate, complex person hungry for life.
- It reveals our lack of control over what matters most, and throws us into a storm of unexpected vulnerability and vitality.
- It separates us from our past.
- It teaches us to commit to a relationship in spite of the possibility of loss.
- It teaches us to let go of the controls and give ourselves over to love. People prove to themselves they are lovable by giving love, not getting love.
- It prompts us to value the parts of the world that no one can explain.
- It fires our imagination and expands our possibilities.
- It pushes us to believe in ourselves.
- It gives us a strength called by many names—an inner certainty that is stronger and more important that outside events.
- It prepares us for a lifetime of love.

~

Taking all these things together, it seems to me that the love of a lifetime is for many of us the one time in our lives when we experience life in its pure, raw form. The guardian angels Common Sense, Reason, and Decency desert us, and we are left alone to suffer the desire to be alive in its most intense and most heartbreaking form. We discover for ourselves and in ourselves a force of immense power—a vital, resonant desire that is amplified almost unbearably when we connect without restraint to another person, and that reaches through that person to everything else. We realize then that the treasure bestowed by the love of our lives is not only the enjoyment of the beloved, however wonderful that may be, but also the expansion in our hearts that makes everything under the sun precious to us.

There is no way to enter this meaningful world without giving ourselves over to an experience that means everything to us yet can neither be controlled nor explained. The Dutch theologian Henry Nouwen said that nothing of importance is accomplished by anyone until and unless they embrace this experience and feel welcomed by the world. Katharine Hepburn learned that we don't experience love by figuring out what we want, but by discovering what we can give—which must be everything. Rumi said that a lover's food is the love of bread, not the bread. And I say, don't discount the love of your life if it does not conform to our culture's narrow picture of easy, endless love. True love is complicated, and its lessons, both bitter and sweet, are too valuable to be lost. To embark upon a lifetime of love, you must first embrace the love of your life—your heart's most courageous journey.

Postscript

Almost a decade has passed since I picked up the phone on a winter's night and heard a voice I did not think I would ever hear again. That moment has not faded. I remember exactly where I was sitting, what I was reading, and how my blood turned to bubbles when I heard his voice. I remain unequivocally glad that I had the opportunity to fall for the love of my life.

At first I worried that my life without this man had been a long detour. In living without him, had I missed the life best suited for me? At the same time, I had to admit that at nineteen I had not been ready for a great love. It seemed I needed to take detour after detour until I finally got the message: what counts in life is full engagement, yet no one can choose the form this engagement will take. Love almost never comes to us in the way we believe it should. Looking back, of course I wish I'd understood this sooner, and I wish I'd had the confidence and resources to jump into love at nineteen. Nevertheless, I did not miss the point of my life. My detours taught me exactly what I needed to know in doses I could manage, and like so many of the men and women I describe in these chapters, I gradually gained enough assurance to take the plunge.

After falling for the love of a lifetime, I have found that everything worth undertaking is worth doing as if it were my only concern. How I write and what I write about has changed. How I practice therapy has changed. My friendships have shifted in one way or another as have my relationships with colleagues. In all areas, I try to show up, pay attention, and tell the truth with the same attentiveness and fearlessness I brought to the love of my life. The consequences, I have learned, take care of themselves. In short, no more detours. Everything counts. I don't know how many people get to this stage in life in their twenties, and how many require more time. But frankly, who cares? I couldn't ask for more.

About the Author

Susan Baur, Ph.D., is a licensed psychologist with graduate degrees from Harvard University and Boston College. She has written six other books, *The Edge of an Unfamiliar World: A History of Oceanography*; *On Almost Any Wind: The Saga of the Oceanographic Research Vessel* Atlantis; *Hypochondria: Woeful Imaginations*; *The Dinosaur Man and Other Tales from the Back Ward*; *Confiding: A Psychotherapist and Her Patients Search for Stories to Live By*; and *The Intimate Hour: Love and Sex in Psychotherapy*. She lives in North Falmouth, Massachusetts.